Captains and Commanders

Memoirs of a Scottish West Coast fisherman

Tommy Ralston

Mallaig Heritage Centre

"Captains and Commanders" is a revised and greatly extended version of "My Captains", which was published by Scottish Cultural Press in 1995.

Published in 2010 by
Mallaig Heritage Centre
Station Road
Mallaig
Inverness-shire
PH41 4PY

ISBN 978 0 9565853 1 8

Printed and bound in Scotland
by Robertson Printers, Forfar

Acknowledgments

During the long process of compiling and writing this book I have been conscious of the fact that a very large part of it has been gleaned from fisherman, most of whom are no longer with us. I would like to dedicate this book to the men, mostly gone now, who pursued the herring shoals in the old way. Their like will never be seen in this world again.

It is also dedicated to my long-suffering wife, Ina. Where would I be without her?

Some years ago I spent an afternoon yarning with Pat Croan and George (Dodie) Alexander. When, on the way home, I commented on how much I had enjoyed the yarns, Dodie told me, "Mak the best o' it Tommy – there soon winna be onybuddy left that kens whit ye're talkin' aboot."

How right he was – and they have both left us now!

I am reluctant to acknowledge help given to me by individuals simply because I am sure to miss some out, but I really must pay tribute to Lachie Paterson, of Carradale, who willingly gave me access to his priceless store of old photographs and allowed me to use some of them. Lachie has invested a huge amount of time in rescuing and preserving old material. He gives freely of his time and energy showing his collection to fishermen all over Scotland. For that, and for the use of many of the photographs in this book: "Thank you, Lachie." Thanks also are due to Gary Voce for his valuable help with photographs.

Thanks to Willie Tait of Fraserburgh, the incomparable exponent of the art of purse-netting for his time, and for the use of his photograph, and to Willie Whyte, also of Fraserburgh, whose time is now freely given to the less fortunate of this world.

To my cousin, Angus Martin, I give thanks for being allowed to include his hugely evocative poem, "The Captains".

Thanks also to Malcolm, curator of Mallaig Heritage Centre, for his patience!

Contents

Preface

While I was still writing ‘My Captains’ some years ago, my immediate concern was whether or not I would get it published. I sent a sample to a publisher and to my delight, she accepted it. I then wrote ‘finis’, and that was that. Since then I have realised that I was far too premature in closing it; there were many more tales that could – and should – have been told, and it needed much editing.

This realisation has been with me for many years, but until now I have done nothing about it. Two events stirred me into action.

The first was when it was my turn to give a talk to my Rotary Club. I thought that I would tell them of the days of the herring fishing, a subject that I felt sure they would know little of. My forays to the local library resulted in my amassing an absolute confusion of figures; hundreds of boats, thousands of men and so many tons of herring that when I reviewed what I had written, I realised that the boring liturgy would send them all to sleep!

A return to the drawing board – or more accurately to the computer – led me in time, to realise a staggering fact that I simply hadn’t thought of.

When I left school and went to the fishing from Campbeltown in 1950, there were approximately 40 herring boats fishing from the port. Each boat carried 6 men. There was no prawn fishing in those days, so the entire years’ earnings of those 240 men had to come from herring fishing alone.

How many jobs ashore are required to service one man working at sea? The answers that I found to that question ranged from 5 to 9.

A bit much that, I thought, until I thought further!

There were the men who built the boats and the engines; the men - and women - who made the nets and the ropes; who fashioned the corks and the lead sinkers; the men who made the boxes and the baskets; the lorry drivers; the people who worked in the processing of the herring; right down to the shop assistants who sold the end product! Yes, it was all much clearer now!

For the purpose of my talk, and because it made for easier counting, I chose to multiply the 240 fishermen by 5. That, if you add on the original 240 men, gives a total of 1440 jobs.

Let's round it all down to 1000, I thought, and then no-one can accuse me of exaggerating.

So, in 1950 there were a minimum of 1000 jobs in the United Kingdom that were totally dependent on the fishing efforts of the Campbeltown fleet alone. This total is, of course, greatly increased if one takes in the other Clyde ports, Carradale, Tarbert, Dunure, Maidens and Girvan, and does not bear thinking about if one takes in the Moray Firth fleets of drifters.

1000 British jobs funded from the herring fishing efforts of Campbeltown in 1950. Today, less than 60 years later, I do not think that there is one single job in the U.K. that is totally dependent on the herring fishing efforts of the entire British fishing fleet! This is a shocking statistic and one that spurred me into action.

Further to that is the fact, gleaned from the Kintyre Antiquarian Society magazine, that in Campbeltown in 1772 there were; "seventy-eight sail, from twenty to eighty tuns burthen, all built for, and employed in, the herring fishery; and about eight hundred sailors (sic) are employed to man them."

The second event took place not long ago when I was on holiday in Sharm el Sheikh, on the Red Sea, with my wife and a friend. We were in the departure lounge at the airport, waiting for our flight home, when I fell into casual conversation with a man who was perhaps 10 years younger than me. He told me that although he had lived and worked in the Channel Isles for many years, he had been born in Whitby.

When I told him that I had spent several seasons fishing for herring from that port, many years ago, he surprised me by rather forcefully asking if I had been on the ring-net boats. When I replied that I had, he told me that he had been 'adopted' by the crew of the *Nobles Again*, a well-known Campbeltown ring-netter. Here I should explain that it was common then for young Whitby lads to frequent the boats, running errands and generally helping out where they could. There was some competition among them to be accepted by certain boats and they strutted around the pier in great delight when 'their' boat caught more herring than their pals'.

This man hesitated, then looked me straight in the eye and said, very forcefully, "I wish I had met you earlier. You are very privileged indeed to have been part of that culture. I remember Jock Taylor, the skipper of the *Nobles Again*, very well. He was an outstanding man by any standard but I can tell you that I have never met finer men in all of my life than the crew of that boat. They were gentlemen, every one of them. I think of them often. You should thank God that you worked with such men!"

He then apologised that he couldn't spend more time with me as his flight had been called, and he left. I do not know his name. All I know of him is that he worked in Jersey.

That this man remembered Jock Taylor by name after an interval of at least 40 years was very telling, and this chance encounter pushed me to complete this work, a work that is really meant as a tribute to him, to many of the fishermen of that time and to others who impressed me greatly.

What, if anything, was so special about the skippers and crews who manned the boats that were known as ringers – or indeed, any of the boats of that era?

Well for a start they were, in common with all fishermen, individuals. They went their own ways, in their own times and they were, in many respects, masters of their own destinies. To a large extent now, choice has been taken from their successors who are bound by rules and regulations that are drawn up by people who have absolutely no understanding of the sea, the fishing or of its traditional values.

They learned how to handle their boats – boats that were by today's standards tiny, in weather that was just as bad as it is now and learned how to nurse them through the storms that have today sadly defeated much larger and more powerful boats. This skill was not learned in a conventional classroom. That it was learned well is borne out by the fact that I have no recollection of any of these boats being lost as a result of bad weather. This despite their having to cross the Minches, one of the most dangerous stretches of water in the U.K., loaded and light, time and again, in winter and in summer, in good weather and bad.

They learned the ways of the herring; how to find them and how to kill them, using only the senses that God had given them. Most of this knowledge is now lost. A friend recently referred – with some justification - to modern day fishing skippers as, "Carpet slippered screen-watchers." Deckhands were dubbed, with equal justification in my opinion, "shelter-deck labourers." Today, he could add that it is now a fact that not many of the crews can speak English, as Eastern European and Filipino workers are commonplace now! Where are the Scottish skippers of tomorrow going to come from?

Very soon there will be no-one left to tell the tales of these ring-net men; tales that need to be told from a first hand view. Second hand stories invariably, in my opinion, leave much to be desired.

These men were truly the last of the Seekers and the last of the Hunters. I have now done my best to try to recognise their worth here. This will be the last - I will not write more of them.

None of them remain fishing now.

The Captains.

A poem from Angus Martin.

To aid understanding of the following poem I offer the information that the skippers and crews of the Campbeltown herring fishing fleet often gathered and yarned at the head of the old quay in Campbeltown. When the weather was bad they sheltered behind the old weighing house and in the lee of the Christian Institute building, hoping for a lull that would allow them to go to sea.

Angus sees the ghosts of some of these men long dead. He is not alone in mourning and wondering at the knowledge - hard won - that died with them. Do please read it. Re-read it, think about it and try to understand it. I believe it is one of the most evocative poems I have ever read!

Receiving the captains into my home
required no preparation; they came
with the gait of men accustomed
to straddling water on the thin
comfort of drunken planking,
and rolled themselves politely through the door.
There was whisky for one hand and cake
for the other, and a window beyond
the clock face and the hanging light,
and they gathered there before the glass
seeing themselves reflected, and remembering
the outer space of wind and sea.

What is it out there that could
freeze you now, draw a sweaty film
to your palms and bug your eyes?
Only the living, by God, the living,
unmet, unfathomed to a man
where the inky hills are in their
old proportions and hissing ridges
of the water loom between the shores.
Who is out there? No one that you know,
captains, so cry in the night;
"What ship, and where bound?"
All bound where you are come from.

Loitering, aimless, at the Weigh-house,
A storm on the roof of the
bulking Christian Institute
beyond MacEachern's funeral cross,
a medieval intricacy of stone,
heavenward mystery uncommented on
over the clash of rigging and the lash
of harboured waves. The captains
pace in blue among the casual
knots of crew, pausing to train an eye
on the black well of the weather,
and almost - almost - saying: "We'll go home."

Let me shake your hands. Goodbye, captains.
Be careful out there, where you are bound.
Perhaps you have forgotten certain dangers -
fingers of gloomy shore and sunken teeth of reefs -
and remember there are new lights everywhere.
You'll manage, I dare say, but do not tell me where
you're going, or I may wish to go with you,
a passenger just - no skills to serve you with -
sitting below, hearing the tongues of the sea
and the creaking of the skiff's old bones,
a boy in the bilgy dark, hunched at a mug of tea,
far from home, my captains, very far from home.

Now I invite you to come with me on a journey back in time, and be introduced to some of the remarkable characters I met during my career on the West Coast of Scotland firstly as a fisherman, then later as a lifeboat coxswain, and fish buyer.

In our explorations we will travel North to the northernmost outposts of the Outer Hebrides, South to the Isle of Man, and then East to Whitby - but the bulk of my stories are from the West Coast of Scotland in general; Mallaig and the Clyde in particular.

As this is not an autobiography, I was for some time puzzled as to how to link together the random memories of a lifetime spent among the pioneering giants of the fishing profession until my cousin, Angus Martin, sent me a copy of his poem - which he has very kindly allowed me to reproduce above. This superb poem, led me to visualise these men - or their shades - gathered together around the ghostly fireside of Angus's dream. What a gathering that would be!

As I wrote, I became aware that not all of the great characters I met were fishermen. There were very many ancillary workers, the salesmen, the processors and the buyers and of course, the indispensable hard working, ordinary people who made everything possible.

The poem also gave me the title for the original book and for this, and for all his help and encouragement; I will be for ever in Angus's debt.

The 'Captains' in Angus's poem arrived at his fireside unannounced and uninvited. My guests have all been invited by me and although not all of them rank as Captains or Commanders, they were – and in some cases still are well worthy of recognition.

It is not my wish or my intention to hurt the feelings of anyone alive, nor to harm the reputation of those who are now dead.

The formative years

Gayfield Place was a good community to be born into.

There were over one hundred people living in this three storey high, grey tenement building on the western extremity of Dalintober; once a fishing village in its own right but now considered by most – but not by all - as being a part of Campbeltown. Recently demolished and the site still lying undeveloped, Gayfield Place then glared at the town as defiantly as it faced the all too frequent south-westerly gales.

I was born there in December 1935 – if I had held on for just two days, I'd have made my appearance a year later, in 1936 – so I was only three years old when World War 2 started. This war probably played a large role in making Gayfield Place a very closely knit community. Many of the men folk were far from home, serving their country, so those left behind were called upon to help out with tasks that were beyond the skills of the women, whenever necessary.

I have no memory of the beginning of this War, and the fact that it deprived me of my father's company almost from the outset, was not of any great importance to me then. Time brought the realisation that this deprivation must have had a lasting effect on me. A fisherman, my father volunteered for the Royal Navy soon after war was declared and his Naval postings, to firstly Milford Haven and later to Lamlash on the Island of Arran, meant that my mother, of choice, joined him at these places for well over a year in total, taking me with her.

Another important facet of his absence from home was the fact that my mother had to try to fulfil the roles of both father and mother – not an easy task, particularly given the food and cash shortages that were a direct result of the conflict. There is also a probability that the War against Hitler was indirectly responsible for the fact that there is a six year gap between my brother and myself, an age difference which meant that we were not as close as we might otherwise have been. This is a source of much regret to me, and no doubt to him also.

I remember very little of my time in Milford Haven, but I do remember more of the year or so spent on Arran, although I was very young then.

My father was Coxswain on the *Silver Grey* which vessel had in civilian life been a ring net fishing boat in Campbeltown, referred to in knowing circles as a ‘ringer’, but which had been commandeered on to the Admiralty list as the *R3*, and was now rather optimistically referred to as an ‘inshore patrol boat’! One of my mother’s brothers, Angus, was engineer on the *R3*. He was destined to father my aforementioned cousin, Angus Martin.

Their task was to monitor and patrol the anti-submarine booms that had been laid across the two entrances to Lamlash Bay. This duty was carried out with diligence for some time but when it became apparent that this was not ever going to be a death or glory mission, but rather a long drawn out boring routine with little chance of the action they then craved the crew - who were all ex-fishermen - convinced the Lieutenant in charge of this diminutive warship that they could combine their patrolling duties with a little bit of trawling. After all, they argued, they should do their bit to help feed the hungry in a war-torn nation. That they used the money earned from selling the catch to augment their meagre naval pay was of no consequence, of course!

They usually landed their catch in Lamlash and I remember my father telling the tale of the man who came one day to collect some fish from them. This buyer had a small truck which had a flat back with no sides and his intention was to set off around the island, selling the fish door-to-door. The crew lifted the two boxes of fish – their entire catch – on to the back of the truck. The driver then offered what was a derisory sum in payment and a row broke out. This fellow jumped into his cab, threw some money on to the ground and took off. My father grabbed the two boxes of fish and held on to them. They slid off the tail of the truck and landed at his feet. The driver – wisely - didn't stop, nor did he ever come back. They sold the fish to someone else, so with hindsight, that was a good day's work!

I distinctly remember being afraid of 'funny noises' in the night, and being shown where they originated from - a sink full of plaice. These poor fish took a long time in dying and were left to flap around, noisily, for hours.

Another and very welcome product of this trawling was the 'sea coal' that they dredged up in reasonable quantities. Whether this coal was deposited on the sea bed by natural methods or if it was being deliberately sought in an area where the men knew a 'puffer' loaded with coal had sunk is a question that will not now be answered. I recall that my mother was not too happy with its burning qualities – she said that it sparked badly. It was free, though!

I believe that these fishermen were also responsible for brainwashing the officers in command at Lamlash into believing that they should have a test firing of one of the two depth-charges which were (more in hope than in anger, I am certain) mounted on the stern of the boats.

This test was conducted off the Cock of Arran where the water was considered deep enough to safely detonate the charge, which had been adjusted for the occasion to explode at its deepest possible setting. It was a lovely sunny day, I was told, and they worked the *R3* up to its somewhat inadequate top speed before dropping the weapon over the stern. The lieutenant in command had taken up his post - chosen, he assured his crew, for its overall view of all that went on. That it happened to be right up on the stem of the boat, and was therefore as far away from the action as it was possible to get, was no doubt purely incidental! The corpses of the fish which were the only result of this experiment, floated to the surface where they were gleefully gathered in to be sold, the amount being added to the week's beer money.

I had often heard repeated the story of how a dead rat had been put into the sea boot belonging to one of the crew, a very excitable man who had been christened James Robertson but who rejoiced in the nickname "Gipsy". This unwelcome rodent had been spotted several times, but had evaded all attempts to get rid of it. One night my father and my uncle, Angus Martin, were on watch together and as the time approached for them to be relieved, Angus went below to make cocoa. He surprised the rat in one of the lockers he opened, and despatched it with a well-aimed wallop! When he told my father of his success, the pair of them hatched the idea of putting it in one of Gypsy's boots.

Gipsy was called to stand his watch, and when he drowsily pulled on this boot, and then grumpily shook it to remove the obstruction which his foot had encountered, the drowsiness and grumpiness were forgotten when the corpse of the rat flew out of the boot and landed on the deck. He then battered the remains of the poor beast around the cabin, bellowing like a bull as he attempted to 'kill' the offending corpse!

I had always thought this was a lovely story, but could not swallow the part of it which alleged that poor Gipsy thought that he had in fact been successful in killing this rodent and had a photograph taken as a memento. I was completely amazed and delighted beyond belief in May 1994, to find a photograph in the excellent Scottish Fisheries Museum in Anstruther of Gipsy on the foredeck of the *R3*, proudly holding his 'kill' by the tail!

There are many tales of adventures shared by fishermen during the War and one of them stands out in my mind. A fisherman, whose surname was Morrans and who probably took little joy at being called 'Shitey' for a nickname, had reached the rating of Petty Officer. He encountered a fellow fisherman in Portsmouth and the pair adjourned to P.O. Morrans' ship for a yarn. While they were there a pipe came from the tannoy, requesting the presence of P. O. Morrans in the wardroom.

Not much to laugh at there, you say? No, but his surname was not well known to our English cousins, so they pronounced it MorrANS, with the accent on the last three letters whereas in Campbeltown, the accent was on the first four letters. He probably quite liked his new name, and so took no steps to correct it but his guest, the fellow Campbeltonian roared; "P.O. MorrANS be fucked – better known as Shitey!"

This outburst led to the poor man having, unusually, two nicknames, from that moment on!

Of course it is common now to adapt surnames. For example a recent M.P. whose name was LAmont (Lamont), preferred to be called LaMONT. Don't think I care for RalstON, though!

It was in Lamlash that my long-suffering mother had what was no doubt one of the worst experiences of her life to date. I had gone down the pier on my way home from school to see if my father was around, and had succeeded in falling into the water. An alert sailor recovered me, none the worse for my ducking but my companions - most of whom were much older than I - insisted on wheeling me homeward in a wheelbarrow.

One of them was sent ahead on his bicycle to warn my mother that her offspring was being taken home, and that he was wet.

This messenger rounded the corner below the house we were renting in Hamilton Terrace, saw my mother sitting with her knitting, enjoying the sunshine, on the wooden bench outside the house, and called to her, "Tommy fell into the water. They're bringing him home in a wheelbarrow!"

He then shot off back to the rest of the gang, leaving her distraught and being comforted by neighbours as she awaited the arrival of the 'corpse' of her son!

I went to school in Lamlash and I do recall a book that was given to me whilst there. It contained many illustrations that 'popped up' when the page that contained them was opened. My late mother filled in my recollection of this book.

"Oh yes," she said, "a class in a school in England adopted the *R3* and the children wrote to the boat. Your father was very zealous in writing to the children in return and when he told them that you were around their age they – through their teacher - sent this book as a present. You insisted in taking it to school to show it off but when your teacher asked where you had got it, you told her, 'my daddy's girl-friend sent it to me'! She got a lot of fun out of telling me this," my mother concluded.

As a stranger to the island I was, of course, subjected to a degree of reserve by some in the class, and bullying from one lad in particular. One fine warm day, when several of us were making our way home from school, along the shore, I managed to haul in a wee punt that was lying close to the shore, tied on a running mooring. I had always been attracted to anything that floated so I boarded this boat in high glee. The bully followed me and we untied it and then set off seaward, using wee bits of wood as paddles. Of course, the owner of the punt arrived on the scene and started roaring at us to come back, telling us where he was going to plant his boot when we did so. We were scared stiff, but I had enough wit to agree to come back if he promised not to hit us. We did this, and he made a token gesture at us as we set off at high speed along the shore. When we thought that we were safe, we slowed down and considered our position. Only then did I become aware that my companion had pissed his trousers in fright!

He became my bosom buddy and protector from that day on in return for my not disclosing his 'accident'!

Returning with my mother from our visits to Milford Haven and Arran, the rest of the War years were spent back in Campbeltown in the safe haven that was Gayfield Place, whilst my father was serving abroad.

Ring-net boats in Campbeltown in the 1950s

Campbeltown is built around the head of a beautiful horseshoe-shaped loch which is almost landlocked. Access to the open sea is gained via the narrow channel to the north side of the island of Davaar.

Davaar is only a part-time island, being easily accessible dry shod across the shingle isthmus called the Dhorlin, for around half of the tidal period.

The loch is sheltered on the north and the south sides by high hills: a low gap to the west leads to Machrihanish, a sandy plain which until recently housed an important military airfield. This harbour, on the east side of the peninsula of Kintyre, was ideally situated to be used as a base for the naval units delegated to guard the entrance to the Firth of Clyde in time of war. The local Grammar School was commandeered for the duration of the war and was named HMS *Nimrod*, an important training school for users of ASDIC, the latest submarine detection gear.

The town had reached the peaks of prosperity in the early nineteenth century when it supported in addition to its farming, shipbuilding, and fishing communities, some thirty or so distilleries and all their allied trades. A coal mine at Machrihanish five miles from the town was the catalyst for the construction of a rail link between it and the pier in Campbeltown. At the time of my birth however, the coal mine had closed – although it reopened again briefly - the railway had been scrapped, the number of working distilleries had shrunk to two, and the shipbuilding yard at the Trench Point had also ceased trading.

Now the herring fishing industry, documented as being in existence for over 300 years, has in effect, vanished. My maternal cousin, Angus Martin, relates in his contribution to 'The Campbeltown Book' that in 1820, 435 men were employed in the town as herring fishermen.

Lawrence Robertson and my paternal cousins, Robert and Willie Gillies, retired from fishing, just recently. They are the last men in Campbeltown who went to sea as boys, to fish for herring with ring nets.

Tragically, they were the last in a very long line of herring fishermen in Campbeltown, a line that stretched back for several hundred years. This industry was utterly destroyed in just a few years with the advent of purse-seining and pair-trawling.

Is this the result of a well-governed industry?

My war memories are, as you might expect from one who was then a young child, good ones. It has become obvious to me now that the mind kindly deletes most of the bad memories to the great benefit of the good ones, so that the air raids - fortunately few - that Campbeltown suffered are imprinted upon my mind as times when I was forced to hide under the table of a downstairs neighbour, and was annoyed at not being allowed to watch all the beautiful lights in the sky. Later I discovered that they were tracer bullets! The knowledge, gained in the light of the morning following one such raid, that the Royal Hotel had been badly hit and that a number of fatalities - including a party of Wrens - had resulted, meant only that I was annoyed at not being allowed to view the damage closely.

Sea mines dropped from enemy aircraft and meant for the Loch, but in fact hitting and destroying several houses at the Trench Point, meant the loss of one of the best friends that the Clyde fishermen ever had, Archibald Stewart, a prominent lawyer in the town. At the time however, this was only another source of excitement to me. Sadness is an emotion which I think is either fleeting or is totally absent in the young, whose interests are usually completely self-centred.

It is worth while noting that Mr. Stewart was buried in Kilkerran graveyard on the south side of Campbeltown Loch. His grave is marked by what is to me by far the most impressive headstone in the cemetery. It is not large. In fact it is quite small. It is certainly not the most expensive. It was however erected, with the permission of his family, by the Tarbert fishing community and inscribed - “In memory of a true friend.” Surely a tremendous and possibly unique compliment to a man who was legal adviser to them, and to all of the Clyde fishing fraternity, for many years.

My maternal grandparents rented half of a semi-detached cottage at Ballochgair, about six miles north of Campbeltown, on the road that led to Carradale. It is my recollection that this was done after one of the air raids, in order that they be away from possible danger.

My mother and I spent some time there with them and I remember my grandfather watching boats ringing one night, just below the cottage. I know now, that he would have given a lot to have been aboard with them!

Gayfield Place was, in my opinion, a good place in which to spend one’s formative years.

There was a strong community spirit there, fostered no doubt by the lack of material wealth coupled with the need to stick together in what were difficult times. I fondly remember the all-too-few occasions when the tenants of this building got together and hired a bus, which took us to picnic on one of the many beaches of Kintyre. One of the few buses available for hire was a so-called ‘utility’ model, which differed from the others in that it had wooden seats. Such is the perverseness or 'thrawn-ness', of youth, that I well remember hoping that we got the 'utility' model, which had wooden slatted seats, so that I could relish the scorn heaped by the hirers upon the head of the hapless driver, who of course had no choice in deciding which vehicle was sent to pick us up.

My paternal grandmother, Annie Ralston, was a lady who did not suffer fools gladly. She went, during one fine summer spell of weather to ask Mr. Craig, owner of West Coast Motors, for a bus to take the people who lived with her in John Street, on a picnic.

"A picnic, you say?" replied Mr. Craig. "Are you aware that there is a war on?" he was unwise enough to reply.

"A war on? A war on, indeed!" replied the redoubtable Annie, stretching herself to her full height of around five feet and raising her voice. "You sit there behind that desk and ask me if I am aware that there is a war on? I have six sons and three sons-in-law in uniform, fighting for their country. Nine of them! No, do you know that there's a war on?"

She got her bus!

There was no television of course, and radio reception was subject to the vagaries of a generally unreliable accumulator to power the equally unreliable radio receiver, yet we never seemed to be bored. Going to the Cinema was a treat that depended mainly upon one's skill at collecting jam jars or lemonade bottles. These were turned into ready cash at one of the many shops which offered payment for the returned containers. The oft-experienced dearth of jam jars, and therefore of money, meant that the Cinema was a rare treat which, with hindsight, was no real hardship.

Indeed, it occurs to me now that viewing one of the then popular films such as 'The Three Musketeers', or 'Zorro', was followed by the frantic fashioning of wooden swords with which we re-enacted the fight scenes we had just witnessed. Westerns meant that for days we rode imaginary horses everywhere, shooting at everything that moved, with our hand-carved 'carbines'. Seeing one of the 'horror' films that were the vogue then; 'The Mummies' Return', or 'Frankenstein' – invariably resulted in panic stricken calls of "Mammy, I'm frightened", when I lay in a dark bedroom after having viewed one of them!

These are facts, but they appear to be at odds with today's purveyors of violence and filth, who produce "experts" to prove that we are not influenced by what we view. Indeed, if we are not influence by what we see, how then does anyone justify the vast sums spent on advertising?

There were then two cinemas in the town, "The Rex", opened in 1939, and the "Picture House". Only the "Picture House" now remains. Built in 1913, it is allegedly the oldest in Scotland, and it is a part-time Bingo hall.

The darker nights brought on the games which seem largely forgotten now, "aleevo", "kick the can", "tig" and the like. They kept us running, hiding, and arguing all evening, and it was only the dreaded call from our mothers that took us very reluctantly to the zinc bath by the gas light in front of the coal fire, then upstairs to bed. I do not recall ever finishing any of these games.

Perhaps they are still running somewhere?

Our mothers were fortunate too in that there was never, I am certain, any need for them to worry about us being abused in any way. Such monstrosities are a product of the civil liberties which we now all enjoy!

I am equally sure, however, that they found other things to worry about. There was for instance, a long spell during the black-out that prevailed in wartime, when adults spoke in hushed tones of "the ghost", which tales we children were not supposed to hear. There was always someone who had heard of another sighting, but I am quite sure that this white-clad figure - who certainly never harmed anyone to my knowledge - existed only in the fertile imagination of a few gossips, who had found a new way to command the attention upon which they thrived.

Apart from the aforementioned air raids, there was one other wartime occasion which engendered great excitement among the youth in the town - the Commando raid. This was a simulated invasion of the town by Commandos. They were opposed by the local Home Guard whose members, of course, were all well known to us. One of the Gayfield boys, Arthur MacMillan, gained great kudos from the fact that his father was not only in the Home Guard but was a wireless operator, and as such carried a most imposing looking radio upon his back.

On the day of the 'invasion', several of us were scouting the hills around the town looking for our new-found heroes, the Commandos, when we chanced upon a well-concealed troop of Home Guards waiting in ambush, complete with the radio operator who immediately told us all in general, and his son in particular, to 'clear off', in no uncertain terms.

This we did and of course, when we soon afterwards found our Commandos, we took great delight in guiding them to the Home Guards' hiding place. I am led to believe that Arthur's father made a remarkable recovery after being killed by the Commandos, and made a valiant attempt to inflict the same punishment upon poor Arthur!

The first Captains?

In Gayfield Place I met the first of my potential Captains.

Donald Brown occupied a room and kitchen on the right hand side of the main entrance "close". This was a bad position to live in as it was vulnerable to the prank played by us youngsters of tying his door handle to the one opposite, then retiring to a safe distance to view – and hear - the result of knocking on both doors!

Donald, or "Brown" as he was commonly called, hailed originally from Carradale, a village some fifteen miles to the north of Campbeltown, and in his earlier days he had been a fisherman there. He was a big soft-spoken man, inclined to stoutness, and fortunately for us he was like most large men, very easy-going and good-natured. To the despair of the ladies who - because their husbands were away in one or other of the Services - made up the bulk of his neighbours, he kept ferrets in his coal cellar. Needless to say, he was not married.

One of my earliest recollections of Brown was the day his chimney caught fire.

This caused a great commotion among the rest of the tenants, some of whom had their weekly washings hanging out to dry directly in line with the soot which fell as a result of the fire. Brown denied all knowledge of this conflagration when he was quizzed about it, despite the fact that his face was blackened and that his house - seen through the tiny crack which was all that he would allow the door to be opened - was redolent of sooty fumes.

As a result of this fire the MacBrayne brothers, who were great friends to Donald, prevailed upon him to get his chimney cleaned and engaged one of the Foster brothers to do the job.

Now the Fosters were well-known to us all, having developed the habit of using a bicycle to ride the length of the hall, when anyone knocked on their door. It was a matter of some honour that the caller should protest that whichever brother answered the door was not the required one, which resulted in this poor man having to turn the cycle around, 'arse over tit' because of the limited width of the corridor, pedal back down the fifteen feet or so of hallway, and then the whole hilarious process would start over again with the 'correct' brother!

The great day dawned.

Davie Foster arrived with his rods strapped to the crossbar of his bicycle, and work commenced.

Brown was on the ground floor of a three-storey building so a lot of rods needed to be screwed together to enable the brush to reach the top of the chimney, a time-consuming job. Brown, an acknowledged expert at delegating work deployed my pal, Cecil Finn, and me to stand across the road from the front of the building to watch keenly for the first sign of the brush appearing from the chimney can, and to report this sighting to him in his house where he was doing that which he was by nature best suited for - supervising the work. Of course the already limited attention span of two young lads is a tiny fraction of that of one young lad, so the first sign we had that all was not well was when there arose from the rear of the building a great and increasing uproar.

It appears that while our attention was diverted, the brush had emerged from the top of the chimney and had bent - of course backward away from us - towards the rear of the building and was currently showering soot freely on to the washing lines which were full of what had previously been nice clean washing!

When peace had been, if not restored then at least contemplated, Davie announced that as a result of the severe bend in the cane caused by the weight of the brush pulling it down to one side of the chimney can, he could not now retrieve it by the normal method of pulling it back down the way it had gone up.

A noisy meeting was convened in the back yard before someone produced a ladder, with which assistance Davie climbed from the top landing of the building, on to the roof, followed by loud and conflicting advice from what was by now a thoroughly agitated convention of ladies. Once safely at the chimney head, he took off the brush, allowing Brown to withdraw the now freed canes back into the house.

Davie, safely back on terra firma, then declared himself not to be satisfied with the job, so he clambered back up on to the roof bearing a heavy metal sphere which was designed to take the brush, suspended on a rope, down the chimney.

He chose the wrong one!

When this ball, accompanied by the brush arrived at some speed - unannounced, but accompanied by a great cloud of free-flying soot - into the kitchen of the house directly above Brown's, a house that was occupied by the diminutive but vociferous Willie MacAulay, better known as 'Cala' – a distant relative of mine - and his sister, the resulting discussion filled in any missing words in our budding vocabularies, and has provided mirth on many occasions since.

I would hazard a guess that the preferred reading of the Foster brothers must have been 'Wild West' tales. If we met either of them approaching on the pavement, it was standard practice to adopt a gunslinger's pose, keeping our eyes firmly fixed on theirs whilst our hands hovered at the ready – one at each hip – for a quick draw. All concerned would turn as they passed until we were backing away from one another. Unless someone 'went for their guns'! This provoked yet another bloodless gun battle on the streets.

One day several of us were walking from Dalintober towards the town, on the seaward side of the Esplanade. There is a low wall –

perhaps one metre high – on the inside of this pavement. We spied one of the brothers cycling towards us, the cycle loaded with the chimney sweeping equipment. We dived over the wall and hid from his view until we judged that he was close. We then stood up and 'opened fire' with a selection of imaginary six-guns, and rifles. We certainly caught him unawares for he immediately relinquished his grasp on the handlebars of his cycle, 'went for his guns' - and fell off the bike!

We took to our heels.

Halcyon days indeed.

I remember another rare night in Brown's house. It was, I think, on a New Year's Eve, when two of us visited Donald to find the MacBrayne brothers already there with their record player. They were all great fans of Country and Western music in general and of Hank Williams in particular, and had a large collection of his records.

The record player was placed on top of a small table just below the only electrical appliance in Donald's living room – the unadorned light bulb that dangled from the ceiling. They had taken a connection from this to the machine. Electrical sockets were a thing of the future here!

As the night wore on, the brothers began dancing around the player. The only way I can describe this dancing is to liken it to the war dances that Hollywood would have us believe the American Indians practised. It involved a lot of arm waving and of course, the inevitable happened; one of the arms caught on the wire and brought down everything, plunging the room into darkness!

"Now then, boys," said Donald, calmly. "We'll hae tae move intae the kitchen. Jeest take yer time, there's nae hurry."

This was done, the record player was reconnected to the power from the light on the roof in Donald's kitchen - and the celebrations recommenced.

I sat on the end of Donald's bed and, as my foot swung in time with the music, it connected with a bottle which clattered into another one before it fell and rolled across the floor.

"Now then, ma boy," Donald chortled. "Jeest lee that yin alone – it's no due tae go off tae daylight comes in!"

Of course I, who was around 12 years old at that time, was home and tucked up in bed, long before daylight appeared.

Donald Brown provided a happy and a safe shelter to us on many occasions, and his harmless tales of his time as a fisherman whetted our appetite for the life, and taught us a lot about the sea. He taught us how to mend nets, and it was a matter of some pride to me and also to my pal, Cecil, no doubt, that we were reasonably proficient in this sphere when at last the time came for us to leave school and start our working lives as apprentice fishermen. We also had to make our own mending needles from wood that we cut from a boutrie tree, under his instructions. Brown never told a malicious tale about anyone, and one of his instructions was never to be without a knife - "It might save your life, boy, if you get a rope wrapped around your leg and it is pulling you into the water". Although thankfully this never happened to me I still heed his sound advice. This small pocket knife, the only tool which a fisherman was expected to carry, is still so important to me that my wife has on more than one occasion taken it to me when I inadvertently left it at home. It caused me grief when on one occasion I forgot to pack it in our luggage and as a result had it confiscated, when boarding an aircraft.

A Captain?

Well, why not? My Captains do not easily attain that rank, but Donald Brown was a great character none the less, and he is one who should not be forgotten. I, and many of my contemporaries remember him well, and with fondness but I am certain that none of us have any idea who the Town Provost, or any other local celebrity of that time, was.

More schooldays

It would not do to leave school and to embark upon serious life without mentioning some of the long-suffering teachers who tried to instil some degree of learning into our largely unresponsive minds.

In Mr. Banks, 'Kublai Khan' to us all, I recognise - far too late - a man who had a great love for the English language and who must have despaired of us ever grasping its rudiments. He was a superlative teacher and I owe him a great deal. Why did I not pay more heed to his teaching and to his great love of the classics?

I recall the last time I spoke to him, some years after I left school. My mother had been working on a crossword puzzle and was stuck with one clue that referred to the 'Fourth Estate'. I called Mr Banks on the telephone and after introducing myself (to my delight, he did remember me!) I asked him about the 'Fourth Estate'.

In that never-to-be-forgotten schoolmaster's voice he announced, "Oh yes, boy. That is a reference to the Press. The Four Estates are, in order, the Lords Spiritual, the Lords Temporal, the Commons and the Press. You should have known that!" He did not, as I suppose he could have, introduce the words I had heard him utter so often – not always to me – "Oh boy, what a fool you are!"

"Big Bob" Graham instilled in us a degree of knowledge of the French language, with a kind word to boys who struggled with English. He was undoubtedly ahead of his time in that he achieved success by showing kindness toward, tolerance of, and concern for his pupils. Others less gifted attempted, unsuccessfully, to bully knowledge into our skulls - Big Bob coaxed it in. In short, he treated us as human beings! I left Big Bob's class nearly sixty years ago, but thanks to his teaching skills I can still make myself understood to French people in their own language. Indeed, on a holiday on the French canal with my wife and 'Dod' (more of him later) both of whom had been duxes of their respective schools, and who had taken French, both instantly called upon me for help, when approached by anyone who addressed them in French. I never aspired to being dux, but I had a superb French teacher!

I now express to Mr. Banks and Mr. Graham the debt of gratitude I owe them, which should have been acknowledged while they were alive. I deeply regret this thoughtless omission of mine. What wonderful men they were! The grounding they gave me in their various subjects will never leave me.

While on the subject of languages, it may be of interest to comment on local dialect. Strangers to Campbeltown are almost certainly bemused when they hear the word 'wild' being used in place of 'very', but pronounced 'wile'. For example, it would not raise any eyebrows in the town if someone referred to a dog saying; "that's a wile tame dog," or, "it's a wile nice day!" The word 'hoor' is local dialect for whore, of course but if, for example, one was to refer to a young lady as being a "hoora nice lassie", that would be considered as being a great compliment to her! Although I would translate it as being 'whore of a', somehow it – in Campbeltown - means, once again, 'very'.

These words, and many others like them, were the topic of conversation one day when my cousin Robert and I visited the late Ian Stewart in his home. His wife, Ailsa, who is English by birth, volunteered the following tale. "When I became pregnant for the first time," she said, "Ian employed a local lady to help out with the chores in the house. We had coffee in the morning of the first day and when we had finished this lady said, 'Ah'll jeest syne oot they cups an' lee them in the ja'box'. I hadn't a clue what she meant, wondering why and how she was going to 'sign' the cups. It wasn't until Ian came home and I questioned him that I discovered that 'syne' meant 'rinse, and that the 'ja'box' was the 'jawbox' or kitchen sink!" The lady was simply going to rinse the cups out and leave them in the kitchen sink.

Ian then volunteered one tale that I still think of as being a beauty! A Campbeltown born man who had served for a long time in the Indian Army, on his retirement as a colonel bought a large house in Dalintober. His wife, who had been used to having servants in India, employed a local lady to help out in the house but made the mistake of thinking that she could order this lady around as she had done with her previous help, in India. The obvious result was that no-one remained in her employ for very long. One day a message boy arrived with the day's grocery order and went, as usual, to the back door where he rang the bell. As the lady of the house had – once again – lost her daily help and was alone in the house, she opened the door herself. The young lad, not recognising her, assumed that she was the new help and said: "Hello, you must be new here. You'll no' last very long either – she's a hoora hard wumman to get on wi' so naebuddy'll stay wi' her!"

Back to the tale! No mention of the Campbeltown Grammar School would be complete however without a word about "Wee Mickey", as we knew Malcolm G. MacCallum, the music teacher.

He was, as his nickname might convey, a small man with a florid complexion who sported a small bristling moustache.

His temper was legendary, and I will never forget his tantrums toward us when I was taking part in the usual end of term School concert - my last - in the now demolished Lochend Church. I was in the 'changed voice choir' - all boys of course - and at our last rehearsal held in Lochend Church on the morning of the concert, he was so incensed at our efforts that he literally screamed with temper, and swore that we would not be allowed to sing that night.

We were petrified, certain that he would carry out this threat, but the night came and we, who had the last spot in the programme, were of course allowed to perform. We sang "Star of the County Down", "Land of Hope and Glory", and "Jerusalem". We sang our hearts out, and the audience would not let us off the stage until we had given two encores of "Jerusalem".

I will never forget Wee Mickey standing there facing us with tears streaming down his cheeks, at the end.

He had dragged us to heights unknown.

His success with the Campbeltown Gaelic Choir has not, unfortunately, been matched since he retired, and he is no longer with us.

Incidentally, I only recently discovered that the stained glass windows which once adorned the Lochend Church, where Wee Mickey was organist for so many years are now safely and beautifully installed in St. John's Presbyterian Church in Willis Street, Wellington, New Zealand. My wife and I visited this church some years ago and I sat quietly gazing at them for a long time. What lovely memories they brought back to me.

Teachers promoted to captains?

Without any doubt!

The final major happening which I recall prior to leaving school concerned Neil Campbell, the gentle man who tried against all the odds to teach me and some of my contemporaries, including Cecil Finn, to play the bagpipes.

Neilly Campbell also lived in Dalintober. He was a master painter, a tallish, very placid man with an inclination to stoop. Not content with painting and papering houses, his oil paintings of Kintyre scenes are well known locally, and are quite collectable.

I may well be the only person who ever heard him swear.

Joe Brown, Tommy Ralston, Cecil Finn, Hamish Wareham, ca. 1950

Joe Brown, Tommy and Ina Ralston, Hamish Wareham, May 2010

The bag on Cecil Finn's pipes had rotted beyond redemption so some of his deceased father's workmates fashioned a new bag - which was more innovative than successful - by vulcanising together the ends of a section of an inner tube from the wheel of a lorry, cut roughly to size and holed to accept the drones, chanter, and mouthpiece.

This contrivance had several faults.

One, it was too big for the tartan cover. Two, it was a lurid pinkish colour and three, it was almost impossible to blow. Indeed Cecil was the only one who was able to keep the pipes up, and then only for a very limited time. He had, however, one fault; he did not appear to be able to differentiate between the beat and the off-beat.

There came the day when Neilly, as he was affectionately known, entered us in the junior competition for piping, at Kintyre Park in Campbeltown. I had fallen and had cut my wrist quite badly just a day or two before the event, and couldn't take part but I joined Cecil and Neilly on the day, and our demoralisation was completed by the unkind comments of our contemporaries on seeing us in our kilts – skirts they called them – borrowed from who knows where for the day.

Neilly puffed nervously on his beloved pipeful of baccy as he tuned Cecil's drones to the best of his ability and coached him on the ritual of 'placating the judges', which had to be undergone before being allowed to play.

The moment arrived. Cecil marched with apparent boldness to where the three ancient judges sat - seemingly asleep - halted in front of them and, upon seeing a possible movement from one of them, saluted smartly.

This salute was belatedly acknowledged in a desultory hand wave by the senior judge, who then demanded to be apprised of Cecil's name.

This given - and received with only a derisory snort - Cecil had then to tell them which tune he would play. This information was duly noted by the only judge who gave any indication of being alive but his scornful reaction gave the impression that such a tune was well beyond the capabilities of this candidate who had dared to approach him, and a casual wave dismissed the competitor who was by now in a state of pure terror.

Cecil saluted again, turned, and marched to where he would begin his offering, leaving the judges apparently asleep again.

This scene of somnolence was destroyed when one of the judges, perhaps he was the one currently on watch, suddenly sat bolt upright and abruptly shook the other two into awareness of the sight which was now unfolding before their bleary eyes.

As Cecil blew into the bag which had hitherto been hidden by being stuffed into the too-small tartan cover, there started to appear from its hiding place this lurid, decidedly phallic tube!

This appalling sight was obviously beyond the comprehension of the combined experience of the poor men who were now apparently in the first stages of shock, and who were seemingly unable to give the command to start. Our piper, whose endurance, remember, was somewhat limited, watched them intently.

Time the great healer did its work; the signal to begin was given, and Cecil started at last.

On the off-beat!

Poor Neilly's pipe almost caught fire, and that was when I heard him swear, but all was not lost - Cecil was one of the prize-winners.

Neil Campbell is another gentle Captain whose presence around the fireplace of Angus's dreams would indeed be a delight, and whose playing would give much pleasure to many.

⚓

Cecil and I could hardly wait to join the bands of those we were desperate to emulate, the young fishermen who flaunted their worldly knowledge before our envious eyes. They had seen places we had only dreamt about; Castlebay, Lochboisdale, Stornoway,

Mallaig, Peel, Whitby. Their tales of these far-flung ports, we listened to with awe.

I remember while still a schoolboy, sitting with two others of like mind in a café in Campbeltown one evening, when to our astonishment we were joined by a young fisherman whose attraction for the ladies was the envy of many, especially we pubescent lads whose combined experience of the fair sex totalled absolutely nil, despite our bravado. This brave fellow, whom we will call 'Bill', was well aware of his reputation with the lasses, and he flaunted it. He exuded confidence that we could only aspire to. On this evening 'Bill' actually deigned to sit down with us, youngsters who were usually ignored and deemed to be low life and unworthy of any sort of recognition by such as him, and started to talk.

"What is it like in the North (at the Minch herring fishing)?" we asked him.

"Well," he replied, "it's hard work but it can be great fun too. We had a good shot of herring in Oban the week before last. Aye, we got a good price, too. That was on the Friday, and it was late when we finished discharging so we didn't go back out that night. I went to a dance in the Corran Halls where I met a girl. God, but she was beautiful!" He then launched into a detailed physical description of this young lady's physical attributes, which had us all transfixed and drooling in anticipation of things which we felt were yet to come. We had hit the big time!

"After the dance I walked with her to the farm," he said. "This was her home, and we went into the barn, a cosy place filled with hay. There was a full moon that night and the spot where we lay on the hay was fitfully lit by moonbeams coming through a window high on the wall. We kissed passionately".

A long pause followed, and then he slowly described to us how he had caressed her lovingly, and had removed all of her clothes, silken piece by silken piece, until her beautiful body lay in his arms clad only in the soft moonlight. We dwelt on his every word, drooling at the mouth.

“She lay there, her eyes wild and wanting,” he continued, “then she arched her nubile body against me”.

“‘Hurt me Bill!’ she cried desperately, her nails clawing my back”.

By this time he had us totally engrossed and we were as desperate as she was alleged to have been, for the consummation of this tale.

‘Bill’ waited. He waited for what seemed to be an age, sipping reflectively at his tea.

“What did you do?” someone eventually called in a strangled voice.

“What did I do?” concluded ‘Bill’ as he stood up and drank the last of his tea. “What do you think I’d do? She wanted me to hurt her, so I gave her a right good slap on the face!”

We never seem to learn.

As young boys we were desperate to experience anything connected with the sea, an obsession that must have caused our parents much worry on occasion. When a kindly old gentleman named James O’Hara bought several dinghies which had small petrol driven engines, to hire out to holidaymakers, we pounced on this opportunity to get our hands on any kind of boat by offering our ‘services’ as boat minders and general helpers, free of charge. Our persistence bore fruit in that we got a great deal of pleasure when our duties involved moving the dinghies around the harbour for any reason. This gave us a lot of experience of boat handling at a very early age, though our fertile inventiveness in coming up with good reasons for having shifted the dinghies must have stretched his patience to the very limits.

Whenever two or three of us got the opportunity we would motor off down the Loch. One of us was perched forward with a rowlock, ‘chapping’ it on the dinghy’s rail.

“Stand by!” he would roar when he saw – in his imagination – a spot of herring in the phosphorescent burning below the boat (this in broad daylight!)

The ‘skipper’ at that moment was required to turn the dinghy and surround the place where the imaginary herring had been seen. The third boy had at regular intervals to throw overboard the oars and anything else that would float. These were to mark the positions of the five buoys that were on a ring net.

Many times we filled the fleet with the imaginary fruits of these adventures!

The apprenticeship

The long-awaited day arrived. I left school in December 1950.

It was time to start work.

Being a fisherman then was much more of a pleasure than it is now. Financial and political pressures have placed such unbearable demands upon the men pursuing this career, that it is now a very highly stressful and therefore, in my opinion, life-limiting occupation. The political ineptitude of successive leaders has ensured that the future, if indeed there is a future in the fishing industry, is not a rosy one.

There was, for example, more time for leisure and more time 'for a yarn'. One of the many songs I learned as a youth was the fisherman's alphabet; this was often sung when relaxing while lying at anchor somewhere. The name of the composer is long lost. As I recall it, and with much – anonymous - help from the 'Kintyre Forum' web site, this is how it went.

Now A's for the anchor that hangs on the bow,
And B's for the boy that gets in a row.
C's for the cable, a good friend and true,
And D's for the deck that shelters our crew.

Chorus: So merry, so merry, so merry are we,
For we are the boys of the Clyde fishery.
Hard Eastward, hard Westward, you're right through our net,
You're the stupidest fisherman I've ever met!

Now E's for the engine that goes very well,
And F's for the forecastle where we do dwell
G's for the grub that we all like to eat,
And H is for herring, they cannot be beat

Chorus.

Now I's for ideas, they're not very plain,
And J's for the jumper that keeps out the rain,
K's for the kettle we use every day
L is for loaves that we all stow away

Chorus.

Now M is for meshings we all like to see.
N is for nets that we cast out to sea
O is for the oil that we burn or we waste
P's for the pump that we oft grab in haste.

Chorus.

Q is for the quarter that our gear run out o'er
R is reef points, not used as in yore
S is for sail, it's not used much of late
T's for the tiller that steers our boat straight.

Chorus

U is for urchins we take out for a treat,
And V is for vomit they spew at our feet
W is for winch, for which we all pine
And X, Y and Z I just can't get to rhyme!

In the time of my 'apprenticeship' life was quieter and men were able to take the time to lavish upon their boats the attention that they deserved.

These boats were beautiful in their own right. The swooping curves of their lines were a joy to behold, and the varnished wooden hulls reflected the care taken, by the fishermen themselves, to keep them looking as they did. These boats were hunters – and they looked the part.

Mistakes were occasionally made, of course, in the care lavished on them. These men were fishermen first; being painters came further down their list of priorities! One unforgettable source of joy came about when a boat's crew diligently scraped off the boat's registration letters and number. Stencils of the boat's number and of the port of registry, C.N., were cut out of stiff cardboard. The skipper leant over the bows and stern of the boat in turn, starting with the port side and pinned the stencils in place before chalking around them. One of the crew, a young lad, was sent down on to the beach to ensure that they looked to be in the correct place. He did this but when the skipper moved around to the starboard side, the lad had, I presume, lost interest in the proceedings so he called, "Aye, that's fine," when the skipper asked if they were in place properly.

Now if you look at a boat's port side, the 'C' of CN is nearest the bow whereas on the starboard side, this letter is furthest from the bow – you always read from left to right. The youngster was apparently quite happy to see the 'C' nearest the bow on the starboard side, as it had been on the port side!

The letters were painted in before the mistake was realised, and for ever after this poor skipper boasted the nickname "NC"!

The crew of another boat erased the waterline, but had the foresight to first of all mark the top side of it in heavy pencil. The waterline had to be painted in place before either the varnish or the anti-fouling paint was applied.

Two men took on this task. One started aft on the starboard side, the other forward on the port side. One of the painters used the pencil mark as a base line. Unfortunately, the other used it as a top mark so when they met …!

The 'ringers' as the boats were called, took their name from the ring-net which they were designed to carry. This net, of which more later, was first used in Scotland, specifically in Loch Fyne, in a very primitive form in the early 1800's when several drift nets might be laced together to form a longer net that could be –

and was – used to trap shoals of herring in bays on Loch Fyne , although versions of it were almost certainly used in Scandinavian countries well before that time. Indeed, some people would have it that it was a ring net that was in use on the Sea of Tiberias when our Lord told some of His disciples to cast their net on the right side of their ship – and they got a big shot!

Brailing a shot of herring aboard *Watchful* BA124

The boats were built of wood - usually larch, Oregon or pitch pine planking, on oak frames. The length varied between forty-eight and fifty-eight feet, with a beam the classic "one third of the length", and their draught was in the region of six feet when light.

They were powered by diesel engines varying in size between the 66 horse-power of the old favourite Kelvin K3 model and latterly, the then unbelievable 152 "horses" of the Gardner 8L3. A far cry from the three and four hundred horse power required by similar sized boats to tow the gear they now use.

The configuration was always the same. Accommodation for the crew of six was forward, the hold amidships, and the engine room aft. When I started my time, the wheelhouse, which by today's standard was small and basic, contained only a steering wheel, a compass and controls for the engine. It was situated above the engine room, the back of it being about ten feet from the stern. Incidentally, when coming on watch whilst the boat was on a passage the first thing one did was to feel for the spoke of the wheel that was warm to the touch. This was because the man you were relieving would, during the three hours or so of his watch, have settled on what position the wheel was to be held in order to compensate for the effect of wind and wave on the desired course. No automatic pilots then!

These boats were designed purely for the pursuit of that king of fish, the herring, and again, when I started, were used almost exclusively for that purpose. The ring-net was so called simply because it was shot in a circle, or ring, around a shoal of herring.

They would carry, dependent on size, from one hundred to well over two hundred crans of herring. A cran is a liquid measure, but would weigh approximately twenty eight stones or 180 kilos, and contain on average around nine hundred fish.

The bigger boats would therefore carry well over 30 tonnes of herring when loaded. The purse-seiners, when they came on the scene, often arrived in port with well in excess of 100 tonnes and they were tiny in comparison with the super purser/trawlers in use now.

The cran measure was used to quantify the catch on all of the fishing grounds, with the exception of the Clyde. There the measure of the basket - which was simply one quarter of a cran - took over. A catch of 400 baskets in the Clyde area was described as "400 baskets" but anywhere else that we fished the same amount would be described as "100 crans".

I do not know why this was: perhaps someone somewhere can tell me!

These ancient standards have both now been superseded by the unimaginatively named 'unit', which is a metric measure of one hundred kilos, foisted upon the industry by the faceless bureaucrats of the ubiquitous E.E.C.

The boats were almost without exception, varnished, and every spring when they were scraped to the bare wood, they were sanded and then re-varnished, five coats being quite commonplace. There was great rivalry to see what crew by what device could make their boat the best looking one in the fleet!

This 'spring-cleaning', was done by the crew of the boat at a time when the fishing was naturally quiet, and although they were sometimes – but not always – able to claim unemployment benefit, this essential work was undertaken with the knowledge that they would not be paid for it in any way by the owner. Try that now!

As the use of a ring-net required two boats, loose partnerships were formed by skippers of similar personalities. Your partner boat was called your neighbour. The nets which each of these boats carried were in the region of three hundred metres long and about forty-five metres deep. They were "shot" around a shoal of herring in a semi-circle. Corks were attached at regular intervals to the 'back rope' of the net for flotation and were augmented by either three or five regularly spaced buoys of around two feet in diameter. These buoys, pronounced 'bows', were made of tarred canvas that was invariably painted white for visibility when I started fishing, but were latterly made of plastic. The bottom of the net, or 'sole rope' was weighted with the lead rings through which the sole rope was threaded.

When shooting the net one man was positioned aft where he not only saw the net safely over the stern, but called out the progress of the shooting action for the benefit of the skipper who was of course fully involved in other matters. This time honoured chant seldom varied. "First bow, second (or shoulder) bow, centre bow, second last (or second shoulder) bow, last bow, ease her" - (this if he thought the boat was moving too quickly)". The call, "Net's away!" concluded this ritual as the last of the net disappeared overboard.

The neighbour boat picked up the end of the net which had been dropped by the shooting boat, and after a short tow (perhaps only a minute or so) to get the net properly into shape, the two boats turned towards one another. The circle was completed when the neighbour boat's crew jumped aboard the shooting boat taking with them their end of the net, and a towing rope. While the two crews hauled the net on the port side, the neighbour boat pulled gently on the tow rope which was attached amidships on the starboard side of the shooting boat. This was done in order to keep her vulnerable propeller and rudder clear of the net.

Not long ago I visited Thailand and on a remote island there I found some fishermen on a sandy beach doing repair work on what was without doubt a small version of a ring net. When - with the help of our guide as translator - I questioned them on how they worked it, I was puzzled when it became apparent that there was only one boat involved in its use. Further questioning revealed that they - instead of pulling the net onto one side of the boat, half forward and half aft as was done here - used each shoulder of the boat. One half was hauled on to the port side, and the other on to the starboard side. The boat was able to go astern slowly, thus keeping the potentially snagging propeller and rudder well clear of the net. Why did we not think of that?

It is probably worth recording the duties of the engineer on these boats.

He was not required by law to be technically qualified, but was usually interested and thus, to a degree, gifted in things mechanical. This extra work, which involved doing running repairs on a day to day basis and keeping the engine and its environs clean, was not financially rewarded in any way. He was paid the same as the other deckhands. His only bonus – if it can be called that – was that he usually remained aboard his own boat with his skipper when his neighbour shot. They towed the boat whose net was in the water while, of course, his shipmates hauled the net.

There was a time, long ago of course, whilst the mechanisation of the boats was in its infancy when technical knowledge of engines was difficult to come by. This period was marked by one or two amusing incidents.

On one occasion the petrol/paraffin engine on one of the boats was not running properly and as the crew were unable to correct the fault, the services of one of the few available 'experts' was called upon.

He went down into the engine room and, after due deliberation, recognised that the air to fuel mixture was not correct, and that therefore the carburettor needed adjustment. The diagnosis made, he told the skipper that the engine was not getting enough air.

The relieved skipper rounded on the anxious crew who had all gathered around the hatch leading into the engine room, and roared, "Hear that boys? Stan' back an' gi'e her air!"

The first engines were called 'go ahead' engines for the simple reason that there was no gearbox, and therefore as soon as the engine was started up the boat drove ahead. Reverse gear was a luxury still to come, and it became a matter of great pride if not of honour, that this engine be stopped at exactly the correct time when entering a harbour so that the boat coasted gently to a halt at her designated berth. To this end, the engineer was positioned in the engine room hatch waiting for the order "Stop her!"

One skipper, taking his boat into Campbeltown harbour and having given the order to stop the engine, looked at the pier – which was crowded with onlookers – and suddenly became aware that he had left it too late, that she was carrying far too much way (was going too fast) and would not stop in time to avoid damage.

Panic took over from reason.

"Stop her!" he cried in desperation.

"She's stopped!" squealed the equally horrified engineer, who was also aware of the skipper's mistake.

“Well, stop her more!” was the last order from the skipper before bedlam was let loose!

Returning to the ringers, which I was describing, the engineer, because of his dirtier job, suffered more than the rest of us from the lack of personal cleaning facilities. My late uncle Crawford, a very meticulous man, was engineer on my father’s boat and he devised a method of cleaning oily boiler suits, part of which process involved towing them behind the boat when under way. One day, when entering Lochboisdale after a trip across the Minch, he hauled in the rope to find that his boiler suit was no longer there. He was not amused to hear a wag suggest that a basking shark had taken it!

There were no wash basins on the vast majority of the boats, except for the enamel basin in which we washed to the best of our abilities. Baths? Well, we had a bath before we left, and this had to do us until we got back home – an interval of four or five weeks when fishing in the North! I asked ‘Dodie Icey’ (of whom more later) how they fared on the drifters who spent as much as three months away from home when fishing from Yarmouth.

“Weel,” he mused. “We wis affa parteeclar aboot that. Ye aye hid a bath afore ye left tae ging Sooth. Aye. An then ye hid anither een faniver ye got hame again!”

On a more delicate subject, although the newer ringers had the luxury of marine toilets, on the older boats this most basic of facilities was limited to a metal five-gallon drum. This was made usable by having the top cut off and the resulting ragged edge covered by a piece of hose which was split lengthways and lashed about three-quarters of the way around the drum. Toilet paper? Copies of newspapers were jealously guarded whenever we were fishing in areas where they were difficult to come by!

I hear that prisoners and ex-prisoners are being awarded quite large sums of money in compensation for their having to 'slop out' whilst in jail. I think that is a brilliant idea; can I claim for having to do the same thing while I was aboard the *Golden Fleece*? Any good lawyers out there? You can have half of whatever you get for me!

These then were the boats in which we hunted.

I am at a loss to explain to anyone the mystique of the pursuit of herring. That there is some sort of mystique is beyond doubt.

As evidence of this, I offer the fact that there are literally dozens of poems and songs about the herring. I know of none praising the cod, haddock, whiting, or prawn!

The pursuit of herring with a ring net in these days required that the men were much closer to nature than is the case now in the days of computers and sonar sets. An East Coast fisherman told me very recently that he remembered as a young man lying one fine spring afternoon on the pier at Pooltiel on Skye, in the company of an old fisherman, gazing down into the sea. "D'ye see anythin' odd aboot this pier?" asked the old chap, "somethin' that probably means the herrin' fishing'll be late this year?" My informant admitted that he couldn't see what had come to the notice of the old man, so he was told that he should have spotted the absence of barnacles on the wooden legs of the pier. Their absence meant that the seasons were running late, to the observant eye.

In the time of which I write, before the invention of echo-sounders or sonars, all of the senses bar one - that of taste - were used. Touch was used to feel the herring which were struck by the fine wire that was trailed behind the slow moving boat with a heavy lead weight attached. Herring could be heard when they jumped clear of the water - perhaps in an attempt at evading a predator, or when they indulged in the frenzy of 'playing', which unexplained behaviour meant that on a quiet night the rushing sound made by a large shoal as they splashed madly on the surface, could be heard literally miles away.

Sight was used in a great many ways to track the herring. Looking for a gannet 'striking' or diving on a shoal, or merely 'looking well', or "two ply" – the lovely description used when a gannet was seen peering intently downward from a high hovering attitude. We used to chase the poor gannets which were seen sitting heavy in the water, as they would then, in a panic, spew up the contents of their stomachs in order to lighten themselves enough for flight, thus revealing what they had been feeding on.

"Sailfish" or "Muldoans" as we called the basking sharks then, fed on the same plankton as herring, so whenever we saw them - and they were relatively common in those days - we cruised among them hoping that there was a shoal of herring there also.

When Tarbert fishermen spoke of sailfish, they called it a 'sholter'. That is my version of the phonetic spelling of a word that is, in fact, derived from the Gaelic word 'seol', meaning 'sail'; therefore sholter, or seolter simply means 'sailor'.

Muldoans could cause a lot of damage to the nets if accidentally caught, so a necessary piece of equipment was a can of diesel fuel kept ready for instant use when we thought that they were around. When shooting the net in a semi-circle, the diesel was poured sparingly into the water in the hope that the beasts would dive clear of the foul-tasting stuff, and so clear of the net also.

Seeing herring gulls sitting contentedly on the water in the evening, was a sight interpreted as a sign that herring lay deep below them. We watched intently for a 'change in the water' at night in the summer months, a change brought about by the movement of fish causing a revealing phosphorescent glow. This was usually referred to as "seeing them in the burning", or "seeing them in the water".

Finally, yes, they could be smelt! A very distinctive raw smell in a loch meant that there was a heavy concentration of fish there.

My late uncle Henry Martin was taped by my cousin Angus, relating the following tale.

Henry Martin

One lovely summer evening they were lying alongside 'Jimmy the May', whom they were then neighbouring, in Corrodale Bay on the east side of Uist discussing what their next move should be. "There's naethin' here," cried Jimmy, "Whaur d'ye think we should go?"

Henry's skipper Willie MacIntyre, better known as "Screich" , called forward to where Henry sat watching a gannet low in against the cliff face, "Ye're afa' quiet up there Mertin, whoot d'ye think we should dae?"

Henry stated that in his opinion, anyone who left here was going away clear of herring, because, he said, he could get the "Raa' smell o' herrin' in the air". There was much scoffing about this, Jimmy the May saying, "Well, if ye can smell herrin', that's a new yin on me. I've heard many's the thing, but I never heard anybody sayin' they could smell them!"

"So we waited", said Henry, "an' they started jumpin' in the darknin', an' we shot an' got a good ring, jeest as close tae the rocks as we could get. Jimmy went haywire. 'There's a man can smell them!' - he says".

"Well a funny thing. We cam' back there the next day, an' it so happened the fishin' was slack, but there wis a fleet there, boats ringin'. Ye know that smeltins ye get in the watter, an' the smell o' the oily smeltins? Well, the place wis polluted. Jimmy cam' alongside an' he says, 'Mertin, there's nae doubt,' he says, 'the smellin' business is aa right - are ye smellin' that?'"

"Says I – 'That's gleshins (young saithe) ye're smellin', that's no' herrin'.'"

"Now that wis a chancer ye see. I thought the smell wis aafa' strong right enough. Well the Nobles an' the *Silver Grey* shot an' got a hunner baskets o' gleshins. That killed him!"

"Years later", he continued, "I mind o' bein' in the fo'c'sle o' another Ayrshire boat wan day when the talk wis o' herrin' as usual, an' a young lad pipes up, 'I heard tell o' a Campbeltoon man that could smell herrin' miles away. Is that true?' - but I jeest held ma peace an said nothin."

Henry had a very distinctive deep bass voice, very easy to listen to, and hearing a recording of him reminded me that he had what I would describe as the last Dalintober accent - as opposed to Campbeltown, just half a mile away - that I ever recall hearing.

'Nothing', in his accent came across as 'nawthin', a Campbeltown accent would say 'naethin'. 'Came' was pronounced 'cam' - for example, "He cam fae Tarbert". A Campbeltown accent made it sound more like 'kim'. He pronounced 'aboard' as 'aboord'. He also used 'fornenst' instead of 'in front of'. For example - "Ah was stannin fornenst the winch". A wonderful old man, with a wonderful memory. Why did I not think to tape some of the tales I heard him tell?

Henry was an extremely independent man, one who would not accept anything that he thought was offered in the name of charity. I remember once, some years after his wife had died, calling on him with a gift of kippers that I had taken from Mallaig. I was really taken aback when he refused them. The next time I called I again took some kippers and, instead of offering them to him I showed them to him and asked him if he could guess where the herring had been caught. He felt them, sniffed at them and then offered the opinion that they were very like the summer herring that he used to catch at Canna. Now I didn't know where they had been caught, but I expressed amazement at his having guessed correctly, telling him that they had been swimming round the Stack at Canna just three days before. I left them with him, and he later told me how much he had enjoyed them. I reckon that this deception of an old man was forgiveable and well worth while!

Another maternal uncle, Dunky, told me a true story which is well worth repeating even if it is a wee bit out of place here. I will alter the names but not the content.

He had, Dunky told me, been in school with "S--", a local worthy who was only sober, in my opinion, when he had no money for drink. As he was not a very savoury character at all, I was surprised to hear my uncle confess that he had always had a soft spot for him. This surprise was lessened when he went on to explain to me that he had been schoolmates with "S--", and had always felt that given half a chance, the poor man would not have ended up in the gutter. Dunky continued the tale by telling me that he had never passed this fellow by, but had always given him the time of day, although he was more often drunk than sober and therefore probably didn't recognise Dunky, his old school pal.

One day he met the reprobate, who told him a story which he promptly dismissed as pure fantasy. "S--" had been on his way back to the hovel he called home, and was by his own admission, drunk. His path took him past a certain establishment from which emanated hymn singing. Dunky quoted him as saying - "Ah felt somethin' pullin' me in tae this place, so in ah went, an' sat doon at the back o' the Hall beside a nice young couple. This pair looked at me, an' shifted aweh clear o' me wi' their noses in the air. Ah didna' wait, but jeest went aweh hame."

"The next day," he continued, "'B' (a prominent local business man who worshipped regularly in this hall) cam' up tae my hoose, wi' his big car an' he asks me whit wey ah didna' stay in the meetin', an' he offers tae come for me an' tak' me tae the next meetin' in his car."

"No, says I, whoot ah wis lookin' for wisna' there. Ah'm no' gaan wi' ye."

Shortly after that, he told Dunky, he had been passing the Salvation Army Citadel in the centre of the town, in his cups again, and had been drawn into the hall by the singing he heard coming out of it. This time, remembering his reception in the last place, he had gone in very reluctantly and had stood in the passageway at the back of the hall.

"There was a man wi' a uniform on, he was the Captain o' this Army, an' he was singin' doon at the front o' the hall, an' dae ye know this, Dunky, he cam' up tae me, pit his airm roon me - drunk an' dirty as ah was - an' took me right doon tae the front wi' him. They gave me tea an' sandwiches, an' took me hame that night in a car. Ah'll nivir touch drink again as lang as ah leeve, Dunky, that's it!"

"Now I had heard him say a thousand times that he was feenished wi' the drink, an' this was only a year or two ago when he wis an old man," Dunky told me. "But d'ye know this, fae that day tae the day he died, jeest last year, he wis a reformed character. There wis nivir a night went past but wan o' they good folk cam' up tae see him if he wisna' able tae go tae the meetin', an' he nivir pit a fit wrang!"

Back to the tale.

One Campbeltown skipper, more noted for the noise he made than for his prowess in catching herring, made his reputation almost immortal by calling to his crew from his place in the wheelhouse, "Look and listen with all the eyes and ears God gave you boys, for my home's in a deplorable condition!"

Another skipper joined him in the ranks of the 'oft quoted', whilst they were fishing at the Brown Head, on the south-west coast of

Arran. It was a cold, raw night, and there were no herring to be seen in fact, none of the fleet had shot a net when two young lads, who would much rather have been at the dance that was taking place at that time in Campbeltown commented, in rather a loud voice, that there was a big ring round the moon (this was a sure sign of bad weather to come). When this brought no response from the skipper the youngster said again, in an even louder voice, "Aye, there's a big ring roon the moon the night - there's a lot o' win' tae come." The skipper stuck his head out of the wheelhouse window and answered, "There'll be a big ring roon your fuckin' eye, if ye don't shut up!"

These were typical of the feelings of many of the men who were at the job then. There was a feeling - totally unjustified in fact but understandable none the less - that we were hunters, and as such were superior to those who used drift nets to catch the same species we sought but who, in our completely erroneous and biased opinion, simply shot nets and hoped for the best!

The men themselves were, in the days of which I write, a quieter, gentler breed, and I am sure that they had much more concern for their fellow-fisherman than seems to be the case now.

I believe that the reason that there was so much more companionship between them stemmed in part, at least, from the fact that there was a lot more time spent lying alongside one another. It was not possible to use the ring net in the bad weather in which drifters, seine-netters or trawlers could work. In the bad weather that often prevailed in the winter fishing in the North, boats shared anchorages or lay at piers in remote locations. There they sought out their fellows in order to swap reading materials, to play cards and to exchange the latest gossip.

That they were not angels however is borne out by the oft-repeated tale of the disappearing petrol, which phenomenon occurred in Campbeltown many years ago.

In the early days of engines, the fuel used was paraffin, but a bottle of relatively expensive petrol was carried for the starting procedure. The bottle full of petrol had been stolen from a particular boat on several occasions.

This persistent pilfering had to be stopped, so cunning was put to good use and one morning the crew whose petrol was disappearing, stood at the head of the quay until all the boats except theirs and one other had left for the fishing grounds.

They then wandered quietly down the pier and silently watched the efforts of the other remaining boat's crew to start their engine. Eventually one of the men on the quay shouted down to them, "If ye dae get that engine started, yer fortune's made. That bottle's full o' watter!"

This then was the occupation into which, all starry eyed, I entered to become an apprentice to the men I thought to be a breed apart, the ring-net fishermen.

It was customary at this time that the youngest man on the crew was delegated cook.

Cooking was by far the most onerous job on the boat, and I now feel sure that the practice in place then was only accepted by the cooks because the hapless youth was unable to wield enough clout to alter it.

My first trip, on which of course I was cook, was in January1951, right after I left school at Christmas. We went to the North, which involved going round the Mull of Kintyre, up inside Islay, Jura and Mull, round Ardnamurchan then North again past the west coast of Skye. Through the Sound of Harris we went, to our final destination, West Loch Tarbert in Harris. This Loch is completely exposed to the west, and I was horrified at the enormous swell which rolled in on us from the North Atlantic. I had been seasick all the way, but this did not bring any sympathy from anyone, and I was expected to simply get on with my work. Anyway, the crew ate their dinner (such as it was) going through the Sound of

Harris, then I had to set to and wash the dishes, although I am quite certain that - after three days of vomiting with an empty stomach - if a doctor had seen me, he would have had me in a hospital. This washing up chore meant filling an enamel basin which I had put on the table, with hot soapy water. I had just started the dishes, when our neighbour, the Morag Bhan, shot, so I put the basin and dishes on the floor where they could fall no further, pulled on my oilskin or doaper as we called it then, and went on deck to help haul the net. Back aboard the *Golden Fleece* after this vain attempt to catch herring I took off my oilskin and went below to finish the washing up. I promptly stood on the basin, and flooded the forecastle floor with what was by now cold, greasy water. I don't mind confessing that I sat down and cried, and if I could have got on to a pier anywhere, that would have been the end of my fishing career.

Older hands agreed that the only sure cure for seasickness was for the sufferer to sit below a tree, for an hour or two. It took me some time to realise what they meant by that!

The cook, in addition to having to take his full share of all the everyday work, was expected not only to cook for six men - having had no formal training – but also to keep the living space clean and tidy. This living space, the fo'c'sle, measured about fifteen feet long by around twelve feet wide at the after end. It tapered to a point as one went forward toward the stem.

In this tiny area six men lived, ate, and slept for periods of up to five or six weeks, without respite. Personal belongings and some clothes were stored in suitcases kept in the individual bunks, except of course when the bunks were occupied. Then they found space on the platform, as we called the floor of the fo'c'sle. Making breakfast was not made easier by having to clamber around the suitcases while the men remained in bed.

The newer boats were much bigger, and some of them actually had what then seemed to me to be the ultimate in luxury, individual lockers for each man to store his personal gear in. They also had that most wonderful addition, a gas cooker!

My cooking efforts were accomplished - if that is the correct word - on a coal stove which had a very small oven to one side of the fire, with the additional back-up of a single-burner Primus cooker.

This paraffin-powered Primus was set in operation by heating the burner with highly inflammable methylated spirits, and on one occasion the cook on a boat that will remain nameless, was so dazed by lack of sleep that when he was wakened – after a couple of hours in his bunk - and was told to light the primus and put the kettle on, he poured the meths on to the hot coal stove. The resulting conflagration woke him up quickly!

Washing-up was done in one of a pair of different coloured enamel basins. The other one was for washing oneself in.

Of course, stores also had to be kept in this tiny living area, and when leaving home for the Minches - which adventure we called 'gaan tae the North' - the boat had to be provisioned bearing in mind that no food of any kind would be available in the more remote lochs, for periods of time which no one could predict. Woe betide the poor cook who ran out of any of the basics, no matter what the circumstances.

I myself spent Christmas Day of 1952 storm bound at anchor in a tiny bay near the entrance of Lochmaddy, in North Uist. There were three boats tied together, each with chains and anchors out. The wind was howling from the South West and, as was usual with this kind of gale, the rain was driving past us in horizontal torrents. I remember sitting alone in the cold draughty wheelhouse with the radio tuned to a B.B.C. outside broadcast which came from a children's hospital somewhere, listening to the sounds of merriment and wondering, as I looked at the scene of desolation all around, just why I hadn't listened to my Mother's pleas to get a job ashore!

At about eleven o'clock in the morning, we slipped our chain aboard one of the other boats and went to the pier at Lochmaddy. There was too much motion to lie alongside the exposed pier without doing damage to the boat, so with my uncle Crawford at the wheel, we put our stem to the pier, and my father jumped ashore. He soon returned, bearing three bottles of whisky, we again approached the pier, he jumped aboard, and we were off back to the anchorage again where he passed a bottle to each of the other boats.

The Christmas dinner on that day was a steak pie made with tinned steak and covered with pastry made by my father who was quite a good baker, having worked in a bake house for a short spell when he first left school. He thought up some pretext to get the rest of the crew on deck, swore me to secrecy and used his shaving brush to paint tinned milk on to his pastry to glaze it!

Tinned soup, steak (of the tinned variety) pie, potatoes and tinned peas, followed by tinned rice and tinned fruit was the feast that day, and was pronounced "great" by the unsuspecting crew. Then, before we ate, my father produced our bottle of whisky and emptied it into six cups (you didn't expect glasses aboard a ringer, did you?). He then looked long at me, pronounced, "One in the family is enough to be drinking," and scoffed mine along with his own!

Just a year or so later there was another incident with whisky. We were lying in Corrodale bay one evening, waiting for our neighbour to return from market. It was almost dark and I decided to pass the time by doing a spot of fishing. I tied an old rusty great line hook to a length of twine, baited it with a bit of herring, made fast a three-quarter pound lead as a sinker, about 6 feet above the hook and swung it around my head in order to get it clear of the boat. When I let go of the line, the flying hook hit my hand and set itself very firmly into the fleshy base of my thumb. The lead carried on and broke the line, leaving me with around 6 feet of twine hanging from the hook in my thumb!

My father examined my hand and decided that it would waste valuable fishing time if we went south to Lochboisdale and the doctor there decreed that I had to be taken to the hospital in Daliburgh, so he took me below into the forecastle, saying that he would take it out himself. He felt below the mattress in his bunk and retrieved a half bottle of whisky. Good, I thought, I'm going to get a pain-killing dram! He opened the bottle, took a goodly slug out of it, hauled the offending arm up, jammed it under his oxter and twisted the hook free. Then he poured a little of the whisky on to my badly bleeding hand to kill the germs, took another slug out of the bottle and disappeared up on deck, taking the half empty bottle with him. James McNaughton, one of the crew, came below at his bidding and put a crude bandage on to my hand. This 'bandage' consisted of a somewhat unclean handkerchief that was taped into place using black insulating tape. Did I get the night off because I had a sore hand? You must be joking!

Yes, I was cook on my father's boat, the *Golden Fleece*.

This carried no privileges. On the contrary, if there was a defect found in the engine room I was usually blamed though I was the cook, and might have been busy at the stove at the time the fault manifested itself!

The storage of water for drinking was a big problem. The tank, which was quite small, had to be filled at every opportunity from a tap on the pier, or from a convenient well or burn if there was none available on the pier. This was done by carrying the water to the boat, in a flask which held about five gallons. This again was the responsibility of the cook, and the task of carrying this heavy metal container was expected to be shared with the cook of your neighbour boat. Presumably this job was considered to be beneath the dignity of the crew, or perhaps they had done enough of this kind of work when they were cooks themselves! We also failed to recognise, or else ignored the possibility that there could be a dead sheep lying in the burn from which we sometimes had to fill our tank.

At some point in the *Golden Fleece*'s history, a length of hose had been lost into the water tank. This hose had been attached – not securely enough – to the filler which was not long enough to reach from the deck to the hole in the top of the tank. As a result, every time the boat rolled, the pieces of ancient, disintegrating rubber were stirred up in the tank. This did NOT help the taste of the tea! We tried tying a piece of cloth around the tap in an attempt at filtering out the worst of the gunge that contaminated the water, but this wasn't really successful. Why did we not all succumb to some of the diseases that seem so common nowadays? Health and safety?

The 'boy', as the cook was invariably called, was also charged with the job of knowing where his neighbour was at any time during the searching part of the fishing operation, and had to watch this boat very carefully.

This was a very important task because when the neighbour boat was about to shoot her net, the end of it - which was marked with a very small lit buoy called a 'winkie' - had to be picked up immediately. Your skipper therefore had to be informed at once.

The only indication of this imminent activity was the sudden appearance of a light on the fore end of his wheelhouse, a light which was not easily seen. This tiny light was called a winch-light.

The flashing of any bright lights was considered to frighten the herring so, if the dim winch-light was not spotted at once, and the shooting boat had to draw attention to her activities by using a searchlight flashed at her neighbour (before the days of radio) then the poor offending boy was in trouble once more!

This watch was relatively easy to keep in the lonely lochs of the North, but became very difficult in the crowded waters of the Manx or Whitby fisheries where many boats worked in congested areas. This difficulty led to the addition of very many and totally illegal versions of navigation lights, which were designed solely to make the task of recognition easier. I often wonder just what went through the minds of the skippers of coasters when they were confronted with the myriad of double stern lights and the vast variety of multi-coloured masthead lights of a fleet of ringers.

In the Isle of Man, and the Whitby fisheries, where we worked among boats from the East Coast, life was further complicated by the fact that the East Coast ringers worked their nets from the starboard side, whilst we used the port side. This meant that if a boat was seen by its lights to have its net in the water, one never knew which side of that boat to pass, in order to keep clear of the net which he had shot and was now hauling.

The boy was only relieved from his watching task when he had to make a cup of tea.

This tea was normally all that was required by the men during the short hours of darkness at the Isle of Man or Whitby fishing. On more than one occasion I used the pretext of making a cup - always acceptable to the crew - when I had lost our neighbour.

I would say to one of them - "Watch our neighbour, that's him there. I'm going to make a cup of tea". A vague pointing gesture in the general direction of the most crowded bunch of lights visible, and then I would scuttle below before he could ask any questions!

I love the tale, which I was assured was true, of the Greenock based skiff in the early days of ringing that was owned and crewed mainly by West Indians. They were, as was common then, short of cash and were forced to use old petrol cans – the square type that tapered to a point on the top that had a screw attached, instead of buoys. "If ye wur workin up a Loch ye could hear them shottin' miles aweh, wi' the racket o' they tins gaan oot ower the stern! Aye, an' their neebur hud lost them wan night when they wur shot so they roared tae another boat, 'Catch wir end, it's a petrol can!'"

Another task, though not solely that of the cook, was to question other boats' success or lack of it if they passed closely enough to be hailed. This was of course before the advent of V.H.F. radio, which refinement meant that news spread very quickly.

This querying is interesting when one looks back, because it all happened in a language used by Clyde fishermen, the nuances of which would not be understood nowadays. The interrogatory call, "Puckle the night?" would be answered according to the luck – or more often lack of it - of the crew questioned, and the replies ran thus.

"No, no!" meant nothing at all. "A wheen o' baskets," was less than a "Puckle o' baskets," which in turn - strange to relate - was somewhat less than "A wee wheen!" The reply "A wee puckle," was shouted in a rather smug tone, signifying that Lady Luck had smiled upon the questioned boat. Finally, "A good puckle" meant that the informant would soon be off on his way to market, as this was a well-fished boat.

There were also of course the definitive replies, e.g. "A hunner baskets".

On one occasion when a large fleet were meeting with very little success, the bored crew of the *Almanzora*, when questioned by the skipper as to what the replies were, changed them so that it appeared to the poor man that he was the only one who had caught no herring. Their arrival in Tarbert the following morning brought the realisation that this lack of success was by no means unique, and provoked another famous row!

John - 'John the Shore' - McConnachie, of Carradale, himself a very successful skipper of many years standing, found it impossible to hide his glee as he recalled the occasion when a pair of Carradale boats were fortunate enough to have caught more than a thousand baskets, early one evening. They almost immediately discharged this fine shot to a 'klondyker' - the fishermen's nickname for the trawler-sized boats that followed the fleets around, buying up the catches on the grounds, either boxing and icing, or salting the herring into barrels before taking them to market. When they finished discharging – the final tally was a thousand and fourteen baskets – they dropped their anchors for a few hours sleep before resuming fishing.

They had just got under way when they encountered a pair of Campbeltown boats in the dark hour before dawn and were hailed with the question, "Puckle the night?"

In all innocence the man forward on the boat so questioned replied, completely accurately, "A thousand and fourteen baskets."

John fairly chuckled as he recalled that there was nearly a riot that morning because the Campbeltown man was able - even in the dim morning light - to see that the boat being interrogated was not loaded. He also knew that no-one would ever answer with an exact figure like that and so was led to believe that the Carradale fellow was being sarcastic, which did not go down well!

Questioning the crew of a successful boat as to just what method had been used to find the herring which they had caught provided another example of a form of language which no longer exists.

The query, "How did ye feel them?" would on occasion be answered by what to the uninitiated would appear to be the sarcastic reply, "We saw them in the watter!" This simply meant that they had seen the herring in the 'burning'.

Seasickness - from which I suffered quite badly for what seemed to be a long time - was just one more cross which had to be borne, and was not accepted as an excuse for not cooking.

Payment of the crews was, and still is, strictly by results. No fish meant no money!

When fishing away from home, crews were often given 'subs' at the weekend, this being a cash advance geared to the skipper's estimate of the amount earned that week. From this, each man was expected to send money home to his wife, and of course to buy cigarettes etc. for the coming week. When fishing at home, the skipper 'divided' the net earnings every Saturday. There were at that time eight and a half shares in this computation in a boat which carried a crew of five men and a boy - one for each crew man, half for the boy, and one each for the boat, engine, and nets.

When I started fishing the boat's weekly expenses were almost always just under £100 per week. Indeed, there was an 'inquest' held if the £100 barrier was broken! This was made up of the fuel, food and the boat's insurance. I have no idea what the expenses of a similarly sized boat would be now, but the figure I have quoted would hardly cover the bread bill alone!

Crew wives spoke to one another about the earnings - or lack of them - so there were not many opportunities for the few men who were inclined to 'skin off' a few pounds for a dram or two, but one enterprising chap who had married a girl from outwith the fishing community, hit upon the idea of deducting a pound or two every few weeks, telling his unsuspecting spouse that it had been his turn to buy the baskets which were used to discharge the catches. These baskets were in reality, of course, paid for out of the gross earnings.

This scheme worked well until the man got a bit too greedy, and his wife complained to the skipper's wife about the obviously deteriorating quality of the baskets, which now seemed to have to be replaced almost every week. That was the end of that little scheme!

I was talking to Bob McCutcheon, an eminent skipper from Dunure just recently. He had been asking another acquaintance, not long before the conversation I am speaking about and had asked who had bought the Girvan boat, *Jeannie 2*. I was able to tell him that it had been bought by my wife's late father, Willie Sutherland and had been taken by him to Mallaig. Shortly after they arrived, 'Big Willie' had suffered a heart attack. He died four days after taking this boat to its new home. My wife has the deed of sale and I was able to tell Bob that the boat had cost Willie £2,750.

"Whit?" said Bob. "D'ye ken somethin', ye couldna fill her tanks wi diesel fur that noo!"

Practical jokes were commonplace then as now, and I well remember hearing of the cruel trick played upon an old chap whose eyesight was so bad that he had shipped on his latest boat as cook, feeling that he was no longer fit to be a deckhand. He had laid a fry of plaice on the wooden floor of the hold clear of the attentions of the hungry seagulls, until it was time to cook them. One of the crew, seeing this, later nailed the flat fish to the floor, reducing the poor old chap to the verge of tears when he later tried to lift them! I remember in my youth being sent to a joiner's yard in Campbeltown to get a 'long-stand', but was probably too late, as electric lights had taken over from the paraffin variety, to fall for the joke of being sent to the chandler's shop for a gallon of red paraffin for the port light, and a gallon of green for the starboard one.

Another trick which did not immediately end in laughter was played not too long ago in Eyemouth. Two brothers who owned seine netters and who fished very well, decided to treat their hard-worked crews and their wives to dinner when they stopped fishing for Christmas. This dinner became an annual event which was relished by all concerned. One day one of the crew had started celebrating in the afternoon, and went home somewhat the worse of wear to find his wife getting dressed for the big event. She was not at all amused by his lapse, and told him so, in no uncertain terms. Dressed, they set off for the hotel which hosted the dinner, where they were ushered into the cocktail bar to meet the rest of the guests. This poor man sat down, and promptly fell asleep. When they were called to go to the dining room, his wife - still incensed - would not allow anyone to waken him, so he was left where he sat, sound asleep. One of his crewmates however went back to the bar on some pretext or other, unzipped the fly on the poor chap's trousers, and therein placed the neck of a turkey, which he had purloined from the hotel kitchen, in such a position that it protruded from the fly.

The wife, having eaten her soup, then suffered a fit of remorse, and went to waken her spouse. She went into the bar just in time to see the hotel cat, which had climbed on to the lap of her sleeping husband, chewing on the turkey neck. The poor woman screamed and fainted, cutting her head on one of the tables as she fell!

These men worked hard, and played just as hard.

I well remember when I was about sixteen, having three Lancashire miners who were on holiday on the Isle of Man, come out with us for the night to see what our job was like. One of them, who was quite small in stature but built very broadly, was extremely sick all night, although the weather was fine.

I did my best to look after him, mainly because I knew only too well how he was feeling. They went ashore at Peel in the early morning, this guy feeling very sorry for himself, but he returned in the early evening before we sailed, bearing a gift of sweets for me by way of thanks. He gripped me by the hand, and said in the most heartfelt tone, "There just isn't enough money in the world to pay you guys - I just couldn't do your job, no matter what the pay."

This came from a man who with his fellow miners had described to us how one of the coal seams they worked was so lacking in height that they actually had to lie on their sides on the wet stone whilst wielding their picks!

Not enough money in the world?

There was another momentous occasion which springs to mind about taking visitors to sea with us, but this time the location was Whitby. A local lady who ran a fish and chip shop was in the market for the occasional cod which was caught among the herring, and as this was a welcome source of pocket money for the young lads, she was well known to us all. One day she asked me if her daughter could come out with us some night. She was, the lady explained, an actress, and was appearing briefly in the local theatre, the Whitby Spa. Hearing that the subject of the request was an actress - with all the stories we had heard of actresses - guaranteed the trip.

The appointed evening came around, and the fish and chip lady appeared with a stunning beauty, whose appearance confirmed all of our wildest hopes. We watched intently as she climbed down the ladder in her billowing skirt but when she was safely aboard, she won the hearts of all as she drifted around wafting behind her the most exotic perfume we had ever smelled. We danced attendance upon her every whim, and when she eventually declared that she was a little weary and desired to rest for a time, one of my older and infinitely worldlier shipmates beat me to the punch and offered his bed for her to lay her weary head in.

I hated him!

When we arrived back in Whitby and the beauty had gone home to her mother, taking our hearts with her, we prepared for bed ourselves. Great was the delight of this shipmate (who will not be named), as he elicited to us in great detail the dreams which were in store for him when he laid his head on the pillow which, as he demonstrated, was redolent of her perfume.

Even greater were his roars when he eventually clambered into his bed to discover that it was soaking wet. He never lived it down!

There was a self-imposed ban on Saturday and Sunday fishing which meant that work for the week was finished as soon as the Friday night catch had been discharged on the Saturday morning, and the rest of the weekend was free for leisure pursuits. This was the rule everywhere, with the exception of Whitby where the locals decided that as the season was very short, they could not afford to give up a night's work. Because of this weekend ban on fishing, the Isle of Man was a favourite place with all the young unmarried men. It was quite common then for one half of the pair of boats to set off home on a Saturday morning with all of the married men from the pair on board, leaving the other boat to go into Peel with the young single lads.

It was in Peel that I first heard the legend that the Manx people, having made soup or broth, would eat the meat that made the stock, first. Others would eat the soup, followed by the meat but the Manx were allegedly afraid that the marauding Scots would fall upon them and steal the food, so they ate the meat, the most valuable part of the meal first!

It was also in Peel that I first tasted 'dourkey' trotters. There were only three of us left aboard on this weekend, my father, myself and the cook from our neighbour boat. My father went ashore to buy the food we needed and returned with these three horrible looking things. He announced that he would poach them, and make soup with the liquid. They were put in water, and left on the stove until we two youngsters returned aboard. My father was at a ceilidh aboard another boat. My friend and I opened the lid of the by now cool pot and decided that the contents now looked a wee bit better, maybe even edible.

We scoffed the lot, but you can only imagine the complaints when the old man returned to find the pot empty!

Dancing was the 'in' thing then, and if one was to have any success with the fair sex, it was essential to be reasonably accomplished in the art of ballroom dancing. We all fancied ourselves as budding Fred Astaires, and it came as something of a shock when my wife and I met an old acquaintance of mine from these days, only for her to say to my wife, "He thought he was a good dancer then, but we hadn't the heart to tell him otherwise!"

This need to be a reasonably proficient dancer meant that it was foolish to take too much to drink. All we usually took was enough to give us Dutch courage to make that dreaded long, lonely journey across the dance floor from the 'man's side' of the hall, to the other side where - dressed in their party best - stood the aloof

girls pretending they didn't see us coming! Anyone the worse of wear stood little chance of being accepted as a dance partner, and so would not be able to pose the vital question, "Can I see you home tonight?" to the girl of his choice. Another lonely walk back to the boat was all that was left to the unfortunate fool who drank too much.

After the 'last waltz' the National Anthem was always played and almost without exception, everyone in the hall stood to attention. The same applied in cinemas then, the audience stood where they had sat until the Anthem was finished. Nowadays, in pubs and clubs at any rate, the majority of people are too drunk to stand to attention and are probably too busy fighting in any case. The girls appear to be at least as bad as the men now. This is progress?

Not much of my time was spent fishing around Campbeltown then, this was left mostly to the Carradale boats, which meant that few of us experienced a home life worthy of the name. We got home from the North around one weekend per month at most, but from the Isle of Man we got home weekly if we had herring on the Saturday which merited a trip to Portpatrick, thus taking us halfway home. It was rare indeed for anyone to get home from the six weeks or so spent in Whitby. The years toil began in May when all the boats - looking beautiful after two months of varnishing and painting - set off for the North. This fishing, one of the few conducted in daylight when the herring were up feeding on plankton on the surface, lasted until the early part of June, when the Manx season began. In late August we set off through the Forth and Clyde Canal, to Seahouses and Whitby.

The Forth and Clyde Canal runs from near Grangemouth on the Forth, to Bowling on the Clyde, and en route skirted Falkirk and Glasgow - exciting country for young lads. I remember looking for the landmark of the clock - which was then reputed to be the biggest in the World - above the Singer factory in Glasgow. The canal was closed for many years but was recently reopened, at great cost. It should not have been closed in the first place, in my opinion.

The Yorkshire fishing lasted until late September, and the return to Campbeltown meant a quick touch up to the varnish and a bottom clean before setting off again for the North where we remained until the end of February or the beginning of March. There was then a short spell fishing for spawning herring around the South end of Arran, or on the Ballantrae Banks off the Ayrshire coast before it was time for the boats to be beached in Campbeltown to scrape and varnish before another year began.

This lack of time in Campbeltown did not bother me, a young single man, but must have been a strain on a marriage where for a great part of the year the wife had to be a father to the family in addition to her normal motherly tasks.

The Men

At this time, I was in the company of one of my Captains, although I did not realise it then.

Jock MacKenzie, or "Kenzie" as he was known, was just about the most expert and dedicated fisherman I ever worked with.

He was a round sturdy man, not very tall, with very fixed habits and ideas. An individual who, for example, would not eat a fried egg which had not been salted in the pan whilst cooking, and for whom herring - a staple food - had to be boiled for exactly twenty minutes! They were, in my opinion, grossly overcooked if given that time and it was my habit, if Jock wasn't watching over me, to consider them done when I had finished making the toast that invariably accompanied them when they were cooked for breakfast.

He never left the deck at any time when fishing was taking place. Prior to leaving the harbour, Jock would fill all of his pipes with baccy, make sure that they were all drawing to his satisfaction, and then stow them carefully bowl up, at the side of his bunk. When he felt the need for nicotine, the dreaded call "Light my pipe, boy" arose!

He would not strike a match himself, as this would destroy his night vision, but many times in my imagination I destroyed much more than his vision, such was my loathing for these foul-tasting abominations, especially when I was feeling seasick!

During the short summer nights he lay on the starboard side of the bow with an old wooden mallet in his right hand, with which he would strike the top rail from time to time. This blow sent a shock wave through the water, which startled any herring which were too deep to be disturbed by the boat's passing.

He demanded a mallet for this work, being convinced that nothing else – a hammer or the like – would do the job.

The movement of the herring which resulted from this shock-wave stirred the phosphorescence in the water, causing a faint glow deep down which revealed their presence. This task demanded total concentration and a very keen eye, as well as great experience. "Ease her down!" he would call to my father in the wheelhouse, then in an aside to me, "Did you see that, boy?". "Aye Jock," I would reply - but on many occasions seeing the dim glow deep down took far more experience than I had gained. It would also be fair to say that my eyes were closed in fitful sleep more often than not when lying on the foredeck, because the fleshpots and bright lights of Whitby and the Isle of Man were a sore temptation to a young lad who should have been sound asleep in his bunk!

He was the only man I ever knew who called for the net to be shot in the month of January, in the Minch, saying that he had seen a "wee scatter in the burnin". We, who knew that no one could possibly see any herring in the winter months in the 'burnin' as we called the phosphorescence, were put firmly in our places when the first herring was spotted meshed in the wide wings of the net that had been shot as a result of his observation!

At the Whitby fishing, the fleet used to leave harbour in the early evenings en masse on their way to the grounds between Whitby and Scarborough, and the quay would be thronged with holidaymakers viewing what must have been a wonderful sight.

One evening my father had fallen by the wayside, and was still in the pub long after the last boat had left, leaving only us and our neighbour the *Glen Carradale* still tied to the pier.

The skipper of the *Glen Carradale*, "Wee Alec" McBride, would much rather have been fishing around the Pluck (a point of land close to his home in Carradale) and the absence of my father was all the ammunition he required to re-state his objections to being so far away from home.

He rolled up and down the deck of his boat, his burly figure swaying from side to side exaggerating his anguish, calling to all from whom he thought he would get sympathy. "He's a hellova man that Tommy Tit. Up there boozin' and us lyin' here wi' the rest o' the fleet at the sea. We'd be far better off at hame than lyin' here lik' this. Aye, ye'd be far better off lyin' at the Pluck, than lyin' here. Oh my God, is this no' jeest terrible!"

On and on it went, with myself feeling most unhappy at his seeming miscalling of my father, yet too young and inexperienced to do anything about it, until at last my father rolled down the quay and we were able to go to sea .

It was dark now of course, but as soon as we had cleared the harbour, Kenzie was up at his usual station, although everyone knew that no one caught any herring until they had reached the grounds which were at least eight miles from Whitby.

Everyone that was, but Kenzie.

The herring were there that night, not too far past the buoy that the fleet had rounded earlier, but they had all passed over them in daylight.

"Stand by," roared Kenzie from his post at the bow.

We shot, and two hours later were back in the still-deserted harbour, with the night's quota safely stowed below.

"Aye, ye're a hellova man althegether, Tommy," was now the cheerful call from Wee Alec as he strutted up and down the deck grinning from ear to ear, all thoughts of the Pluck gone. "Ye've the luck o' the Devil right enough!"

Kenzie was not given proper recognition for his professionalism by me, till many years later.

A Captain? Oh yes indeed.

One of the most disagreeable facts of life at the fishing in the summer time was having to put up with 'scowders' (called scalders by some), the stinging jellyfish which were the source of much pain to all.

When hauling, the nets became liberally coated with the highly irritating tendrils of the scowders. These tendrils became airborne when the net had to be shaken to get rid of the herring that were meshed in it.

The stinging which resulted from these airborne particles hitting exposed skin was really quite painful. There was no guaranteed way to get rid of the pain, although some swore by washing the afflicted parts with methylated spirit.

I have seen men wear plastic false-faces when hauling in a vain attempt at escaping the stings, and it was not unknown for a piece of monish, the soft laid heavy cord that was used to attach the net to the ropes to be attached to the relevant place on one's anatomy, to avoid being stung there when answering a call of nature!

Different nets were used for the winter and the summer fisheries. When one fishery was finished, the net (in those days made of cotton) which had been in use was steeped in a preservative called bark or cutch, which was derived initially from the bark of Acacia trees and latterly from a distillation of the wood of the same tree, was melted in hot water to make a brew which looked like very strong tea.

The nets were afterwards dried thoroughly by hanging them from poles erected for this job, or from fences and were then stored until next required.

So persistent was the sting of the scowders that, when taking the net from the store after perhaps eight months, the dust from the nets stung just as badly, and gave us a wee taste of what we were now about to face again!

Whilst on 'medical' matters, I recall hearing of a wonderful truth uttered by a famous - or rather infamous - local worthy who revelled in the nickname of "Doosan". He looked in one night on the local consulting room, where sat the sick in mind and body, waiting to be consoled by one of the doctors on duty.

Now if you have a good look around the waiting room of a similar establishment when you are next there, paying particular attention to the demeanour of the other occupants, you will see very few smiling faces. Doosan looked around the twenty or so patients carefully, then roared, "What a miserable lookin' shower o' buggers. There's no' wan o' ye but what a good shite wad dae ye the world o' good!"

He was probably spot on in his observation.

In the days when I was cooking, a great source of information was from one's watchmate.

There were few boats equipped with radio transmitters or receivers in the first year or so of my apprenticeship, so the hours spent on watch during a passage were made less wearying by yarning, or rather in listening to the yarns of the older men. In fact the best watchmates were invariably the best yarners!

One such was "Lofty" McIntyre, who I always remember with a great deal of pleasure.

Quite a tall man, of a spare build, he always seemed to have a wry grin on his face, and was in his element dispelling gloom with a cheery word.

I dearly wish that I had kept a diary in those days for I have forgotten most of what I was told, but I remember Lofty telling me some of the adventures which befell him during the War.

He had been, he told me, a Seaman/Gunner aboard a mine sweeping trawler for a time during the war, and one day was on duty as Quartermaster, steering the mine sweeper, when she was strafed by an enemy aircraft. This aircraft was spotted approaching from the starboard side with its forward gunner firing as the aircraft approached.

“Man the port Oerlikon, McIntyre!” was the shouted order from the Officer on watch.

Lofty obeyed this order, understanding that the idea was for him to open fire on the aircraft as it climbed away from its attack, using one of the guns mounted on each wing of the bridge. However he looked back into the wheelhouse just in time to see the Officer, who had grabbed the steering wheel from him, drop to the deck behind the dubious shelter of the binnacle.

Lofty surveyed his own totally exposed position and decided he didn’t like what he saw, so he immediately jumped down on to the engine room casing where he got equally dubious shelter behind the funnel, from the incoming hail of bullets.

As the aircraft pulled up and away on the ship’s port side, the rear gunner opened fire on the trawler, using tracer bullets.

The Officer obviously risked a quick glance, and on seeing the tracer, made the mistake in the heat of the moment of thinking that Lofty was firing. Ducking back behind the binnacle he roared, “Bloody good show Lofty - I can see them going right up his arse!”

One foggy night as we were approaching the Mull of Galloway en route to Portpatrick with a shot of herring, I commented on the lack of visibility – this was before any of our class of boat was fitted with radar. Lofty said - “This is no’ right fog. I mind wance when I was on the Murmansk run, bein’ sent up the foremast tae the crow’s-nest tae keep a lookout for German battleships. Well I was up there so long that when I cam’ doon, the boat was gone!” He also told me that the seas were so enormous in the Arctic, that they were three days running off the back of one wave!

The risk of being killed or drowned in action was probably higher on the mine sweeping trawlers which had been commandeered from the fishing fleets, than on ships which had been specifically designed for warfare, so in order to preserve some of the lives at risk, the wearing of lifejackets was at all times rigorously enforced.

Lofty told me that for years he had worked, eaten, and slept with this lifejacket around his neck. Burdened with this lifejacket, like the Ancient Mariner with the albatross, and loathing its presence just as much, he was allowed to take it off only when leaving the ship to go on shore leave.

He was he said on watch keeping duty whilst the ship was at anchor in Portsmouth harbour, when the official statement came through that the war in Europe was over.

The lights came on ashore, there were the sounds of celebration from all around, and Lofty having celebrated modestly (he was on watch remember) returned to his lonely post on deck.

There he leant on the rail seeing the lights, so long darkened and now reflected in the black waters below. Nostalgia took the place of euphoria, and his memory went back over the long weary years of war: the good friends he had made and lost, all the waste of killing he had witnessed, and then casting around in his mind for some positive way of marking what should be a joyous occasion, he remembered the hated lifejacket.

He removed it. Looked at it long. Permitted himself a few more moments of pure delight, and threw it in a last gesture of defiance, down into the sea below.

"The fuckin' thing sank!" Lofty concluded.

Lofty might not make it to Captain, but as a Commander his company and his yarns would grace those around the fire in Angus's dreams, and if I was there, I'd listen more carefully this time.

I also heard some lovely tales about the early days of the war from my mother's nephew, Jim McAuley, who had served aboard a cruiser at that time. Jim's younger brother, Duncan, was aboard the same ship. The Spithead Review was held just before the war started and as the Navy needed some extra manpower at the time, Naval Reservists were asked if they would volunteer for a few weeks.

Work was short and money was scarce in Campbeltown in this time of depression, so around 20 men answered this call. They would be paid and fed whilst they were away and they looked on it as being a bit of a holiday. While they were aboard the cruiser to which they had been drafted – I think that she was HMS Dispatch – they were asked if they would like to stay for a few more weeks, as the ship was going off to the Caribbean for a cruise. To a man, they agreed. A cruise in the sun – and being paid into the bargain – that was a deal they could not resist. War clouds grew, their ship stayed in the West Indies, and they got out again in 1945!

At that time membership of the RNR was not dependent on the man being of a seagoing persuasion and one of their number, Pat McAllister, 'The Hoadler' by nickname, was well known for his wicked sense of humour. Jim roared with laughter as he recalled the Hoadler being relieved as quartermaster (steering the ship) whilst they were steaming in company with several other ships, in line ahead. He gave his relief the course, which the luckless man repeated and then, as the relief uttered the words, "I relieve you," the Hoadler put the wheel hard over and left the bridge at the gallop just as battle commenced and the officer of the watch took issue with the poor man who was now busily trying to get the ship back into line!

Jim also told me of the day, after the news had been broken that they were "in for the duration". He was leaning on the rail looking dejectedly at the scenery around the anchorage when the Hoadler appeared.

"Well, Jim," he roared, clapping him on the shoulder. "How would ye like tae be a wee bit o' paper, blowin' roon the heid o' Dalintober Pier jeest noo!"

Another favourite watchmate from my very young days as a fisherman was Dennis McKay, better known as 'Old Dubs' for some obscure reason. He was a lovely singer and the long watches seemed to flash past when listening to his old songs or stories from his younger days.

One day we were going round Kilmory Point which is at the north most tip of the Island of Rum, and which was better known to the Clyde fishermen as Dirty Point because a reef of rocks runs, not as one might expect, straight off the point but at an angle to it. Dubs then told me that long ago a couple had lived in the ruined cottage which is still visible on the green sward above the beautiful beach which lies inside the reef. They had, he told me, seven children. These children were taken from them one at a time by the then deadly diphtheria, and after burying them just behind the cottage, the distraught couple had left the island, never to return.

The story seemed to me to be confirmed when, looking at an old Admiralty chart of the area I saw, marked just where Dubs had indicated, the legend 'Graves'.

Many times when rounding Kilmory, my mind turned to what he had told me, and I imagined the utter despair which must have been felt by the poor parents as they helplessly watched their children die. No telephone, no doctor, no helicopter, no lifeboat - just the deaths of their children in a lonely place. What, I wondered, were their thoughts as they left, and where did they go? At the back of my mind remained the hope that the story was not correct, and that the graves were not of the children.

About twenty years ago there appeared in the Scots Magazine, a monthly publication, an article on Rum. In it the writer described visiting Kilmory and related the story just as I had heard it. Reading this brought back all the despair I had felt but worse still, removed all the forlorn hopes I had entertained that it was not true.

A couple of issues later my delight knew no bounds when I found a letter from a lady in New Zealand who said that she had greatly enjoyed the article about Rum, but that she wished to correct the writer on one detail. The children at Kilmory had not all died.

Four of them had survived the ordeal of illness, and the subsequent migration to New Zealand. There the parents had another three children, bringing the total back to seven.

This she knew for certain, she wrote, because her grandfather was one of the family which had been born on Rum!

I'd dearly love to be able to tell 'Old Dubs' the happy ending to his tale if I was privileged to meet him at Angus's fireside.

I had only been aboard the *Golden Fleece* for a year or so when my father invested in a radio transmitter/receiver. Nearly all the other boats had Coastal radios but my father, rather unwisely I felt, chose a Pye Dolphin. It was installed in the wheelhouse and proved a great blessing when crossing the Minch on a dreary winter night, as we could tune it to receive A.F.N., the American Forces Network, which was then transmitted from somewhere in Germany. Our favourite programme then was 'Grand Old Opry', which played an almost non-stop selection of Country and Western music. This was long before the days of Radio Luxembourg.

We were not supposed to listen to this sort of stuff, we should have been listening to what other boats were saying, in order to glean information about what herring had been caught, and where, but I am afraid that at my age, the music of Hank Williams and his contemporaries took precedence over that sort of information!

The radio was also, of course, used to receive the shipping forecasts that were broadcast by the BBC and I have fond memories of one announcer – he always seemed to give out the midnight forecast – who invariably ended with the words: "Goodnight gentlemen, and pleasant sailing." His thoughtfulness was much appreciated by many.

Boredom on the passages to and from the Isle of Man was lightened by listening to Radio Eireann, another station that broadcast the sort of music we craved.

On Monday afternoons when there was quite a fleet of Clyde boats headed back towards the Isle of Man, more often than not an impromptu concert would break out on the 'trawler band'. Many singers contributed to this but without doubt the star performer was Dick Andrews, skipper of the May Queen. Dick had a really good voice and one day a Fleetwood trawler called him to tell him that he had developed a large group of fans among the wives of the Fleetwood fishermen. These ladies were in the habit of listening to the trawler band on their radios where they often heard messages from their loved ones. They had soon figured out that there was good entertainment to be heard from the ringers on Monday afternoons.

Thereafter, Dick always included a special song for the 'Ladies in Fleetwood'!

Around this time, I arrived at the age when National Service reared its head.

As fishermen, we were not obliged to do the two years in one of the Services, which was the lot of others less fortunate. We could opt to join the Royal Naval Reserve instead. This meant doing an initial training period of 28 days, followed by 14 days every year, for ten years. Of course, we all jumped at the idea of 'paid holidays' every year, and I must say that I did enjoy my time there.

Later on in my time in the RNR I was asked if I knew the difference between the RNR, the RNVR and the RN. At that time the RNR were drawn from seamen, either merchant or fishing, and the RNVR were men who were drawn toward the Navy, but who had shore jobs. This no longer applies.

My questioner was an ancient Chief Petty Officer – I felt that he had probably sailed with Noah – and I knew that his question required an answer, which would, if I waited, come from him! When I said that I didn't know he enlightened me thus. "RNRs are seamen trying to be gentlemen, RNVRs are gentlemen who are trying to be seamen and RNs are neither, trying to be both!"

My initial training took place in the Naval Barracks in Chatham, and I went in company with Jackie McGeachy from Campbeltown, whose father Sweeney owned the *Margaret Newton*, and that tremendous character who sadly died very young indeed, Archie "Baldy" Black, from Tarbert.

We arrived in Hawke Block of the Royal Naval Barracks in Chatham, at what I later discovered was a bad time - mid-afternoon on a Sunday. This was the time when regular sailors were sleeping off the effects of their lunch time tot of rum.

The Petty Officer who dealt with our entry into Service life was not amused at having his siesta spoiled, and found great difficulty in coping with Jackie's surname, a difficulty which was shared by almost all of his fellow Englishmen! When in reply to his query as to where we had come from, we answered "Campbeltown", he threw his pen on to the floor and bellowed, "I don't want any of your bloody tricks here. I've had enough of you people".

The reputation of our predecessors had obviously made a big impression on him!

Baldy was a little older than Jackie and me and was vastly more experienced in the ways of the world, so was more able to cope with the pressures of life there. This became obvious when we went on our first parade.

On the hallowed parade ground!

Regular Naval personnel marched on to this parade ground to be reviewed, but it had obviously been discovered that fishermen could not readily cope with marching, so we were ushered quietly into our designated area long before the others, told to stand to attention and not to move nor speak.

In due course, the rest of the parade was marched smartly into place to the strains of the Royal Marine Band, and the Captain appeared, followed by his retinue of attendants.

To the justifiable horror of the Petty Officer in charge of the squad of Reservists - around 20 in number - the Captain made a beeline for us.

As he approached, I for one became more petrified with each step which brought them nearer, amazed by the array of brilliant gold braid, and dazzled by the glittering drawn swords of his escort.

He paused in front of Baldy, and in a very cultured accent inquired as to where he hailed from. On being told, "Tarbert, Sir", he then said, "Oh, Tarbert, Loch Fyne. What a beautiful place. I sailed my yacht there often."

Then, no doubt wondering just what kind of fishing our hero pursued he asked, "And what were you before you came here?"

Baldy instantly replied with a guileless grin, "I wis fuckin' happy, Sir"!

The Captain's escorting party froze, their faces reflecting the horror they felt at hearing the Captain being addressed thus, but the great man laughed heartily as he moved on and certainly must have had a good sense of humour, as Baldy heard no more of it.

Years later I attended the Petty Officer's training School, H.M.S. Royal Arthur, which was oddly situated many miles from the sea in Corsham, a lovely little village in Wiltshire. There I heard one of the great characters who were the backbone of the Navy then. On Church parade, or Divisions as they were known, denominations other than the Church of England were invited to leave the parade ground before the service started, by the time-honoured call, "Fall out R.C.'s (Roman Catholics) and other denominations." This character, a Chief Gunnery instructor, would bellow from his position on the dais which we faced, "Fall out R.C.s, Parsees, Hottentots and Church of Jocks." I suppose that some do-gooder would object to this now as being an invasion of human rights, or some other such bullshit!

Royal Arthur was an extremely well run establishment, and I learned a lot in my short time there. We were kept busy at all times and on one occasion, when we were to be taught how a talk or lecture should be given, we got a real shock. My squad, which consisted of around a dozen men, had seated ourselves in the classroom when the door burst open and our main mentor and teacher, a Chief Gunnery Instructor came rushing in. We were shocked at his appearance! His cap was perched precariously on the back of his head, his jacket was undone, his tie was all awry and one of his trouser legs had parted company from the gaiter that should have contained it.

He rushed up on to the stage and started, "I'm here to give you some idea on how to …" At this point he stopped, fished a piece of paper from his jacket pocket, looked at it and continued, "How to give a lecture." He then turned away from us and scrolled down a revolving blackboard, muttering to himself as he did so. A very short time of this sort of behaviour was enough to convince us that there was something seriously amiss!

Unseen by us our class officer, a Commissioned Gunner, entered the room.

"What do you think you are doing, Chief?" he called.

"I am trying to teach these men how to give a lecture, sir."

"You aren't making a very good job of it, Chief."

At that the Chief threw his chalk on to the floor and shouted, "If you think you can do any better, fucking well get on with it!" With that he jumped off the stage and rushed from the room.

We were totally shocked. This man had gained our respect and admiration. He had blown it now, big style, we thought.

The Commissioned Gunner took the Chief's place on the stage. He was absolutely immaculately dressed and looked to be totally at ease.

"That," he began, "is how <u>not</u> to give a lecture. Be properly dressed, know your subject, and face your audience at all times."

These men were expert at grabbing – and keeping – the attention of their audience.

During my time in Royal Arthur we had to take part in an exercise that involved us being taken out in the back of a covered lorry from which we were dropped off in groups of three on the road at intervals of a mile or so. We couldn't see where we were going in the lorry, so had no idea where we were when we were dropped off and the Chief in charge simply told us that the camp was bearing so-and-so, and gave the approximate distance. We had to get back to the camp as quickly as possible and were, as we were supposed to be escaped prisoners, being hunted by members of the camp staff. We were clad in just trousers and a shirt – no cap – and wore an armband which was to be removed by our captors when we were caught. The hunters were wearing jackets and caps. We knew that we had an hour or so of a start so had some time when we were reasonably safe.

After a short discussion my two companions agreed that they were going to take the direct route across fields, but I didn't agree so they set off running down what they thought was the correct bearing. I was quite young then and was reasonably fit, so I set off trotting on the road. Before long I passed an old workman who seemed to be clearing the ditches at the side of the road and shortly after, I saw that a bicycle, obviously his was lying on its side in the ditch. It had what looked like his lunch bag, tied to its crossbar. I stopped and thought about it – for a couple of seconds then hauled it onto the road, removed the bag and left it there, then mounted the bike and set off at a good lick, pursued by angry roars from the workman!

I made good time for a few miles and then abandoned the bike at the roadside, in plain view, continuing running, but now keeping a very sharp lookout, until I came on a lovely little pub. The day was warm, and I was thirsty, so I went in, and ordered a pint of best! This quaint little pub had, I was certain, been a house in the past, and there were a number of rooms, all connected by short passages so I sat myself down and relaxed in one of them, with my pint.

I hadn't been there very long when I heard some other customers arrive in one of the other rooms and very shortly afterwards the barmaid who had served me appeared at the door, holding her fingers to her lips, and gesticulating over her shoulder. I soon discovered that the newcomers were three of the guys who were supposed to be looking for the 'escaped prisoners'!

With the help of the barmaid, who of course knew all about the exercise – good barmaids know just about everything - I got out of the back door and set off again down the road that led, she told me, to the camp. I was only a couple of miles from safety!

I had two more close shaves and then arrived at the main gate – the second prisoner to arrive! I had a shower and spent the rest of the afternoon relaxing quietly.

The Chief G.I. sought me out in the early evening and, looking me straight in the eye, asked if I had stolen a bike that afternoon. I had anticipated that the owner might well complain, but had decided that no, I had not really stolen it – just borrowed it for a time, so I looked him back just as he had looked at me, and denied it! He turned away and then stopped and looked back: "Well, whoever did nick it left it where it would be easily found, so we'll let the matter drop for the time being. Be careful, young man – just be careful!"

Several of my training stints were spent at HMS *Lochinvar*, in South Queensferry. Sadly, it was closed down many years ago. I was in the Chief's and P.O.'s mess there and it was one Sunday afternoon that I witnessed something else that today, would be totally unacceptable.

It was a warm afternoon and most of us, the duty Petty Officer included, were relaxing in the mess. Our tots had been drunk and this, aided by a heavy lunch, conspired to send most of us off into the land of Nod.

The peace was shattered by a tannoy announcement: "Duty Petty Officer required in the guardroom!" This came from the guardroom, which was just across the road from where we lay in our armchairs.

We were all wakened by this announcement and watched with amusement as the man thus summoned put on his jacket and cap, and strode off in the required direction. He, unlike us, was definitely not amused. He crossed the road and went into the guardroom from which, a few moments later, there came a fearful uproar. This was followed by the emergence of a fellow wearing civilian clothes, very red in the face, who almost ran down the road toward the entrance to the base, around half a mile away.

When the duty PO returned he told us that when he arrived in the guardroom and asked what was wrong, he was shown the civilian and was told that he was a sailor who was 'adrift' (absent without leave). When he asked this poor fellow how long he had been adrift, the chap replied, "Four years!" confessing to a potentially serious crime that would take many hours of form-filling to sort out.

When the gravity of the situation permeated the alcohol, food and sleep befuddled PO's brain he immediately howled: "Fuck off you silly bastard. Come back tomorrow, when I'm not on duty!" and evicted the totally bemused ex sailor.

Having finished his story, he took his cap and jacket off, and resumed his relaxed position in his armchair and closed his eyes. As far as he was concerned, the incident was over!

I never did discover the end of this tale.

I was in H.M.S. *Vernon*, in Portsmouth, years later and witnessed an incident that taught me much. A frigate had been sold to the South African Navy – this was whilst apartheid was at its worst - and a South African crew had been sent to exercise with her before taking her to her new home. Several of these men arrived in our mess for lunch but when they saw two black sailors in our company, they refused to eat there.

This situation we were later told was taken to the duty officer who, fearing political repercussion from on high, took it to the Captain. He, when he had ascertained all the facts, asked what the problem was.

"Well, sir," the duty officer said, "These men are refusing to eat in our mess in the company of our black sailors."

"So, what is the problem? If they don't want to eat there, they don't have to. Don't bother me with this again, please."

They went hungry that day!

Could lessons be learned from this very wise decision?

One branch of the Navy which made an enormous impression on me was the gunnery branch in general, and the instructors in particular. Their bearing and turnout was immaculate in every respect, and a visit to the hallowed ground which bred these martinets, Whale Island, was a revelation.

No one walked anywhere within this establishment at any time. They ran or doubled, as they would have it. The parade ground was sacrosanct, and the only time anyone put a foot on to it, was when they were on parade.

One day when running from one class to another, thinking I was not being observed I took a shortcut across a corner of this parade ground.

There was an unearthly eldritch screech from a Chief Gunnery Instructor across the square: "Come here. You, sailor!"

In terror I ran around, and halted in front of him.

"Who told you to halt? Double mark time! Who gave you permission to cross my parade ground? Don't speak to me you horrible sailor!" (This when I tried to explain).

This tirade was delivered from beneath the brim of a Guards-style cap, with the wearer's nose about six inches from mine - in a high pitched scream which could have been heard miles away - and which served only to complete my total demoralisation.

"That is my parade ground and I only allow one person on it apart from me," the screams continued. "The other person is God, and I only tolerate Him because I can't see Him!"

No doubt Baldy Black would have been able to think of an answer, but I was alone and greatly afraid.

I think it was Baldy who told me of one of the MacDougall brothers, famed ring-net exponents from Tarbert Loch Fyne, who was called to serve in the Royal Navy during the war. He was sent to train in the Patrol Service, which branch of the Navy had been formed to man the fishing boats which had been requisitioned into the Fleet.

On hearing that MacDougall had been in charge of the engine on his boat at home, it was ordained that he, in company with a few others, should take an exam which, if completed successfully, would mean his advancement to Petty Officer Engineman.

He duly, but reluctantly took his place in the examination room, the question papers were handed out, and the examinees were told to begin work.

The invigilator, a Lieutenant Engineer, curious at the seeming lack of activity from our candidate, approached, looked over the man's shoulder, and saw a sheet of pristine paper.

On enquiring into the reason for this inactivity, he was treated to the loud statement, "Ah've been drivin' engines for fifteen years, Jeck, an Ah nivir needed a bit o' paper tae start wan o' them yet!"

Many years later we had a visit, as part of the Mallaig Fisherman's Mission Gala weekend, from a naval fast patrol ship – I cannot recall her name. I made contact with a few of her crew and had them home for a meal. One of them told me a tale, which is relevant today when there is so much controversy over the rights, or otherwise, of the Ghurkhas to remain in the UK after their service days are over.

My new friend had been a Petty Officer aboard a Ton class minesweeper that was based in Hong Kong – this was before it was handed back to China. Some sort of dispute had broken out amongst rival Chinese gangs, a dispute that led to some bloodshed and much civil unrest.

Our hero had been made part of a small group of sailors, led by a naval officer whose task was to help the overstretched Army to keep the peace. Before they went ashore they were issued with rifles. Now to hand a rifle to a sailor is a very dangerous thing to do – dangerous for the sailor, that is. They are much more likely to shoot themselves, than any perceived enemy!

They were flown by helicopter to the summit of a small hill on the outskirts of the city. This hill overlooked the road that led through a village that was less than a mile away. Before the helicopter left them, the army officer who had accompanied them, and who was now flying off in the chopper, gave them their final instructions. They were not, under any circumstances, to try to resolve any disputes that might break out between the inhabitants of the village, he told them. If there was any trouble, they were to use the radio they had been given to call upon the Army, who were used to dealing with such problems.

All was quiet, he told us, until late afternoon when large crowds of rival villagers began to gather on either side of the road, howling what sounded like insults at one another. The Naval party was NOT happy!

The temperature of the dispute grew until their officer decided that something had to be done, so he wisely radioed for help. Shortly afterward a small helicopter appeared, landed and disgorged an Army subaltern who was leading a group of four Gurkhas. The subaltern watched the warring factions for a few moments and then spoke quietly to the Gurkha sergeant, in his own language. This little fellow saluted, drew his kukri which he then held up before his face, and set off at a rapid trot down the hill toward the village. Alone!

The sailors watched this in amazement, and in fear for the fellow's life.

He set off down the hill and trotted, kukri held vertical before him, straight down the middle of the road. As he approached the howling mob, it became silent, and parted before him – "Just as the Red Sea did for Moses," my new friend said. He reached the far end of the village, turned, and retraced his steps back through the now silent Chinese, and climbed the hill to rejoin his companions.

"Do you know this, Tommy," he said. "The little bastard was hardly out of breath!"

The subaltern then told them that he didn't think they would have any more problems and then led his troop back to the waiting helicopter.

"Trouble?" said my friend. "Anybody that looks for trouble with these little bastards deserves what they are certainly going to get!"

Tarbert and Carradale

There are, I think, remarkable similarities to be seen when considering the Ayrshire and Kintyre fishing communities. There are three fishing villages, or towns, on each side of the Clyde. The north-most ones, Tarbert in Kintyre and Dunure in Ayrshire, are similar in size, and their inhabitants tend to be more garrulous and aggressive than their immediate neighbours to the south, Carradale and Maidens. The last named are the central villages on the western and eastern shores of the Clyde respectively and their residents tended generally to be quieter, gentler, and more softly spoken than their noisy neighbours on either side!

Tarbert is also home to a great many odd turns of phrase, quite often a mixture of words from the days when Gaelic was commonly spoken, and English. On a recent visit I telephoned Ian McAlister, brother of Donald. They run a small kippering plant where they make what in my opinion are the best kippers in the country. Ian's wife answered and when I explained that there had been a mix up in the day when I was to pick up a stone of kippers to take home.

"That'll be Donald," she said by way of explanation, "His heid's as runkled as a bag o' hammers."

Don't ask me for an explanation, but it sounded brilliant!

The two remaining towns, Campbeltown and Girvan, are by far the largest on their respective coasts. They are the south-most fishing settlements, and their populations shared the dubious distinction of having a much harsher sounding accent than their

Northern neighbours. They also in my opinion, tended generally to be much more noisy and quarrelsome than any of the others.

Tarbert Loch Fyne must be the first port of call in our rounds of fishing strongholds, mainly because it is probably there that the ring-net was first developed in the pursuit of herring in Scotland.

A small village on the narrow neck of land which marks the northern boundary of "God's Country" - Kintyre - it has been blessed with what must be one of the best and most beautiful natural harbours in the world.

I recall being told often – as a young lad – the tale of the lady in Tarbert who earned a few shillings in an extraordinary way. She would make her way to the pier when the herring fishing was at its height and perch on a bollard above the boats that were discharging. Then she would alternatively open and then close her legs chanting, as she did so, "Now you see it, now you don't. Perhaps you'll hit it, perhaps you won't!" Of course, the men below would have a worm's eye view of what was being revealed and would throw herring at it. I was assured that she had a fair few boxes of herring to sell, before all the boats had finished discharging!

Tarbert has also been blessed with more than its fair share of what can only be called 'fishers extraordinary'.

The MacDougall brothers of Tarbert - Donald, Archie and Peter - referred to in the last chapter, who owned the *Mairerad*, and the *Fionnaghal* must be immediate candidates for Captaincy.

They were commonly known as the "Ghosts". This collective nickname of theirs was derived from their habit of using paper to lessen the brightness of their navigation lights.

This was done for several purposes.

Firstly that the brightness should not scare the herring off the shore where it was hoped that they could be trapped, secondly, that it would lessen the chance of destroying the night vision of the skipper who wanted to get as close to the shore as possible, and finally it had the bonus of not betraying their presence to their rival fishermen! It was said of them, "Ye'd need a light tae see their lights!"

The favourite hunting ground of the Ghosts when fishing in the North, was Shepherds Bight, a small bay on the east coast of South Uist about two miles south of Loch Skipport.

The Ghosts

On more occasions than I care to think of, the fleet would race out of the usual anchorage in Loch Skipport as darkness approached in the winter evenings in the 1950's, and try to beat one another into all the favourite herring haunts - south along the east shore of the Uists towards Loch Boisdale.

The Ghosts took part in the beginnings of these races, but always seemed to drop out early.

In fact they turned their backs on the mad scramble to the south just as soon as they could and wandered unnoticed back north, and when they could crawl, dead slow, on their own terms into their preferred Shepherds Bight, they did so. In the early mornings when the reports of the efforts of others began to filter through, very often we heard that, “The Ghosts are away full up fae somewhere north”.

They were also noted for their habit of making their own anti-fouling paint with which they would paint the bottoms of their boats. The recipe for this was kept secret, but was generally thought to consist of any unused paint, gloss or flat, mixed up in an old barrel. To this was added sheep dip, the ingredient which killed off the unwanted ‘galbhin crechachs’ (I think that is how it is spelt) - barnacles to anyone not of Tarbert extraction.

They spent just about all of their idle time lying at the pier in Loch Skipport, and it was usual for them to leave Mallaig as soon as they had finished discharging on a Saturday, headed for Skipport. Others were keen to stay to see what delights the fleshpots would offer, but not the Ghosts!

If only they could be invited to tell their secrets at Angus’s fireside!

Around 1999 I went on a trip to the Hebrides, taking Ina with me. We left the main road through Uist and took the side track toward Loch Skipport. I had it in mind to visit the MacLeod family who had lived there in the times of which I write. At that time there were two brothers and two sisters living with the father in a house not far from the pier. They owned the house and a fair sized croft. Opposite the house stood a small wooden structure that served as the Post Office cum shop – which they ran. They looked after the pier and were the agents for David MacBrayne, the owner of the shipping line that served the Hebrides. Goods delivered to Skipport were stored on the large shed until they delivered them in one of the lorries they owned. They ran a taxi service, a school bus and in their spare time, looked after the croft!

My first shock was when we reached what remained of what had been a busy pier. There remained only some of the upright wooden supports! The entire decking had gone and there were only the foundations left of what had been the MacLeod’s store. It was a sad sight indeed!

When we turned around, I was mystified when I couldn't find either their house, or the shop. Had my memory played a huge trick on me?

We arrived back at the main road and turned north again. We had not gone very far when fortunately, Ina spotted a wee shop at the roadside above which we saw the name board, 'MacLeod Brothers'. I went into this shop and immediately recognised James, the older of the two brothers, although I hadn't seen him for almost forty years.

I spoke to him, but did not introduce myself and to my amazement he recognised me, after a few moments thought. After a few minutes talking, he suggested that we accompany him to his house for a cup of tea. It was early afternoon, and I knew that customers could arrive at any time so I said: "But you can't close the shop, James!"

He looked at me for a moment then said, in a rather puzzled voice: "Why not?"

Yes, I was back in the land where they had their priorities right, I thought.

In his house we met his sister, Mary, and his brother, Ian. The only one of the family who had married – I think her name may have been Katie – had died very young, but had left a family.

They talked fondly of the Ghosts who had spent, they said, many happy hours at their fireside in the house at the pier. Much of the conversation they shared had been conducted in Gaelic. This house had burned down, they told me, and they had demolished the shop.

We exchanged Christmas cards for a few years then their niece wrote telling me that both brothers were now dead. Another link with the past was broken.

Tarbert was home, I think, to another skipper – whose name honestly escapes me – but who added another famous chapter to the folk lore of herring fishermen. He had run his ringer onto a rock one black night and could not get her off by going full astern. The boat was firmly stuck, and was rolling from side to side, bumping each bilge in turn and threatening to do herself severe, if not fatal, damage. He flashed his searchlight at his neighbour – this was before the days of radio – and as soon as he judged them to be within earshot he roared, "Boys, ye better hurry up an get this boat off or we'll aal be in maternity"!

***Village Belle* Leaving Girvan, 1968**

It would not be possible to leave Tarbert - which has, as you will see, a deserved reputation for inventing nicknames - without mention of that other family of fishers supreme, the Jacksons, who latterly owned the *Oak Lea*, the *Village Maid* and the *Village Belle*.

Their father, Willie "Baillie" (pronounced "Biley") Jackson was one of the legendary fishing partnerships in Tarbert that consisted of Tommy "The Bear" Jackson and Alec "Calabour" Jackson. The first boats they owned, as far as I can ascertain, were the *Flora* and the *Sweet Home*.

The Baillie had six sons of whom perhaps the best known were Willie "The Count" and Neil, "The White Fella".

Neil told me of being at sea as a very young lad with his father, the Baillie, in the *Village Belle*. She was powered by an 88 horse-power Kelvin. Their neighbour was the *Village Maid*, a slightly smaller boat with a Zulu stern that was powered by a 44 h.p. Kelvin. After fruitlessly searching for many long, weary and boring hours on a bitterly cold January night, to the freezing and exhausted crews' relief they dropped anchor at Bear Island, near Newton, which is opposite Furnace, in Upper Loch Fyne.

They had barely crawled into the warmth of their welcoming beds, however, when The Bear dropped into their forecastle and announced that they were getting under way for Crossaig, which is some way south of Tarbert.

They all got dressed again, lifted the anchor which in Neil's words, "was hardly in the watter lang enough tae get wet," gave a tow rope to the slower *Village Maid*, and set off south. Three hours later, when they arrived at Crossaig with daylight just coming in they shot, and got 350 baskets of herring – the only ones landed that day.

Neil was genuinely puzzled as he asked: "What on earth got into that man's heid – how did he know there were herrin' there?"

There was a token wheelhouse on the *Village Maid*, but The Bear wouldn't use it - it was just a store for old oilskins and tins of paint. He stood out in the open air - rain, hail or gale, on a beam behind the wheelhouse and steered the boat with a tiller. He wanted to be at one with nature hearing, smelling and seeing everything!

Neil told me, between cackles of laughter, of the occasion off the Cock of Arran when The Bear took offence at one of a pair of Maidens boats which was, he thought, coming much too close to the back of their net. He removed the heavy tiller and, waving it over his head, told the skipper of the offending boat just what he was going to do with it as soon as he got his net hauled.

“That poor man took off then, and ah don’t think he eased her doon till he got tae Lamlash!” Neil told me.

The old Baillie used to hire a taxi on occasion if the fishing was slack in the Clyde, and set off for a run west and north from Tarbert, around the head of Loch Caolisport which is on the west side of Kintyre, north of Tarbert. He was looking for an ‘appearance’ of herring and the sighting of a seal might be enough to send the boats through the Crinan canal. These expeditions were often blessed with success but Neil, not much more than a year before he died, told me of a later occasion when his brother, the Count, was in charge and he got the word that there was an appearance in Loch Caolisport. He mustered the crews and without telling any of the crew where they were going, both boats set off through the Crinan Canal. They returned via the same route, filled with herring, taken in one ring at Loch Caolisport.

As soon as the news got to Tarbert, the rest of the fleet set off immediately for the canal, hoping to get a share of what herring were left.

Back in Tarbert the Jacksons unloaded their catches and it was very late at night when they finished work. “Home to bed now, after a wee dram,” thought Neil but no, the Count had different ideas. They set off south, round the Mull of Kintyre, and north again to Loch Caolisport.

They crept into the dark loch as quietly as they could, and with their lights extinguished. They saw the anchor lights of the fleet lying in the outer loch. These boats had searched in vain and, as the area they had to search was quite small, they deduced that the Jacksons had killed all of the herring. Discouraged and tired, they gave up and went to sleep. Neither Neil nor his brother, Willie, could tell me why the herring were in the inner loch when they arrived – probably they came in with the flood tide. They shot, and again caught enough to fill both boats.

“We left them fuck aal but scales!” cackled Neil, as he relived the events.

When I recounted the tale, as Neil had told it, to Willie he said, "Aye, that's right, but did he tell ye that when we finished discharging the first lot I went up to the pub to look for Neil. He was there with Robert Ross and I jeest told him to get to hell back aboard the boat. He looked at me an I could see what he was thinking, but Robert said: 'Ye'd better get oot o' here an dae whit Willie tells ye!'"

"A bloody good job he did, tae," Willie concluded!

Willie also put a large part of his success in catching herring to never giving up, no matter how tired they might be. He told me of dropping his winkie right alongside a pair of Tarbert boats that were lying at anchor. "Ah wid tell ye who they wir, but there's some o' them still alive up there," he said, pointing up the hill. "Ah widny want tae offend them!" One of the anchored boats' crew came up on deck to see what the noise was about and I think that the event was all the sweeter for Willie to recall, as these boats were great rivals of his. "We filled the two boats before their bloody eyes were right open," he said.

He also told me of the time when, frozen half to death and dog tired, they had dropped their anchor for a couple of hour's respite, somewhere near the Skate, which is opposite Tarbert. They weren't long in their bunks when his brother, Neil, had to go on deck to relieve himself only to find that the herring were "playin' the sea dry," all around them. His roars roused all hands. They shot and got over 500 baskets of bonny herring. That was just pure luck!

Their preferred fishing grounds in the early days in the North were Loch Skipport and Shepherd's Bight but they later transferred this preference south to Eriskay, Barra Sound and around Northbay.

They took a lot of herring from an area close to the eastern entrance to Eriskay harbour. It was an extremely 'tight' place to ring, being surrounded by very foul ground that almost certainly guaranteed a tearing if the net was out of place by even a few yards. At this time there was a small group of very successful

Eriskay fishermen, led by Calum MacKinnon. Calum was another gentleman – and I use the word thoughtfully – who tragically died at a very young age.

These men knew that the Jacksons were taking herring right on their doorstep and had tried ringing in this spot several times, each time doing damage to their nets. Neil Jackson went out of his way to show Calum just exactly how to take the ring – another example of the comradeship shown at that time.

In the days when telephones were a rarity indeed, one of the great sources of news was the milkman. He, on his rounds with his horse and cart, got to know all of the gossip in a village, and it was from him that wives got much of the news of the success - or lack of it - of their husbands at the fishing. Tarbert men used to laughingly say, “Aye, ye’ll be namely at the milk kert in the moarnin,” whenever anyone did something of note. Well, the Jacksons were namely on a fair few mornings. It was said of them that, “These men would get a shot (of herring) on a patch of damp grass.”

I stood in such awe of them that I almost believed it!

The Count retired from the fishing at quite an early age, as the ring netting era was drawing to a close. He told me himself that he simply didn’t like having to go trawling for prawns. “That’s no’ fishin’ – that’s jeest pure fuckin’ boredom!” he said.

He moved, to the surprise of all, to Hamilton, where he bought a flat. “There wis a pond that hid ducks an gulls sweemin aboot it, jeest across the green, so I knew ah’d be aa right there.”

A few years ago I was in Tarbert en route to Campbeltown and called, as I usually did, at the small kipper yard that is run – and staffed – by Donald McAllister and his brother, Ian. Donald told me that The Count was back in Tarbert, after several years exile when he lived in Hamilton.

I promptly reversed my course and headed back into the village to see if Willie was in the mood for a yarn. He was, and I spent well over an hour in his company, engrossed by the tales he had to tell.

Willie Jackson, "The Count", in 2008

When I asked him how he passed his time he told me that on most days he drove down to a parking place down past the ferry pier. There he sat, read his paper and occasionally looked out to sea remembering, as he scanned the now barren waters of Lower Loch Fyne, the glory days when he fished there.

On my way back north, on a Sunday morning, I went again to his house, parking among other cars in the space across the road from where he lived. As I got out of my car I saw a head bobbing up and down over the roof of a car a few yards away. When I approached I saw that it was Willie, armed with a shovel, attacking the stone chippings that filled a large canvas container – there must have been a ton in it, at least.

"Aye, Willie," I began. "What on earth are you doing?"

"Whit the Hell does it look lik'?" he replied. "Ah'm shovelling they chips on tae ma parking space. Whit are you efter?"

"I'm on my way home, and I jeest thought I'd stop for a wee yarn, Willie".

"Weel, ye can see ah'm busy, so ye can jeest fuck off!"

I did just that!

Willie Jackson, "The Count", is still alive as I write and I see him as often as I can when I pass through Tarbert. Willie would most certainly, in my opinion, be among the top ten of ring net fishermen!

⚓

Another great character from Tarbert, was Willie "Gorrie" MacAffer. I remember listening one day to a company of what were to me "old men" yarning aboard the *Golden Gleam* in Castlebay, the subject being the bad weather they had severally experienced in their lives at sea.

As the yarns went around, the seas grew greater and the winds wilder. To quote one unforgettable description: "There was a bound," (Kintyre expression for a swell) "aye, a bound up tae the heather". Willie listened to these tales, his pipe drawing well, smiling very gently as the seas and the stories grew taller.

At last a lull developed in the conversation.

Willie, sensing with the unerring instinct of a master that the time was right for the kill, drew deeply on his pipe, fixed his eye on the heavens and said slowly, " Ah mind wan night gaan across the mooth o' Snizort. Aye, the win' was screamin'. South-east it wis."

"Ah had ma heid oot o' the wheelhoose winda there lookin', lookin' for the land. Well -" (a long pause to ensure that the pipe was drawing properly) – "well, she took wan roll tae starboard, dipped ma pipe intae the watter, an' pit it oot!"

As I remember it, the company dispersed quietly then.

I had spent some time with a superb story-teller, and surely a Captain, to boot.

⚓

I mentioned earlier that Tarbert probably had more nicknames per head of population than anywhere else I know of. Chatting to Donald MacAllister, the kipper man, one day, we touched on just that subject. "There wis a man here called 'Cooeedan' for a byename. Hive ye any idea where that might have come fae?" Donald asked. Of course I didn't so he told me that when he was a wee boy this man, whose given name was Dan, was in the habit of rowing across Tarbert harbour to play with his pal, who lived there. When his food was ready, or when it was time for bed, his mother used to go down to the beach and call across the water to her son, "Cooee, Daaan! Time ye were hame!"

Coming south along the Kintyre shore on our quest for the Captains, about whose exploits I never tired of hearing, but unfortunately forget far too much, we come to Carradale.

The Carradale men were often referred to by the collective name, 'The Slants'. This was because they would often, when telling a story, prefix the tale by saying, "Ah mind wan night we got a real good slant…" This simply meant that they had perceived a chance, or an opportunity, and had used it!

This small and beautiful village is about half way between Tarbert and Campbeltown, but until relatively recently when a new pier was built, it did not afford a safe harbour for any of the boats owned and operated from it.

There I instantly think of "Wee Jamie" Campbell owner of the *Irma*, who was probably more in tune with nature than any other fisherman I ever met.

I can still see him as I last did, standing outside his cottage beside the burn at Waterfoot near Carradale - a medium sized stocky man, dressed - as were all the fishermen from this bygone era - in his home-knitted, tight-fitting blue 'gansey'.

These 'ganseys' or jerseys incidentally, were almost all knitted by the men's wives, to their own pattern. This individuality was deliberate, in the knowledge that it might be the only method of identifying the wearer if he were to be drowned, and the body recovered after some time in the sea.

Wee Jamie, 'Buckets' as he was known to all, rarely had to leave home for the other fisheries exploited by so many of his

Mairi Bhan **and** *Harvest Queen* **on Carradale Beach**

contemporaries. He did well enough on his home grounds, and at the end of the year when the 'league table' of financial results were being discussed, he was rarely out of the top ten.

In the time of which I write, the echo sounding devices were in their infancy and fishermen still relied very much upon the traditional methods of fish finding, including the feeling wire.

This was about thirty fathoms of 'piano wire', to which was attached a heavy lead weight.

The device was trailed astern of the slow moving boat, reached down to about fifteen fathoms, and when it was towed through an unseen shoal of herring, the bumps of the herring hitting the wire could be felt by the trained hand holding it. These touches revealed their presence.

Of course, the length of the wire had to be varied constantly by the wireman, keeping it ideally within a few feet of the bottom. Too deep and you ran the risk of losing the lead on a rocky fastener, too high and it might pass over a shoal of bottom-hugging herring.

Wee Jamie would not entrust the vital jobs of either steering the boat or of holding the wire, to anyone else. He stood outside the wheelhouse on the starboard side, his left arm steering through the open window, the wire held in his right hand.

All around the starboard quarter of his boat, the *Irma*, the moulding iron (a metal strip which was fitted to the exposed edges of the wood in order to protect them) was almost cut through in a dozen places. It had been scarred by the feeling wire's constant movement over it. These marks - unique silent testimonials to the eccentric fishing skills of "Wee Jamie" - were looked at and spoken of with awe, by me and my contemporaries.

When echo sounders came into vogue it was noticed that the ping emitting from the transmitter of this device was audible to the human ear when the listener was, for example, in the fo'c'sle of a boat lying alongside the one whose sounder was running.

Wee Jamie hearing this pronounced that, "Them damn things'll jeest frighten aal the herrin' off the shore," and for years refused to have one fitted.

When eventually his son, Jim, insisted on one being installed, it ran only when the son was on deck. As soon as he went below, off went the sounder!

Grieve Gemmell of Dunure told me that while still a young boy, fishing with his father, Sammy, they passed inside the Irma and her neighbour the Watercress who were lying off a bay to the north of Campbeltown one night. Seeing a small mark on the sounder, they shot and got about fifty baskets of good herring.

The following morning, Grieve was on the pier in Campbeltown, listening to some local skippers discussing - as was their custom - the previous night's events.

"We were lyin' off Bobby's Rest," Wee Jamie indignantly piped up in his soft Highland accent. "We were lyin' there quietly listenin' tae a nice play o' herrin' getherin', when that bugger

Gemmell cam' along wi' that sounder bang bangin' aweh. He shot, an' whoot he didna kill, he frightened!"

Grieve crept off quietly, he told me, before he was recognised.

'Wee Jamie' used to take advantage of the time spent ashore when the boats were overhauled in the Spring, by prowling along the shore at low water – particularly in the times of spring tides - in a punt which had an outboard motor fitted. This enabled him to visually survey the bottom for possible fasteners in favoured bays.

Jim, one of his sons, told me of the occasion when his father was ill and confined to bed. Jim skippered the boat but was instructed to report to his father each morning when he returned to Carradale. It was a time of slack fishing but one evening they had gone across to the Arran shore at a place called 'The Rock'. He saw a small spot on the echo sounder but when he turned round, they had disappeared. Thinking that they had been heading toward the shore and knowing that the bottom was very rough in there, he gave up but decided that they should return before daylight, to see if they could get them on their way off the shore again.

All night they searched, but to no avail. There were no herring to be seen at all.

As daylight approached the pair set off toward the Rock again – it was close to home anyway!

They saw nothing at all, and returned to Carradale where James called, as instructed, to report to his father, telling him in full detail where they had searched.

"Whoot time o' moarnin did ye get tae the Rock?" his father interrupted, when James reached the point in his story where they were about to set off for home.

"Oh, about five, or half-past five," James replied.

"What sort o' night wis it – wis it clear?"

"Aye, it wis. It wis frosty, but a bonny starry night."

"Did ye see the moarning star?"

"Aye, we did," replied his puzzled son.

"Ye were too late! Ye needed tae be there an hour earlier. The herrin' come off there jeest as soon as the moarnin' star shows itself ower the hill, especially when there's a clear, frosty sky."

Now this was in the month of January and it is just as dark at 6 a.m. as it is at 5 a.m. so Jim took no great heed of this statement, but went home to his bed.

On the following evening they again saw a small spot of herring in the same area, but again they were gone when they turned on them.

All through the long, weary and boring night they searched, but to no avail.

Well after midnight, Jim called his neighbour alongside to exchange ideas and told him of his father's thoughts of the previous morning.

"Ah well," the reply came, "We might as well try that – we've tried jeest about everythin' else, and it's close tae home anyway."

They arrived at the Rock around four in the morning and shortly afterwards, James shot on a 'wee scatter'. They got over 200 baskets of bonny herring!

Wee Jamie was dead within the week and the bulk of what was an enormous fund of irreplaceable knowledge went to the grave with him.

His son, Jim, has just built a new house near the shore and not far south of Carradale. He has a small conservatory on the seaward side of the house, which has an old boat's compass lying on the window ledge. Jim told me that just around the point that is directly south of the house, is where he rang around 1600 baskets of herring, one night long ago. I know that Jim will spend many, many hours sitting by that window, reliving the events of that night.

Such men are growing fewer by the day!

In the fo'c'sle of the *Florentine* CN 74
In bunk: James McConnachie; Around table: Donald MacAlister, Bill MacMillan, Walter McConnachie, John McConnachie

My wife and I love, on the all too infrequent visits to Carradale, to visit with Archie (Wee Erchie) Paterson, his wife, Crystal and their near neighbours, John (The Shore) McConnachie, whose wife, Ishobel, makes us tea while we are busy re-catching the herring that died many years before!

Archie was the successful skipper of the *Harvest Queen*, a lovely example of a ringer, which had been built by MacMillan of Fairlie whilst John was skipper of the *Florentine*, one of the youngest ring-net skippers ever. They both pine for the days that are gone – but that is common with most, if not all, fishermen.

Campbeltown

My next port of call has to be Campbeltown.

That I know more Captains there, is simply due to the fact that by virtue of having lived there I knew more Campbeltonians than, for example, Carradale men.

The first of my Campbeltown Captains would seem to refute that statement, for although I have seen him when I was very young, I did not know Bobby Robertson, 'The Hoodie', personally.

I have heard and read a lot though, and just this year read an article describing him as having led the way in the revolution in design of the entire Scottish fishing fleet.

He had several boats built here in Fife, the best known of which were probably the *Kingbird*, the *Kingfisher*, the *Kestrel*, and the *Kittiwake*, although a special place in the history books must be kept for the *Brothers*, the very first West Coast fishing boat to have an engine fitted, in 1907.

A book could be written about this extraordinary man, whose foresight and vision almost single-handedly dragged the fishing industry into the twentieth century. He retired early because of the onset of blindness.

I do not think there will be any dissenting voices among any readers of this book who are fishermen, if we promote him exclusively to Admiral. In any company, anywhere, he could only be described as a man of outstanding capabilities.

Several of 'The Hoodie's' contemporaries must be invited to join this elevation to captaincy, John Short, and John Wareham being the first, but we must not forget the Blair family who are credited in many quarters with doing more than any other to further the introduction of the ring net to the 'North', by their pioneering expeditions in their ringer, the *Bengullion*.

I have watched these men in their declining years set off on walks from the 'Wee-us' – which translates into 'weigh-house', at the head of the pier, away down the esplanade on the south side of the Loch. What yarns must have been exchanged on these excursions. What would I give to be able to hear the reminiscences of such giants now?

The 'Wee-us' used to stand in isolation in the middle of the square at the head of the Old Quay in Campbeltown. It was built to house the operators of the weighing machine which was used by carts, and latterly lorries that had been loaded from coasters berthed at the Quay.

On the wee-us wall was fixed a barometer which was consulted every day by the fishermen, but its presence provided shelter from the winds also, so it became a favourite stance for all the worthies of the day.

This barometer bore several legends that helped the observer to get some idea of forecasting what weather was to come. 'First rise after low, foretells a stronger blow'. 'Mackerel skies and mare's tails make tall ships carry small sails.' These are the only ones I can recall now.

This barometer was removed, along with the wee-us, to give greater vision to the drivers of the all-important motor car, when a roundabout was built to aid their passage.

My father was cook on board John Short's boat the *Kingbird*, when she was new in the early 1930s. He told me that one day when they were lying in Rothesay mending a net that had been torn, he approached the skipper and asked him for money to buy some meat for the dinner.

John, a small but stocky character, was at an intricate part of the net- mending operation, and he answered in a preoccupied way - "Ye'll no' need money boy, jeest tell the butcher who it's for. No, ye'll no' need money." This was not a boastful proclamation, but a simple statement of fact. The names of such men were as good as hard cash, and their reputations were beyond reproach.

My father also told me that around this time the four 'Hoodie' boats had been filled with herring in one night in the Kyles of Bute, had discharged them at Rothesay, gone back to sea, and had returned with three of them filled again, all within twenty four hours! I should emphasise that these were not small boats – they were much bigger than the average of that time.

I wonder how many herring could be caught there now.

John Wareham made a valiant attempt in the declining years of the ring-net fishings, to keep the two remaining boats, the *Kestrel* and the *Kittiwake* at sea. Indeed it was said that he spent most of his personal savings in this attempt to help them survive, but in vain. The writing was on the wall by then.

John was not happy unless he was at sea, and the patience displayed by such men in their pursuit of herring was phenomenal.

This patience was not of course shared by all of the crew, and one bitterly cold February night when there was absolutely nothing being caught whilst the fleet was searching the Ballantrae Banks in the biting easterly wind, John's dogged persistence led to a famous incident with his crew.

They had watched the fleet gradually dwindle as other skippers gave up the fruitless search and made their way into Ayr harbour, and were understandably envious of the lucky crews of these boats who were by now sound asleep in their warm bunks.

Soon they and their neighbour were the only boats left on the sea. John, from the wheelhouse, regularly asked the poor man who was slowly freezing as he held the feeling wire which trailed astern, "Are ye feelin' anything?"

Eventually this poor man, tired and cold beyond his endurance, got hold of the broom and fixed it upright into the aft part of the boat, draped his oilskin over it, fixed his sou'wester above this, and sneaked below to the blessed heat of the engine room where he promptly fell asleep.

It was not until daylight started to come in that John realised the reason for the silence which had greeted all of his questions - there was no one there feeling for the herring.

The squeals of temper which accompanied this discovery were spoken of in awe for years. "Yis are aa sacked – every wan o yis!" was the least of the threats – none of which were carried out.

A piece of doggerel sticks in my memory from my early days at the fishing:

> "When the moon wis big an' roon,
> The herrin swam fae Ayr tae Troon,
> An' when the moon wis roon an' fair,
> The herrin' swam fae Troon tae Ayr!"

Just what that signified is beyond me, but I am sure that it was penned to commemorate some event or other in the pursuit of the silver darlings.

"Baldy" Stewart was another whose name should be written large in the annals of the fishing industry. A short, pipe-smoking barrel of a man who was always ready to smile and crack a joke, his jovial face will live forever in the memories of all who knew him.

For many years he skippered the *Boy Danny* successfully, and my most enduring memory of him also reflects the generally high standard of feeling evident in these days for one's fellow fishermen, which has now apparently been eroded beyond recall. This event occurred at the Manx fishing, when the herring were invariably caught south and west of Peel. No one looked on the east side of the Island at all.

The fleet was in Peel one morning after a night which had produced very light returns, when the word got out that Baldy was in Portpatrick with a big shot of herring.

No one knew where he had caught them. No one had seen the lucky pair during the previous night's fishing, so speculation was rife on the quay. Telephone calls to the fish salesman's office in Portpatrick revealed only that the fortunate crews had been sworn to secrecy, but eventually Baldy himself came to the telephone and told his tormentors that he would reveal the secret on the radio that afternoon whilst on his way back to the grounds. Keeping the secret until then meant that he would be in a position to compete equally with the rest of the fleet that coming night.

At the appointed hour he came on the radio and revealed to all that the herring had been killed off Douglas, on the east side of the Island.

The point of this story is that Baldy did not want his competitors to get an advantage over him, but he was not about to tell lies to preserve his position.

That brings to mind an occasion similar to, but on a much smaller scale, involving myself.

We were fishing in the Minch in June one year, and got a small but valuable shot at Muldonich Island at the mouth of Castlebay one Friday, when there was very little caught among the rest of the fleet.

On the way into Mallaig we were all told that we must not disclose to anyone just where we had got them.

On taking the hatches off in Mallaig we discovered a smallish salmon lying on top of the catch. It had been brailed aboard with the herring, unseen by anyone.

I was on the quay prior to starting to discharge the catch, when I was approached by 'Uncle' Jimmy Sloan, another immortal of whom more later. He approached, pipe as usual in the corner of his mouth, and inquired of me in a conspiratorial tone just where we had got the herring.

Now 'Uncle' Jimmy was a man of whom mere mortals stood in awe, especially young lads like the one from whom he was now trying to elicit information, and I was finding it very difficult indeed to withstand his intense questioning, when I remembered the salmon.

"Come here and see what we found on top of the herring when we took the hatches off this morning Uncle Jimmy," I said in a forlorn attempt to buy time, and led him to the edge of the quay from which vantage point he could look down into the open hold. I pointed at the salmon.

"Aw, that's a richt bonny fish boay," said Uncle Jimmy. "Whaur did ye get it?"

I very nearly told him!

Baldy, if I may return to him, had retired from the fishing and lived in a wee flat at the head of the New Quay, alone except for his constant companion, a little terrier dog.

He must have been in his seventies when he went on an excursion to Rothesay on a motor yacht, the *Quesada*, taking his dog with him of course.

On the return trip, the weather deteriorated very quickly. The *Quesada* got into difficulties right at the mouth of Campbeltown Loch and sank, taking with her several young men.

Baldy not only got out of her safely, but took his beloved dog with him!

His son Willie, "Suet" to all, unfortunately died as "My Captains" was being written. Willie was another kind and gentle man who is remembered with delight by me, and I am certain by all of his contemporaries. He had been a Lieutenant Commander in the Royal Navy during the war, and one result of his being in the Officers mess was that on the odd occasion when he took a wee dram, his speech became more 'proper' than normal. So the theory went anyway! One thing for sure, I don't think that anyone ever heard him use foul or profane language at any time, no matter what the circumstances were.

I will never forget him one night in Lochboisdale aboard the *Golden Hind* when there was an impromptu concert in full swing. His turn to sing came around, and as no-one was excused this duty, he reluctantly got to his feet.

"I cannot sing at all well, so I will recite a poetry," he began in his 'proper' accent.

> "Little spider on the wall,
> You ain't got no hair at all.
> You ain't got a comb to comb your hair.
> But you don't care,
> 'Cos you ain't got no hair!"

The 'poem' concluded, Willie subsided slowly back to his previous relaxed position by the table, a beatific smile on his face all the while.

The last time I met Willie was when I was invited to his daughter and son- in- law's house one evening. Willie had been baby sitting for them and, when we arrived, he got up to leave but he stood by the door after he had opened it, turned round and delivered an absolutely cracking soliloquy – word perfect and very amusing. It took several telephone calls to him before he finally wrote out a copy for me.

I will take the liberty of sharing this with you. Willie explained that it was supposed to be an announcement made by the Ringmaster of a Circus. Those of you who were fortunate enough to have known Willie, will be able to imagine him recite it, with that lovely grin on his face as he did so.

<u>The Circus Acts</u>

"Again I have the pleasure of announcing myself on behalf of the Brothers Salvona's Circus, who have done their best to please their audiences in this fair town.

Tomorrow night we will have that famed drama, 'The frozen snotter on the barn door,' followed by 'Who shit in the lodger's stocking.' If time will permit we will have that most laughable and screaming Sketch full of pathos and approbation entitled 'Cheer up Maggie, your mother's diddies have went through the mangle!'

Also, ladies and gentlemen, come and see the spotted wonder; it's got 4 spots on its back, 3 spots on its belly and 1 on its … cock up your heads, ladies and see the greatest dancer in the World. She's very good with the left leg but not so good with the right – but between both legs she makes a decent living.

Come and see the monkeys, they've got hairs from the tops of their heads to the soles of their feet, right round their … can't you see the monkeys?

Now all those ladies and gentlemen who cannot swim will head for the gallery as Boskus the elephant is going to make his water.

Thank you!"

No, thank you, Willie – it was a great privilege to have known you!

Jock Meenan was another contemporary of Baldy's, and for many years he skippered the *Stella Maris*. He was a tall austere man, who thought much more than he talked. He epitomised all that was to be admired in successful fishermen and I know that he was held in very great regard by the late Ian Stewart, a local lawyer and a faithful servant to all the Clyde fishermen.

Jock's son and daughter went to America while still quite young and it was a great surprise to all when Jock and his wife followed, leaving his nephew Jim in charge of the boat.

Cecil Finn, who served his time with Jock and who shared my admiration for the man, told me that most of Jock's time in America was spent watching men sail model yachts in a pond near his new home, which was far from the sea.

In due course he and his wife came back home on holiday, and were aboard one of the Clyde steamers on the final leg of the trip to Campbeltown. The steamer called at Lochranza en route. Jock spotted his beloved *Stella Maris* at anchor in the bay, left the steamer there and then and bribed a small boy to row him out to her. His wife saw him again at the end of the week!

'Captain' Jock was a sore loss to the fishing community in Campbeltown, but Jim Meenan, his nephew, had donned the vacant mantle, and wore it with distinction for not nearly enough years.

I must be counted among the many who had a great regard for Jim – a man who never seemed to see the dark side of anyone's nature, and I remember one day being horrified when he said that another fisherman was in his opinion - "Not very intelligent, but possessing a vast amount of low animal cunning, which is much more important!" I initially thought that this was a derogatory remark - which would have been completely out of character from Jim - but since then of course, I have realised that he was in fact being complimentary to the man.

Jim was skipper of the *Stella Maris* when the stakes became higher, but he never sacrificed his integrity at the altar of financial gain, and the loss to the industry was great indeed when he died, far too young.

Shortly after his death I was in Glasgow, and booked into the Loretto Hotel. This hotel - now closed and the owner long dead - drew most of its guests from the West Coast with Campbeltown and Mallaig featuring often on the guest book pages, and it was rare indeed to stay there without meeting a weel-kent face. When I arrived I was subjected to the usual interrogation about the latest gossip, by the owner Angus Campbell, and I asked him if he had known Jim Meenan. "Yes, of course," was his reply, but when I told Angus that Jim had just died he startled me by turning on his heel and walking quickly away. My puzzlement was resolved when he returned to my room later, and in some distress suggested that when I left, that I should not pay him, but use the money I owed to him to buy some flowers for Jim's widow! I convinced him that this was not a good idea, as I was not likely to be in Campbeltown for some time, so thought that he should send them himself. I do not know the ultimate outcome of this event, but it does illustrate the regard in which Jim was held by even casual acquaintances.

In the days when medium frequency radio was the only means of communicating with one's neighbour when for example, you were on way back from market, it was often difficult to get through the crowded airwaves, so a series of whistles were used by the callers to identify themselves. These whistled tunes would be heard through the most crowded traffic, and meant that the listeners should go to another less crowded prearranged frequency. Jim always used 'Eileen Allanah'. I never hear this tune without thinking of him, and I often wonder if these transmissions are still winging their way through eternal space.

Robert McGown of the *Felicia* was another dedicated man whose integrity was greatly admired by those less gifted. In common with many of the others he did not drink alcohol at all, nor did he smoke and his weekly treat was to buy a half pound of peppermints on a Saturday, so Angus will have to supply something other than whisky for a great many of my Captains!

Moving on to a younger generation, no mention of Campbeltown fishermen would be complete without reference to Duncan

Macdonald, better known as 'Dunky Donal', who skippered the *Golden Hind*.

The last time I met him, he had a small boy by the hand. In response to the prompt, "Tell this man what your name is," the lad replied in a loud voice - "Dunky Donal!" The delight on Dunky senior's face was something to see, on hearing his grandson lay claim to the name. This 'small boy' approached me some time ago and told me that he was the lad in my tale. He was then the harbour-master in Campbeltown.

Ian MacLennan, P. K. McGown (skipper of the *Felicia*), Tommy Ralston senior

I first became aware of Dunky when he was aboard my father's boat, the *Golden Fleece*, before I left school. He was a big genial man, a bluff happy and very popular character who was, when excited, inclined to stutter slightly. He laughed a lot, but was reputedly not too happy in the dark having it was said, in common with many of his contemporaries, an inbuilt belief in 'bockans', or ghosts!

The story was told to me of the time when the *Golden Fleece* was lying in Port St. Mary on the Isle of Man, waiting for a lull in the weather. In due course, the wind went up to the west, and eased. This abatement was accompanied by a very heavy downpour.

The crew had all, with the exception of Dunky, come back aboard before the rain started, but the cook, 'Wee Mo' by nickname - this because of his lack of stature - was sent to fetch the missing Dunky.

Mo donned a raincoat – a demob issue - belonging to my father, which was almost white in colour, and which was much too big for Mo, pulled it over his head, and set off up the south side of the street.

He had not gone very far when, through the murky darkness of the night, he saw the figure of a man, head down against the rain, going toward the pier, on the north side of the street.

Mo stopped, not at all sure of the identity of this person but eventually, after they had passed one another, decided that it was indeed the person for whom he was searching, so he set off in pursuit.

Dunky for his part became aware only of a ghostly white figure behind him, convinced himself – correctly - that this apparition was chasing him, so he set off at a rapid rate of knots down the pier, calling for assistance as he neared the boat!

To his eternal credit, he delighted in telling this story against himself.

The *Golden Hind*, which Dunky later bought, was a large, very powerful boat for her day. She was fitted with a Kelvin diesel, of an almost unheard of 132 horse power. This of course made her very fast in comparison with her companions, and Dunky was very proud of this vessel's speed and manoeuvrability.

One dark January night, Dunky had the misfortune to strike the outside edge of the Stuleys, a small group of unlit islands that lay off the east coast of South Uist, not far north of Lochboisdale. The damage was all underwater, so it was not possible to see just what repairs were necessary, but it was agreed that we in the *Golden Fleece* should escort him to Mallaig where expert help was available.

Dunky's boat was very much faster than ours, so it was some time after he had beached the *Golden Hind* in Mallaig that we arrived.

When the tide had fallen enough Charlie Henderson, the local boat builder, appeared on the scene and accompanied by an anxious Dunky, proceeded to survey the damage.

"What sort of speed were you doing?" was Charlie's first question.

"Full bit," says Dunky tremulously, fearing the worst.

A long pause followed, with Charlie prodding the injured forefoot.

Eventually he spoke.

"Ye've hurt her dignity Dunky," he said quietly.

The roars from the relieved Dunky could be heard miles away - "Hear that," he bellowed to all and sundry, "Full bore on tae the Stuleys, an' aal I did was hurt her dignity. Some ship this, eh!"

At the time when the dreadful disease myxomatosis had been introduced in a vain attempt to control the rabbit population and was headline news in most newspapers, Dunky was enjoying a very successful spell of fishing in the Mull lochs, landing good shots of herring into Oban almost every day. It became his habit to have a wee dram in one of the local hostelries, on occasion.

One day not long after he had come into the bar, he slid on to the floor, his feet waving wildly in the air.

"What's wrong wi' ye, Dunky?" shouted the thoroughly alarmed barman.

"Ah've got mix ma toes!" was the reply from the irrepressible Dunky!

The Minch fishing subjected all its participants to long spells of boredom cooped up in what can only be described as abysmal conditions, when bad weather confined them to anchor in some remote loch. This boredom was relieved in many ways but one game of 'I spy' aboard the *Golden Hind* ended in complete confusion when a glorious character who rejoiced in the nickname of "Neep", had them all baffled with the initials 'L.L'. When at last they had all given in, Neep revealed that it meant 'Lectric Light', and promptly got severely thumped by Dunky for his lack of spelling ability!

There was however one unique event devised by Dunky and his crew.

They would perform a play! They practised this all week and when at the weekend in Lochboisdale the "opening night" arrived, the show was a sell-out. The audience filled the fo'c'sle entirely, and the unfortunates who could not be accommodated below decks were trying to view the fun by looking through the open skylight, from the foredeck.

I do not know who was responsible for the script, but the show went thus:-

Actor No.1 is seen 'sweeping the yard,' at his home in the deep south of America: actually the forecastle of the *Golden Hind.*

Actor No.2 appears slowly from the hold lazily carrying a rifle, (formerly a broom handle) and greets No.1 thus:

"Howdy Paw."

"Howdy son," came the reply, in a drawling Southern American accent gleaned from the Cinema but redolent of Campbeltown. "Where ya bin, son?"

"Ah've bin to the war, Paw."

"What'd ya do in the war, son?"

"Ah done a heap a killin', Paw"

"What ya do ya heap a killin' with, son?"

"Ah done a heap a killin' wi' ma ol' rifle, Paw" (this said brandishing the broom handle), "an' ah done a heap a killin' wi' ma pineapples too."

"Pineapples, son: what's a pineapple?"

"This here's a pineapple, Paw," says the son brandishing a large potato from which protruded a match. "See that there li'l' green shed, Paw? Well, watch this!"

The actor playing the part of the son then pulls the match from the potato with his teeth, counts to five, and throws it into a bunk.

This is the signal for the rest of the cast (the crew) to make as much noise as possible, banging the table, stamping their feet and for lights to be flashed on and off simulating an explosion.

"That sure is a mighty pow'ful weapon, son," says Paw, when the noise dies down. "Ya shouldn' ha' done that though."

"Why not Paw?"

"Because yore Maw was having a crap in that li'l' green shed, Son!"

His slight stutter led to another famous incident. He was having difficulty getting through to Oban Radio for a link call, they were unable to ascertain the name of his boat properly. Eventually Dunky, in a fit of desperation roared, "The *G-G-Golden Hind* , F-F-Francis Drake had wan the s-s-same fuckin name!"

That, of course, was heard loud and clear, and led to a severe reprimand from Oban Radio, in writing.

He was fishing one night at the Brown Head, on Arran, a place where the bottom was so bad that it was nearly impossible to ring without getting a tearing.

After the net was hauled, it was made ready for another ring – a task that would not normally take more than ten or fifteen minutes. If, however, the net was torn it had to be laced – using white twine that was readily visible when hauling again – and this could, depending on the extent of the tear, take some considerable time.

Dunky had suffered a bad tear on the night I am writing of, and his crew had been working on it for a long time. He was not in a good mood.

Seeing his lights on for such a long time, a Maidens skipper called him and asked if he had torn his net – a superfluous question under the circumstances.

"Naw, they're makin a foo-foo machine," Dunky replied.

"A foo-foo machine? Whit's that, Duncan?"

"It's a machine for throwin shite at the moon!" Dunky answered.

Dunky was a successful fisherman, very popular with his fellows from all over Scotland, and is certainly one of the Captains who would be welcome at any fireside.

Modern Campbeltown

A great many of the happier memories of my early days at the fishing are centred on the Isle of Man, with its west-coast port of Peel a favourite among us all. Apart from anything else, it was generally agreed that the Manx herring were the finest tasting ones we could get.

I remember well sitting in a group above the harbour at Peel one fine summer day, when two old ladies stopped to view the fleet of boats assembled there.

"What do these letters on the boats mean?" asked one of them, referring to the registration marks which were painted on the bow and stern of each ringer.

"C.N., my dear, stands for Campbeltown," answered James McNaughton, better known as "Madrala" – another well-loved shipmate of mine. "B.A. means Ballantrae, T.T. is for Tarbert, L.H. is for Leith and P.L. is for Peel."

"How interesting!" replied one of the ladies, "And what does K.Y. signify?" As she said this she pointed to one of the boats from the Firth of Forth, which was registered at Kirkcaldy.

"That means that this boat is from Kentucky," offered the irrepressible Madrala, and off went the old dears, marvelling at the distances travelled in the pursuit of herring!

Two young lads were 'lurking', there is no other word for it, outside a chemist's shop in Peel one Saturday morning. They belonged to Carradale – closer to that in identifying them, I will not go. They were watching to see if the young lady behind the counter would relinquish her post in favour of the male owner, who remained tantalisingly in sight, but not in a position where they could be sure of being served by him. They were, of course, attempting to buy condoms, which were not so easily accessed in the days of which I write.

The chances of their actually needing to use such devices were remote in the extreme, but hope springs eternal …! They had already been in two such shops and as they had been attended by female staff in both of them and were shy of asking for the items they desired, they now had enough aspirins to last them for some time! They were spotted by an older crewmate who deduced what they were after and, sensing the opportunity for a bit of fun, he made a bee-line for them.

"Ur ye efter F.L.s (short for French Letters - condoms to the uneducated!) boys?" he asked.

"Naw, no' really," one of the lads replied, but his scarlet cheeks revealed the lie.

"Jeest come in wi' me, ah'll show ye how tae get them withoot any bother, " said the older man.

They hesitantly followed him into the shop where immediately the young lass stepped forward and asked if she could help him.

"Aye, mebbe ye can. Hiv ye got a jecket fur a hen?"

"Excuse me," said the lass, "I don't understand what you are saying."

"Ah'm efter a jacket fur a hen!"

The shop owner, who had heard this exchange now stepped forward to help and said, "We don't stock what you appear to be seeking. May I assist in some other way?"

"Ach well, if ye hivna got a jacket fur a hen, could ye gie me a coat fur a cock?"

My wife and I enjoyed, a few years ago, a visit from a Manx lady and her husband, who had been friends of mine in those blithe days, and during our recollections of the happy hours spent dancing in the small village dance-hall in Peel, this lady suddenly asked me if I remembered a fight taking place there. Thinking that she was referring to an incident which I had forgotten, I questioned her for more details.

"Oh no," she replied. "I am not referring to a specific fight, I am asking if you remember there ever being an occasion when one took place?"

I couldn't, but since then I have become aware of one of the reasons why there was so little trouble; we were afraid of the consequences of being arrested. Not, I hasten to add, afraid of the Manx Police who were very fair, but no matter how tough we thought we might be the threat of possibly being sentenced to having our trousers taken down and being birched made us think twice before offering violence to anyone. As young men who had, in common with most other young men, a mistaken idea of their own abilities, we raised the dust in most of the many ports of call, but in the Isle of Man we always walked just a little bit smaller.

What say your so-called Civil Rights workers to that, and how about bringing out some Civil Responsibilities workers, to counter their do-good tree-hugging ideas?

At the dance in Peel there was always an interval during which the band went to the nearest Hotel for a drink. I remember one night during this interval, a conga was started up and - led by one glorious character who must remain nameless - it wound its way out of the hall, went all the way along the promenade and back again to the hall, increasing in size by the minute - with never a cross word being exchanged.

It was not very often that nets were torn at the Isle of Man but one night, Dunky Donald tore one quite badly and as a result, had to haul it on to the pier on the south side of the river at Peel, where it was stretched out for mending.

'Neep', as we all knew him, was sent below to the engine room to get a piece of netting from its storage place right aft, beside the steering quadrant. Having taken the netting on to the pier, he sloped off back down the engine room hatch to "tidy up" as he put it. He was missed some time later and investigation revealed him lying in the engine room, sound asleep and full of whisky!

Where did this whisky come from, you ask? On occasion, men who went ashore on a Saturday night for a dram would buy a half-bottle of whisky to relieve a possible hangover on the Sunday morning. If he appeared in the forecastle with this, it would be drunk there and then by his shipmates so very often he would hide it somewhere. It was quite common for the hiding place, chosen by a hazy mind, to be forgotten, resulting in an increasingly frantic search in the morning. If it had been hidden on deck below a bight of net, it very often was not found until a clatter on the deck as the net was being hauled aft on the Monday, revealed its presence.

Someone had obviously 'planked' their carry-out under the spare netting in the engine room where it remained hidden until 'Neep' made his discovery in Peel.

That day Dunky's boat, the *Golden Hind*, had been tied up temporarily with her port side to the pier until the net was hauled ashore. Then she was turned around to lie starboard side to, so that when the tide went out and she grounded, she would lie against her fenders. By the time the net had been mended the boat had refloated and Jim Kelly, one of the crew, suggested to Dunky that he be allowed to turn her around so that the net could be hauled back aboard on to the port side again.

Now Jim was a very good looking young man who had a very muscular body and he often went 'topless' on a warm day. As a result, he was usually surrounded by a bevy of admiring young females. This was the case when he jumped aboard, started the engine and, having let go the mooring ropes, took his place in the wheelhouse.

Jim used the throttle quite a lot as he turned the boat, using his expertise to draw even more admiring stares from the ladies. He did his flamboyant 'three point turn' and placed the *Golden Hind* back alongside the pier. He had her securely tied up when someone, in fits of laughter, pointed out that he had moored her starboard side to once again.

That brought his ego down a peg or two!

I went back to Peel a few years ago with my wife. This was a mistake! What I remembered as a vibrant town had become, thanks to the cheapness of holiday flights to resorts in warmer climes, a pale shadow of its former self, inhabited largely by the ghosts of my memories.

I talked to a fisherman, in Port Saint Mary, on the south east side of the island on a later visit, and asked if there were any herring around – this was at the time of year when we used to fish them. He told me that there were plenty of herring "just out there", but that they were not allowed to fish for them. The fishing licenses, he said, had been bought up by Irish interests and they would scoop up their allowed amounts much later in the year. 'Manx' kippers were being sold in Peel right then and only after much questioning did I discover that they were being bought in from either the north-east of Scotland, or from Norway. Now that may make economic sense to some, but …!

I wrote earlier of the sublime taste of the Manx herring. Breakfast, when we were fishing there, was almost always boiled herring – provided we had caught some, of course – with lashings of toast. We quite often had visitors out for the night and as daylight was breaking and the fishing time was drawing to a close I, as cook, would ask them how many herring they would like for breakfast? They almost invariably would hesitate before declining (after all, who in their right mind would eat *boiled herring*, for breakfast?) They were sat down however, a plateful was laid before them and without exception, they scoffed the lot and were 'instant converts'. A feast fit for a King!

Whitby too brings fond memories, and one night not many years before I left Mallaig for the East Coast, I had a good laugh about these days. I was in the Marine Hotel, in the company of two Lifeboat Inspectors. It was winter and the hotel was quiet, so after our business had been concluded we asked the only other occupants of the cocktail bar to join our company. The young couple were English, and when I discovered that the girl hailed from Whitby, I exclaimed, "Whitby, why that is where I spent many happy days when I was young. I used to fish for herring from that port many years ago." On hearing this the girl, in a rather agitated manner, demanded to see my hands. I hesitantly held them out palm upward, whereupon she said excitedly, "No, I want to see the backs of them!" When I had turned them over for her inspection, wondering just what was going on, she then said in a disappointed tone, "No, it's not you, I'm afraid."

Her husband laughingly then explained that she was always on the lookout for her father who had been a Scottish fisherman, and the only thing her mother could remember about him was that she thought he had a knuckle missing on one of his hands.

Now if anyone reading this …!

I fear that I have strayed too long from the company of Captains, so must return, and in returning, move a little closer to the present day scene in Campbeltown before moving on to other places .

Neil Speed was skipper of the *Moira*, one of the more modern and larger ringers, and must also rate a mention here.

Neil was a very well turned out man, always trim, dapper and smart-looking, with a military bearing, and a very incisive way of speaking. He smoked a pipe almost incessantly. He was another who was lost to us tragically, much too young, leaving his son, also named Neil, to carry on the job.

An award for bravery during the war had been deservedly won by him, but in common with his fellows, when he spoke of that dark period his tales were all light-hearted ones.

Some time after his death I went into the cafe where his widow worked. I had been at the library, and was on my way home with my books which I laid on the counter.

Mrs Speed idly picked them up, and saw that one of them was about Captain Walker R.N., a brilliant officer who had revolutionised the war against the U boats in the Atlantic, and who almost certainly killed himself with overwork in the process of defeating them. Walker had, in pre-war days, been 'passed over' in the promotion league from Commander, to Captain. He had celebrated, in naval parlance, the 'Feast of the Passover'. So successful was he in his wartime anti-submarine career, however, that he was promoted to Captain and had his promotion backdated. This has only happened one other time in the Royal Navy, as far as I can ascertain. He was also renowned for not suffering fools gladly, a fact commented upon in several of the books written about him after his death.

Mrs Speed then told me that Neil had been drafted to Captain Walker's ship as Coxswain.

The Coxswain of a Royal Navy ship is the senior rating aboard, and holds an extremely responsible job.

It was made very plain to Neil, by Captain Walker, that he was not too happy at being sent a 'hostilities only' man for this post. Because Neil had been a fisherman before the war seemed to reduce his chances of being accepted by Captain Walker, but he was assured that he would be given a fair chance to prove his worth.

He succeeded in gaining the confidence of his commanding officer, served with him for over a year, and upon being drafted eventually to another ship, was invited into Walker's cabin on the morning of his departure. There two glasses of whisky were poured, and the two men toasted one another's health.

Neil asked for, and was given the glass from which his C.O. had drunk.

This glass, I was told, had pride of place in the china cabinet in Neil's home.

No-one was allowed to touch it, but Neil took it out at midnight every Hogmanay, filled it with whisky, drank to 'absent friends' and put it back unwashed - as indeed it had remained since his old boss, 'Johnnie' Walker had drunk from it so many years before.

Neil has rejoined his old ship now. I bet the yarn was good when they met again!

⚓

There are of course current contenders for Captaincy among the fishermen of the 'Wee Toon'.

One of the leaders of the pack must be Cecil Finn, my childhood pal, and owner of the *Gleaner*, whose apprenticeship started so long ago in Brown's house.

He is retired now, but played a very active part in the political scene, which has become so important nowadays and was awarded the M.B.E. for his work in this field. This was later followed by an O.B.E.

He is the same age as me, is sturdily built, and until time demanded its toll, he sported a shock of red hair. He closely resembles Amos of "Emmerdale Farm". Oddly enough he and I married girls with exactly the same – quite uncommon – Christian name.

He used a pipe until recently.

I say "used" advisedly. It had become a prop which helped to delay answers to questions which require a bit of thought, but like other stratagems have in the past, so this one backfired on him on one occasion not too long ago. Literally!

I am told by someone who was there, that Cecil had been despatched by his colleagues to 'sort out' the Navy who had announced to the fishermen that they required an area in the Clyde in which to hold a mine-sweeping exercise, and that the fishermen should keep away from this zone while the exercise took place.

It was felt among the fishing community that this was a prime fishing area, and that the Navy should go elsewhere to play their games.

On this 'sorting out' errand he was accompanied by a cousin of mine, Robert Gillies, 'Trapper' by nickname, who is another obvious contender for Captaincy. Robert, with his brother Willie, fished the *Morning Dawn*.

The delegation was completed by the inclusion of Patrick Stewart, a lawyer, and the third generation of his family to hold the post of Secretary to the Clyde Fishermen's Association.

When they arrived in the naval base they were greeted by a 'Four-Ringer' and his staff. These fellows had all been to the naval charm school, which teaches its scholars that most dissenting voices can be silenced by the application of liberal amounts of high powered gin.

The hospitality which they dispensed was being accepted gratefully by all except Patrick. He abstained from partaking of the good spirits on the grounds that he had to drive the others home.

When the naval contingent, experts at the art, decided that the time was right, a chart of the Clyde was spread over the table and the sales pitch began!

"Now then gentlemen, we intend laying our mines heah, heah, and heah, which I am sure you will agree won't affect your fishing efforts at all, don't you see?"

Thus began the aristocratic sounding leader of the naval hosts.

Our two candidates, when they tried to focus on the areas indicated by the pointer wielded by the Captain, realised that they had underestimated the potency of the duty-free gin and Cecil, in order to gain time, produced his pipe and started to apply lit matches to it, sucking noisily as he did so.

Trapper, however, lacking such a prop, viewed the chart through the haze (only part of which came from Cecil's pipe), grabbed the distinguished Naval personage by the lapels, and stated in his usual, very loud, very Campbeltown accent, “Aye, that’s aa’ right Jeck, but whoot if they pit them in the wrang bloody place, eh?”

Cecil was by now very agitated.

This truth of this observation was borne out by the fact that he was still applying lit matches to his pipe although there were actually flames coming from the bowl!

The distinguished Naval person, not at all happy at being grabbed in this manner, shook himself free from Robert’s grasp and in a very hurt tone declared, “ That won’t happen, my officahs are all highly trained navigatahs!”

Trapper re-attached himself to the Captain’s lapels and roared up at him, “Aye Jeck, but whoot if they’re a’ full o’ fuckin gin, eh?”

As this riposte registered in Cecil’s brain, he snorted!

This reaction resulted in burning tobacco being blown over the chart, causing countless fires to break out all over it and the table, and the meeting to break up in some confusion!

What cousin Trapper lacks in stature he more than makes up for in volume, and his habit of referring to all - close friend or stranger, male or female - as “Jeck”, has led to some confusion at times. His use of this mode of address caused a great deal of consternation in a young lady, highly literate in several languages, who was serving as interpreter to him in Brussels on one occasion. Having listened to Robert in full flight for some time, she felt moved to ask in a most plaintive voice, “Excuse me, please, what means this, ‘Jeck’?”

Cecil told me once, that during a holiday in Tenerife he had been brought up ‘all standing’, by local fishermen.

He had made contact with them socially and was aware that they used nets similar to ring-nets, with which they caught anchovies. He was also aware that they did not have even the most basic kind of echo-sounder on their boats.

Seeking to assist them yet trying his best not to be patronising, he tentatively brought up the subject of fish-finding, and told them that their Scottish counterparts used this electronic device to help them catch herring, which had habits similar to those of the anchovy.

When asked if he still used a ring-net to kill herring, he replied in the negative, saying that there was currently a five-year ban on herring catching, this in an attempt to preserve the sorely depleted stocks.

His single-minded attempt to bring these men into the twentieth century came to an abrupt halt when they replied, "No, we will not have this machine. We will keep our anchovies!"

Cecil and Robert were successful fishermen who have also succeeded in gaining respect from their fellows. Not an easy task nowadays.

During the time when herring was the prey, it was not uncommon for crews to go without wages for several weeks at a time. This was accepted by all, simply because there was the chance to make enough in one lucky night, to make up for the lean weeks.

This is not the case now. There is no opportunity to make a quick killing, so it has become one long slog for all concerned. Every day must be made to count, and the resultant pressures of trying to overcome all of the natural obstacles have been compounded by the seemingly impossible task of trying to adhere to the oft-times crazy legislation imposed by the bureaucrats who, in the main, know nothing of the industry which they are trying to regulate.

One prominent Manx fisherman commented to me, "When I started fishing, I fished where I wanted to, when I wanted to, for what I thought I could sell. Now I have a bit of paper which allows me to fish in certain places, at stated times, for specific types of fish - and I'm desperately trying to hold on to that!"

Both Cecil and Robert have now retired from active fishing. Cousin Robert continued until just a couple of years ago. He and his brother, Willie, sold out and quit what has now become a rat race.

Just a year later, they were followed by Lawrence Robertson. Lawrence started fishing at the same time as me and served his apprenticeship as a herring fisherman in the days when men made their entire years' living from catching the silver darlings. When he came ashore, his departure marked the end of a succession of Campbeltown men who had earned their keep by catching herring, a heritage that stretched back for several hundreds of years. Lawrence was the last. The chain has been broken. There is no way back!

This is progress?

The pressure which has been imposed upon men who are already under stress from natural causes, has led to many of them straying from the designated paths of legality, and in so doing being branded as criminals, when all they want to do is to get on with the job in hand, and make a living for their families.

If possible, it is much better to laugh at the results of such 'crimes', and indeed some of them are comical.

Whilst fishing for sprats in the upper limits of the Clyde, one pair who shall remain nameless took a good haul of large herring. Lucky? Well, no. The herring season was over, and to land these herring - which incidentally were now dead - was illegal. By law, they should be dumped!

Our heroes were not about to do this, so they made for a nearby harbour and after a few telephone calls they betook themselves, loaded with herring, to a disused pier in one of the lochs nearby.

In due course, an articulated lorry arrived to take the herring to a processing factory.

As the road to the pier was too narrow to accommodate the large lorry, a small truck had also come along to ferry the catch to the big articulated one.

This operation was well under way, when one of the local householders, who was thoroughly alarmed by this unusual nocturnal activity, telephoned the police.

Picture the scene. A boat is discharging an 'illegal' cargo in a pitch dark, remote loch. Everyone involved is tense and apprehensive. Suddenly, through the trees which line the approach road to the pier, there appears the blue flashing light of a police car!

It was some time before the police decided that this activity did not warrant any more investigation, and left, weighted down with fries of herring. All fears of a holiday in Barlinnie dispelled, the shattered crews were able to continue their toil!

The same pair had a similar catch aboard on another dark night, and it was decided that a furtive visit to Campbeltown was needed to arrange for the disposal of the illegal cargo. A lorry was being taken to the pier belonging to the shipyard, at the mouth of the loch.

The skipper of one of the boats went to bed for some much-needed sleep, and left his brother with the insufficient instructions, "Away ye go for Campbeltown."

Can you imagine the scene when, awakened by the sound of the boat's engine going astern, he came on to the deck to find that his brother had tied up at Campbeltown Quay, with some of their illicit catch boxed and lying in plain view on their deck, just ahead of a Fishery Protection Vessel!

The ropes were very quickly let go and they set off back down the Loch, their hearts in their mouths.

The other boat, being slightly slower, arrived at the mouth of Campbeltown Loch around fifteen minutes after his neighbour. The skipper of this boat had given instructions that he was to be called when they reached Davaar Light, and when he took over the wheel, he asked where their neighbour was, to be told that he had been on the radar, about four miles ahead of them, but that he had been lost when he altered course to go into the loch. I should explain that no navigation lights were being shown.

When boat number two reached the shipyard pier, their neighbour was not there, but the waiting lorry driver told them that a boat had steamed past just a few minutes before and had gone, he thought, to the main pier.

They set off slowly up the loch in search of their neighbour – still without lights and hugging the North shore. Very soon they saw the shape of a boat heading out of the loch, like them, unlit.

They turned off the shore and increased speed until they were right astern of this mystery boat and the skipper trained his searchlight straight ahead and switched it on to make sure they were following the correct boat.

It was their neighbour, but the skipper of this boat very nearly had a heart attack when they were illuminated from astern – that was where the Fishery Protection Vessel lay!

On a slightly different tack, I heard a lovely, though thoroughly alarming, story of a Rothesay man who got himself into serious trouble when on a salmon poaching expedition.

There is apparently a very good salmon river in the Kyles of Bute, which is a great attraction to those who would enjoy a night at such sport.

However, anyone leaving Rothesay on a summer evening and heading west in a motor-boat, was inevitably seen. Their intentions were readily realised, and they ran the risk of having a reception committee awaiting them on their arrival at the river.

Our hero had hit on the ploy of leaving in a rowing-boat, reckoning that no one would suspect that a potential poacher would dream of undertaking to row the considerable distance to the river. As an accomplice he chose one - let us call him Dougie - who was renowned for his strength, but not for his mental abilities. We should also refer to the prime subject in this yarn, as Willie.

This intrepid pair rowed for miles, until nearing the river and hearing a fish jump close to the shore, they quietly rowed in and shot their net - which was about 100 yards long - from the shore out in a semi-circle around the area in which the fish had jumped, then back to the shore.

This effort unfortunately drew a blank, but they decided that they should beach the punt and have a cup of tea from the flasks which they each had taken with them. Dougie handed his flask over the bow to Willie who in the process managed to drop it on top of a rock. The impact smashed it!

Dougie blew his top about this in no uncertain terms and accused Willie of dropping it on purpose. He refused to take the proffered share of Willie's flask, and announced that in reprisal for what he saw as an act of vandalism against him, he would not now row the boat any further.

Willie therefore rowed the remaining short distance to the river by himself, but on reaching it, broke the uneasy silence to ask Dougie to row across the river mouth whilst he, Willie, shot the net. This was reluctantly agreed, the dinghy was slowly backed into one side of the river bank, a heavy stone with the end of the net attached was thrown ashore, and the slow silent shooting process was begun.

Less than half way through this action, Willie was startled to see through the gloaming, a bailiff run down the beach, grab the end of the net and start hauling it ashore. Seeing that the bailiff was alone, Willie stood on the net remaining in the boat - which meant that they were now being drawn toward the shore - and seeking to dissuade the man from hauling, he roared, "Now then Willie, there's only one of them. As soon as we hit the shore, brain him with an oar!"

The bailiff however was made of stern stuff and continued pulling the net, but Willie was mortified when - as soon as the boat's keel touched bottom - Dougie vaulted past him, and felled the hapless man with a blow to the head from the oar.

"Ye telt me tae dae it!" was the uncaring response from Dougie, when the horrified Willie suggested that the man had been killed and asked what on earth they could do now, "So jeest roll his body intae the watter. Naebody'll ever ken what happened!"

Willie then examined the poor man and, deciding that there was no lasting damage done, he started to bathe his bleeding wound.

Seeing the first feeble signs of recovery he told Dougie to gather up the net into the boat, and to be prepared to row for his life.

The casualty was now responding sensibly to questions, and the indications were that his next step would be to open his eyes, so recognising this, Willie stood up and shouted loudly, "Row, Jimmy, row. Back tae Tarbert as fast as ye can!"

"No way, Willie! Tae Hell wi' rowin' tae Tarbert," Dougie yelled in return, "I'm gaun back tae Rothesay where we came from!" It would be better to draw a veil over the rest of this sorry saga.

When I was fishing out of Campbeltown I was completely unaware of the existence of another captain, this one not a fisherman, although his family had strong connections with the industry. John McWhirter, who is still alive as I write, was born in 1918 and worked first with McGrory's, an electrical shop in the town, and latterly with the Scottish Hydro Board.

Anthony McGrory was for many years the Honorary Secretary of the Campbeltown branch of the Royal National Lifeboat Institution but when John McWhirter joined his firm at the age of seventeen he quietly slipped a lot of the work on to John's shoulders, making him what is nowadays called the Deputy Launching Authority when John was only twenty years old.

Apart from the War years, when he served in the Army, John has spent almost all of his life serving the lifeboats as Deputy

Launching Authority, Honorary Secretary and Branch Committee member. He also served on the Scottish Lifeboat Council.

I must stress here that none of these posts earned John any money – in fact, they almost certainly were a drain on his pocket!

It is John's proud boast that he was without fail the first man on the pier when the lifeboat was called on and – uniquely, I am certain – he never left his wee office on the pier until his boat and crew had returned safely. He sat for countless cold, lonely hours by the marine band radio, listening for news of how the search was going.

Alistair Gilchrist, one of his Coxswains, told me of an occasion when the boat, her task finished, had gone into a port in Northern Ireland to refuel before the journey home. It was, he said, around 6 a.m. and the refuelling had not been completed when the crew were hailed from the pier by one of two taxi drivers. John had been informed by the Coastguard of the lifeboat's whereabouts so had contacted a hotel in the port and organised breakfast – and also payment for it - for his men. Then he roused two taxis to take the crew to the hotel. That sort of dedication is, in my opinion, without match in the annals of Lifeboat history.

I experienced his thoughtfulness and kindness when I arrived in Campbeltown after a bad passage late one winter afternoon. John was always on the pier to greet visiting lifeboats. This again was unique among Honorary Secretaries – and this day was no exception. It was blowing a full gale from the south-east and there were heavy snow showers. As soon as we had our boat refuelled and moored, John invited all our crew up to his office. There he produced a number of small 'shot' glasses that were rolled up in a tea towel. I was amazed when John, a lifelong teetotaller, produced – from a locked cupboard, a bottle of whisky.

"I always gie the lads a wee dram when they come back after a bad night at sea," he said.

"You're entitled tae wan as well!"

I noticed that the offer of a dram was not extended to two of the local crew who appeared in his office after us – they had not been at sea!

John occasionally caused me, and others, to blink in surprise at some of his sayings. He had sat on many Scottish Lifeboat Council meetings in ignorance of the fact that another prominent member - I think it was Lord Saltoun – was a cousin of, and was a similar age to our Queen.

"Aye, Tommy," he said in an awed voice, "Ye see, that man had played intimately wi' the Queen, when he was young an' ye'd never hae guessed it!"

I soon figured out exactly what John meant, but the way he put it must have caused my eyes to bulge in amazement, for a moment or two.

"Noo, Jim," he stated to Jim McPhee, another of his Coxswains, "The Ladies Guild are havin' a meetin the night. I think ye should go along an' stimulate them a wee bit!"

"Jeest put yer car ower there, Tommy – park it paralyze wi' Jim's!" This was his instruction when I arrived unexpectedly at the Lifeboat Station one day.

John pronounced the 'A's in 'radar', as in 'apple' whereas everyone else I ever heard pronounced them as in 'day'. This led to a great deal of confusion when he reported to a Divisional Inspector that the boat's radar wasn't working. That was a relatively minor matter, but the poor fellow thought, because of John's pronouncement of radar that he was actually saying 'rudder', which was a much more urgent affair!

John retired as Honorary Secretary in 1983, although he remained on the local Committee. He had, during his time with the

Lifeboats, been awarded a silver badge, a gold badge and then, very unusually, a bar to his gold. Why his going was not marked by the award of some sort of Civil Honour, is utterly beyond me and is, in my opinion, a total disgrace.

He probably didn't kiss the arses of those who decide who gets what!

He never, in my presence, commented on it himself but his late wife, when I talked to her alone one evening, told me of her disappointment at the lack of recognition. I hope that I was of some help when I told her that it was infinitely better that so many should wonder why he hadn't got an award, than have someone ask why he did get one!

A book could – and probably should be written about John's lifelong dedication to the R.N.L.I., but unfortunately I am not the man to do it.

I would not be forgiven if I left Campbeltown without mention of my father.

He was demobbed from the Navy in 1945, and shortly afterwards bought a second hand boat to pursue the career he loved, hunting herring.

With hindsight, the boat which he bought was too small and too old. It was also bought at a time when boats were commanding a very high price, being sought after by many young men returning from the war, who wanted to get a share of the good fishing which had prevailed whilst they were away.

That he succeeded in being among the best earners for a number of years despite the handicap of trying to keep up with bigger boats, is a measure of the man.

He had a lot of fun in him at times, and I often recall his tale of the fisherman who was guilty, in his fellow's eyes, of being a 'mooch'. This fellow never seemed to have any cigarettes,

Skipper Tommy Ralston, Whitby 1952

'borrowing' them from others and as he never appeared to have any money, he was a man to keep clear of in a pub.

One day, with little to do, my father with some of his pals, approached this fellow as he stood at the 'wee-us' at the head of the old quay. They were all chewing busily – on nothing at all – but the mooch, seeing this, pleaded for, "wan o' yer sweeties."

Someone then took an entire bar of Brook-Lax – a chocolate flavoured laxative – from his pocket and, apologising for the lack of paper, gave it to the poor fellow, saying that this was the last of what they had. They then set off 'for a walk' toward the new quay, leaving him chewing busily.

At that time – it is now long demolished – there was a gent's toilet at the head of the new quay. I can remember it vaguely; it was built of what I recall as being cast iron. The stalls had no doors and the waste was carried away by means of a constant flow of water that ran in a trough below the wooden seats.

Our heroes didn't have long to wait until their victim appeared in the toilet, pale faced and clutching at his stomach as he loosened his trousers. He was confronted by my father and his pals, who occupied all of the stalls and who were all reading newspapers!

"For God's sake, boys – ah'm desperate – gie's a seat!"

He took his place on the vacated stall which was, of course, the one furthest downstream and was in the throes of severe evacuations when the lads bundled up all the sheets of newspaper, lit them, and dropped them burning into the stream that flowed toward the poor man. Ring of fire indeed!

Shortly before Christmas time one year, my father bought a Labrador pup in Lochboisdale, and the poor wee animal was subjected to the rigours of crossing the Minch on a poor night, en route to Campbeltown, immediately after the purchase had been completed. It was sick as a dog!

My young brother was still at school then and, as fishermen, my father and I were away from home for probably nine months of the year. Despite the fact that my brother spent a lot of time with the dog and my mother fed him, there was no mistaking who was his master. As soon as my father came home 'Glen', for that was his name, went wherever he went.

We often saw the poor dog sitting outside whichever pub my father had chosen to indulge in his great weakness for whisky, but Glen refused to abandon his vigil for any of us. I was told that in one pub that allowed my father to take Glen in with him, the dog would sleep at his feet. My informant said, "That dog was almost human. If yer faither went tae the toilet an' Glen woke up tae see he wis gone, he wid jump up, pit his two front paws up on the bar an' look tae see if there wis anything left in yer faither's gless. If it had something in it he wid jeest lie doon again – he knew Tommy wid be back, ye see!"

Glen's name was heard often aboard the boat, for whenever anyone made a mistake of any kind, the roar would arise from my father, "My Glen could do better than that!"

On one occasion, my mother refused to accompany my father to the annual Fishermen's Ball until he had promised that he would drink lager only. The hall in which this function was held was adjoining the Royal Hotel, a favourite haunt of his, so he had the barman well primed that whenever he asked for a lager, the barman would surreptitiously add a gill - four pub measures - of whisky to it!

All went well, he was getting his dram, and my mother was happy that he was drinking only lager, until a friend, who was 'feeling no pain', insisted that he would buy my father a drink.

He was surprised to be handed a glass of 'lager' when he had demanded "A dram for Tommy," but when the barman asked him for money far in excess of the expected price of the lager, his surprise exploded into voluble anger. This of course let the cat out of the bag, and signalled an end to that little ploy!

Writing about the annual Ball reminds me of the two acts that appeared each year. James McMillan, 'Sheep', had a very good baritone voice and each year he would sing 'Bless this house', as a grace before the meal was served. After the meal, and to tumultuous applause, 'Pop' Scally would sing 'Just a wearyin' for you', and as an encore, would sing 'Drinking'.

Pop had, by any standard, a superb bass voice. It was so good that I still feel sorry that his voice was not discovered and trained.

My father took great pleasure in buying the *Kingbird* from John Short in, I think, around 1955. He had been cook on her when she was launched at Anstruther around 1930, and I still have a ribbon from the bottle that was used at her naming ceremony. He fished her for around two years and then she was sold to the Isle of Man.

Some ten years ago, I was asked to look at some photographs that were in the Fisheries Museum in Anstruther, to check if they were of the *Kingbird*. They were indeed, and I was convinced, when I looked at photographs of her engine, that it might well be the original 66 horse-power Kelvin. I called Neil Short, the original owner's son, who at that time worked in the stores department in the Bergius Kelvin works in Glasgow, and he was able to tell me that this was indeed the case. She was now lying near Liverpool was still in good sea-going condition, and the old Kelvin still puffed away.

The Museum were keen to have her as an exhibit of a typical ringer but the then owner was asking more money for her than the Museum could afford. I wrote to this man telling him some of her history and pleading, unsuccessfully, for a price reduction. The Museum later obtained a boat free of charge but sadly, this boat is not, in my opinion, recognisable as a ringer.

The *Kingbird* was sold to someone else for a price that I have not been able to ascertain but just recently I had a most distressing telephone call from Brian Ward, of Leeds, who is, I believe, a fanatical fan of the boats of the ring-netting era.

He told me that he had come across the *Kingbird* lying derelict, abandoned and totally neglected. He got her on to a slipway where, believe it or not, he managed to get the old Kelvin running, but the money required to have her renovated was beyond his purse so after many attempts to save her, she was eventually broken up.

He very kindly sent me a piece of wood from the forecastle – which is as fresh as it was when she was built some eighty years ago – and a selection of the last photographs taken of her.

I wish I had never seen them!

This whole affair was a dreadful experience for me and should never have happened. She should have been sitting in the Museum today – just yards from where she was built.

My father was never happier than when among herring, and when it became obvious that the days of the ring-net were over he, like so many others, was unable to put his heart into fishing for any other species.

Like so many of his peers, he also died young, as a result of a drowning accident, and his popularity among his fellow fishermen was well illustrated by the large number of mourners who travelled long distances to pay their last respects at his funeral.

I would leave Campbeltown with a poem written, I have been told, by a schoolgirl whose surname was McNiven, and which was published in the Campbeltown Courier many years ago. It contains the names of many of the old ringers, and was taught to me by my mother.

The *King Bird* fled with the *Fairy Queen* into the *Golden Dawn*.
The *Marie Stella* watched their flight, but the rest of the world slept on.
The *Busy Bee* was the first to awake, so she went to the *Mystical Rose*.
"They have gone," she cried, "What can we do? Perhaps *Bengullion* knows."
"Let the *Frigate Bird* pursue," he cried, "In her garb of *Silver Grey*."
And *Swift* as the *Crimson Arrow* sped the beautiful ship away.
Then the *Blue Bird* cried, "I am as *Swift* as light, *Nulli Secundus* am I,
I will bring them back, or return no more." And the *Falcon* made reply,
" *Nil Desperandum*, I will go forth on this *Enterprise* with you."
But the goddess *Felicia* shook her head, and helped the lovers through.
So they came no more to their old *Sweet Home*, where the *Kingfisher* roams at will
But *Ave Maria*'s sweet notes recall the *Loch* they both love still.

The Ayrshire men

Across the Firth of Clyde, on the Ayrshire coast were fishermen of like minds and spirits to the ones we have been meeting, and it is to there that I now turn to find my next quorum of Captains.

The first village we would come to on our journey south from Ayr is Dunure, a small community living in neat houses which cling to the rocky slopes leading to the tiny harbour. There lived one of the most extraordinary of my candidates, Sammy Gemmell of the *Storm Drift*.

One of five sea-going brothers, Sammy was not a very tall man, but he carried a lot of weight around his middle - almost as much weight as he carried with his fellow fishermen. He was a very successful skipper, but was also probably unique in that he was both a politician and an honest man. These two descriptions are usually a contradiction in terms, in my estimation.

He started his political career early, after one very hard week when the herring which he had succeeded in catching had been more than usually difficult to sell.

It was then common practice that bribes be given to buyers as an incentive to them to buy the herring, but this had got completely out of hand as is common with all such devices, and it was not unknown for the fishermen - desperate to market their hard-won catches - to give away half of the shot.

Sammy went home one Saturday, and on reviewing the past week's work became aware that he had given his crew ten shillings (50p) as their share of the earnings, but had given a buyer three pounds nine shillings, or £3.45, for his 'graft'. This horrified him as much as it should horrify you, but Sammy took steps which no one had taken before, and which I cannot see anyone else taking now.

This bribery, although common practice, was in contravention of the rules which the Clyde Fishermen's Association had written to govern themselves, so he took himself to the then Chairman of the Association and turned himself in, demanding to know how he was to be punished.

The man not surprisingly did not know how to handle this situation, so Sammy in desperation then went to Campbeltown where he confessed all to Archibald Stewart the afore-mentioned lawyer, and secretary of the Association.

The ensuing discussion between the two of them took up many hours, and resulted in the starting of a 'pooling' agreement, which briefly meant that the prices of comparably sized and quality herring were 'pooled', an average was worked out, and this average price was paid to all participants. The pooling system meant of course that there was no longer any gain for those indulging in bribery, and its continued use until herring auctions ceased is a lasting memorial to the man.

Sammy was given a gold watch by his grateful fellow-fishermen from Whitby in an unprecedented gesture of thanks for his help to them, and it was a favourite prank of his to use this watch - which was waterproof - to stir his tea. This was usually done when he had partaken of a few drams, and caused great consternation amongst many when they witnessed it for the first time.

While in the chair at a meeting of fishermen with the Herring Industry Board, Sammy took exception to the long-winded speech being given by Sir Frederick Bell, who was at that time Chairman of the H.I.B. He stood up and interrupted the speech by telling Sir Frederick to - "Sit on your arse and shut up. You hav'na' got it in ye tae be a fisherman onywey!"

I am reliably assured that Sir Frederick wisely followed this advice!

Ian Stewart, the lawyer who succeeded his father as Secretary to the fishermen's association, told me that Sammy - who did not suffer fools gladly - on one occasion interrupted another prominent politician who was running off at the mouth and told him to: "Sit doon an' stop speakin' a lot o' soft shite!"

Ian also told me that whilst attending a meeting in London he had, as he was not feeling too well, gone to bed early, leaving Sammy in the company of several other fishermen together with a handful of politicians.

He became aware, at breakfast the following morning, that there was a strained atmosphere among the company. It took some time, and only after Sammy had left for his room did Ian get the story – from another fisherman. He was told that one of the politicians had 'bad-mouthed' Ian after he had retired to bed. Sammy had jumped to his feet and told this foolish man just exactly what would happen to him if he did not retract his statement immediately. Very sensibly, the man apologised, Ian was told!

His son, Grieve, told me that he turned the boat around one evening as they were steaming south past Bay Harti – a bight just south of Lochboisdale, where herring were often taken.

"Whaur ur ye gaun?" demanded his father, Sammy, who was in the wheelhouse with him.

"Ah saw twa gulls sittin on a rock jeest aff the point, there. We'll hae a wee luk in the bight," replied Grieve.

Sammy disagreed with this action and a row broke out. As Grieve refused to comply with Sammy's demands to "dae whit yer telt an cerry on sooth," Sammy stormed out of the wheelhouse, slamming the door shut behind him.

As he passed the open wheelhouse window on his way forward he roared his final judgement at Grieve.

"Yer naethin but a communist!" This was not pronounced in the usual manner, but thus – 'commYOOnist' – with the accent on the ‘yoo’. This epithet, Grieve told me, was the ultimate insult in Sammy’s vocabulary. Nothing, in his mind, was worse than a Communist.

Grieve shot in the bight and got, as I recall it, 160 crans. Sammy’s reaction to this is not recorded.

I must be honest and admit that I thought, when Grieve himself told me the above tale that, although it was a good story, it had probably been exaggerated somewhat. Just last year, however, Gary Voce of Ballantrae, who had been crewing aboard the *Storm Drift* at the time, told me the same tale and when questioned, assured me that it was absolutely true. Gary, who later skippered the *Marie* and neighboured Grieve, told me that he had asked Grieve why he had shot there when there was nothing showing on the echo-sounder. Grieve replied that he thought that there might be a big overhang – a sort of cave, in fact – in the rock face, below the surface and that the herring had gone into it as the boat passed above!

The gull, Grieve reckoned, knew better!

Sammy served as Chairman of the Clyde Fishermen’s Association with great distinction for four years, and when he retired, was deservedly awarded the M.B.E. by the Queen for his services to a grateful fishing community.

When his successors recently went to London to protest to the Government about the killing of the crew of the *Antares* by a submarine - an action not far short of murder, in my opinion - to my absolute amazement they took with them samples of their produce which they handed in to Downing Street. I can only guess at what Sammy might have done had he been there, but he most assuredly would not have gone bearing gifts

The industry could use a man of his stature now, to lead it out of the mess it is in!

Grieve Gemmel playing the part of an American naval officer

His son Grieve took over the reins from Sammy in the 1960's and continued the successful fishing side of the Gemmell saga. Grieve was very well known and liked among fishermen everywhere, and was probably the last of the ring-net exponents to make a good living at the winter fishing in the Minch.

On a visit to Dunure he told me whilst reminiscing, that his first trip to sea as a fisherman had been through the previously mentioned Forth and Clyde canal to fish herring into Anstruther. This was in 1940, not long after the war had started. They fished there for only three weeks and then left when the authorities closed the fishing because there had been acoustic mines laid around the area in which they had been working, and he thought that the accidental detonation of some of these mines - whilst not resulting in loss of life - had caused injuries to some of the fishermen. They were there for three weeks, and earned just over £300 each for the trip. Big money indeed, in those far off days!

He was just a boy then and, as they had landed big shots on two successive days, he badly needed a rest. "We were lyin' at the mooth o' Anstruther harbour waitin fur the tide, full o' herrin' for the third day in a row," he told me. Ah wis sittin' on the seat locker wi' the fryin' pan full o' bacon, on the Primus. Ah jeest went sound asleep, fell furrit an' landed on the pan. That wakint me up!"

He was there when the big steel purse-seiners arrived on the scene and he recognised with so many others that they heralded the end of the old ways. I heard him on the pier in Mallaig telling a group which included purse-seine skippers that he had been at the boat builder in Girvan on his week-end at home. Asked if he was thinking of building a new boat, he replied with his usual pawkish humour. "No, Ah wis lukkin' fur a big weldin' machine tae weld aw they tin pursers together, so they couldna get oot o' the herbour!"

He also said to me on one occasion, "There's nae herm in a bottle o' whisky. No. As lang as ye keep it in the bottle, there's nae herm in it. It's when ye let it oot o' the bottle that the trouble starts!"

Grieve had a great regard for the fellow creatures of the Earth.

It was common for seagulls to have their feathers completely soaked when they were trying to feed from the bag of herring in a ring-net. The oil from the herring destroyed the waterproofing on their feathers and the poor gulls so afflicted would not float at their designed waterline, and so ran the serious risk of being drowned! On one occasion in Shepherds Bight, Grieve had the wheelhouse almost filled with gulls which he had rescued. He refused to leave for the market until they had all dried off properly, a process that took several hours.

His neighbour, also filled with herring, left immediately.

The wind was just about gale force and the boat which had left early had an extremely bad crossing, but by the time the gulls had dried off the wind had eased somewhat and Grieve, he told me, had a relatively good passage.

They fished very well during their last winter in the Minch, and early in the season they were lying in Mallaig harbour one morning, waiting to discharge their catch when Grieve's attention was drawn to the fact that a cat was trapped under the pier, and was about to be drowned by the rapidly rising tide. He rescued this poor animal, and not only saw that it was fed every day that they were in Mallaig, but when leaving for home, told the oil merchant that he must feed the cat for as long as was necessary. The bill for the food was to be sent to him!

The engine room of the *Storm Drift* was absolutely immaculate - the cleanest by far that I have ever seen anywhere. Its gleaming brightness was not surpassed by any yacht I have ever been aboard, and it was certainly an enormous tribute to the hard work put into it by the engineer, Davie Edgar, better known to us all as "Horsey", who sadly lost a son to the sea, not so long ago. The price of fish!

Grieve told me during one of my visits to see him that Davie was now in the local hospital, and that his memory had just about gone. Grieve visited him faithfully but one morning, Davie greeted him with the news that a local worthy had died.

"When did that heppen?" asked Grieve, surprised that he hadn't heard the news before.

"This moarnin. Aye, an auld Jimmy's deed tae".

"Wha telt ye that?" asked Grieve.

"Ah heard it doon at the herbour!" was the reply.

Now Grieve knew full well that Davie hadn't been near the harbour for months so he looked him in the eye and asked, "Did ye hear onythin o Grieve Gemmell? Is he aa richt, or is he deed tae?"

Davie looked at him in some confusion, so Grieve told me that he threw his arms around him and said, "Oh Davie, Davie. Is this whit we're aa comin tae?"

"We were jeest stannin there wi wir airms roon yin anither, greetin lik bairns," he finished.

Ring-net boats from Ayrshire and Campbeltown in Mallaig Harbour, 1960

When I met Grieve for the first time after he retired I asked him what he was doing to pass the time.

He told me that he helped his wife, Margaret, in the garden then added, thoughtfully, "Some moarnin's I waken up early. Mebbe three or fower o'clock, so rather than disturb my wife, I jeest lie there an' think. I imagine I'm back abaird the *Storm Drift*, lyin' shelterin' in a wee corner in Carnan or in the Kettle in Loch Skipport. The win' eases a bit so I mebbe lift the anchor – quietly, for I don't want tae waken any ither boats that's lyin' there – an' set off doon the shore frae Skipport, intae Shepherd's Bicht, richt doon through Corrodale, by Boisdale an' Bay Harti, an' intae a' the favourite wee holes we used tae get herrin' in. It passes the time fine, an' if we all come back again an' get anither chance at this auld world, I'll mebbe mind aa they hauls, an' it'll gi'e me a heed stert on a' body else!"

"Do you get much exercise then?" I asked.

"Oh aye. Ah goes doon the road ivery moarnin fur the paper an' then ah come back the lang wey – up by the kirk. Ah go intae the kirkyaird an' walk up an' doon ivery path in it. Ah hae a guid look at aa the stones in it an' if ah don't see my ain name on yin o' them, ah jeest come hame an' read the paper!"

Around the same time I spoke to Matt Sloan, who was then the sole surviving fisherman residing in Maidens.

He told me that he now rarely saw any of his erstwhile workmates except at funerals. Just recently, he told me, when attending the third funeral of a fisherman in as many weeks, he stopped outside the church and spoke to Grieve.

"Aye Matt," said Grieve, "the wey things are it's hardly worth gaun hame. We micht as weel bide in the Kirk till oor turn comes - it'll no' be lang noo!"

Grieve lost his dear wife, Margaret, in – I think – 2002. Ina and I went to her cremation service, and arrived early. There was only one other couple in the waiting room and I spoke to them thinking, correctly, that I had met the man before.

He had been a fishery officer, he told me, and Ayr was his last posting before retiring. He told me of his time when the Clyde was re-opened after several years of a ban on all herring fishing. One of his duties was, he said, to ask skippers as they docked what amount of herring they had aboard, and where they had caught them.

"I knew that they were telling me lies, and they knew that I knew they were lying," he told me.

"One morning I met Grieve coming up the pier. I asked him the usual questions, and wrote down his answers. Grieve looked at me square in the eyes for a long, long time. And then he spoke."

"Dae ye ken hoo lang Saint Peter his been stannin at the Pearly Gates?" he asked.

"Not really," I replied.

"He's been there nearly twa thoosan years. Dae ye ken whit he's lookin fur?"

"No," says I.

"Weel, he's been there aa that time tryin tae get a crew o fishermen fur his boat, but lads lik you makes us fishermen tell sae many lees, that nane o us iver gets as far as the Gates!"

Grieve is another definite Captain, but unfortunately he died early in 2004, just before I started this revision. One of the last times I saw him was at his home shortly after he had an operation for a hernia. My wife and I were in the vicinity so I called on him. "It's awfy guid o ye tae call, auld boy," said he. "Don't you worry about me, though. Ah kid last fur weeks yit!"

His daughter, Doreen, told me that when she was sitting by his hospital bed – the bed in which he died just a day or so later – he whispered something to her.

"What was that, Dad?" she said, putting her head nearer his.

"Ah want ye tae bring me a length o licht rope – ye'll get a bit in the garage."

"What do you want with a length of rope, Dad?" Doreen asked.

"Ah want tae tie you up wi' it!" was the reply.

He didn't talk again.

I speak to Doreen occasionally and during one such call she told me that she had just bought two dogs. She named one of them 'Storm', and the other, 'Drift'!

Going south from Dunure and deliberately bypassing Maidens, we come to Girvan, the largest of the fishing towns on the Clyde, which of course had its share of Captains also.

'Jimmy the May' was one such worthy. Jim McCreath, to give him his full name, seemed totally unafraid of any kind of weather, and the tale was often related to youngsters of the night when he and his ringer, the *May*, were caught in the strong tideway off the Mull of Kintyre in a very bad gale. The Lighthouse keepers watched him with great concern for several hours as he tried to make headway, until the wind eased a bit and he was able to continue his passage to Girvan.

When he got in, there was a considerable amount of damage done to the boat and as soon as they had secured the ropes, the terrified crew resigned en masse.

This led to Jimmy saying on many occasions, "Ah don't pey them aff, Ah wash them aff!"

He was at sea at the Manx fishing one wild night when no other pair had ventured out, and had shot his net, resulting in it being brought back aboard with no herring, but suffering quite a lot of damage from the excessive strains caused by the weather. He managed to get his neighbour's crew back aboard their own boat with some degree of difficulty, and their skipper then called to him, "D'ye ken if there's an Asylum fur the insane on the Isle o' Man?"

"Ah don't ken," says Jimmy, "But ah expect there is. Whit wey are ye askin'?"

"Because that's whaur we should be put for bein' oot here on a nicht like this".

Alec McCrindle, better known as "Rin Tin Tin", was skipper of the *Silver Crest* from Girvan, and he was another character who could have a book written about him.

I remember him having a machinery failure whilst fishing at Whitby, which meant that he had to have a new crankshaft delivered to him there. This heavy piece of machinery was encased in a wooden crate which was about six feet long, and when it was being lowered on to the deck of his boat on arrival, this activity caught the attention of many of the holidaymakers who thronged the piers then. The act of getting this expensive load safely on to the deck was accompanied by much shouting and waving of arms. When it had been safely lowered onto the deck, Rin Tin Tin looked up at the onlookers, doffed his hat and loudly announced, “Dust tae dust, ashes tae ashes, and thank you all for your kind attendance here today!”

In the years immediately following the war, many manufactured items were perhaps not as good as they might be, so this led to the words ‘pre-war’, being applied to something which had been manufactured in times before hostilities commenced, and which therefore was expected to be of better quality.

The *Silver Crest* had been on the beach at Girvan having her bottom painted, but when it came time for her to be refloated and to resume her fishing effort, all were horrified to find that she would not float because the tides were weakening, and that she was in grave danger of being ‘neaped’ - that is stuck there until the tides started to increase again in perhaps two weeks time.

Immediately ‘Tarry’ McCrindle - another great character - was called upon to assist, as his boat, the *Aliped*, had the most powerful engine in the fleet, a 132 horse-power Kelvin.

‘Tarry’ sprang into action at once, secured a tow rope to the *Silver Crest* and applied the power. The rope snapped.

‘Rin Tin’ jumped down into the engine room of his stranded boat and emerged soon after with the end of a very heavy rope, announcing. “This’ll dae it”.

It was obvious to all the onlookers that this rope had not seen the light of day for many years and judging by the clouds of dust which arose from it, was well past its ‘sell by’ date, so no one shared his confidence. However, the tow was passed, the towing boat went ahead, but had hardly taken the strain when the rope snapped.

“I canna’ understan’ that. It’s pre-war, I can assure ye,” was the roar from ‘RinTin’, a comment which passed into the vocabulary of all the Clyde fishermen, and which is probably still used when an accident happens through using inferior gear!

Captains Extraordinaire

We now go for our last call in the Clyde to Maidens, which is the place where the idea for this book was conceived.

Maidens is a small village between Dunure and Girvan. This little sandy harbour which once housed what was in my opinion the finest and the best kept fleet of fishing boats in the world, is now utterly devoid of any sea-going activity of any consequence. The superb fleet which once graced this tiny tidal haven is scattered and gone.

It was home in my young days to some of the finest fishermen anywhere in Britain, and they and their boats, were admired everywhere they went.

Some – very few now - of these fishermen are still alive today, and it is to one of a pair of brothers who epitomised all that Maidens meant in fishing circles, that we turn first.

Matt Sloan, who died a few years ago, lived with his wife, Jeanette, in a bungalow in the centre of the village. He still carried himself tall and erect, and displayed the powerful physique which enabled him to haul the sole rope of a ring-net faster than the winch which he was supposed to assist!

Indeed, I remember one occasion when they had engine trouble in Mallaig and had herring to discharge. The lack of engine power meant of course that the winch was not available for the landing operation, so Matt was hauling the full baskets of herring from the hold up to the pier, single-handed. A lift of perhaps thirty feet, and a gross weight of around seven stones

When he was called away to the engineer's workshop in the village, the two men who took over this task from him were very soon struggling, and great was their relief when another boat came alongside and they were able to use her winch!

His brother was Billy, who died several years before Matt.

Billy was somewhat different in build, tall and not so heavy, with a slight stoop. He had an almost schoolmasterish air about him.

These two brothers served as officers in the Royal Navy during the war, and when hostilities ended they returned to the fishing to make up a team which many thought was pre-eminent on the West Coast from the 1950's to the 1970's.

Their strength lay in their differences, in my opinion. Billy was the Cavalier and Matt the Roundhead, to borrow an historical allusion. Billy was the laughing brilliant blade, with a razor sharp intellect, and Matt - though equally clever - the dogged plodder who would never know when he was beaten.

They were born into an already legendary fishing family, all of whom were referred to by any younger fishermen with the prefix 'Uncle', probably as a mark of respect. These famous 'Uncles' - Jake, Jimmy, Billy, and Tommy were men who were unsurpassed masters of their profession, and who would have commanded instant respect in any company anywhere in the world.

It was customary during their heyday at the week-ends, to haul the ring-nets forward from their usual place of readiness aft, to the forward side deck of the boats, where they were spread out to dry. On more than one occasion, when we were berthed near them, one or other of these men requested me to lay out 'hand-holes' for them when we hauled the net 'forrid'. These were small holes in the nets which were not of any consequence, and which were usually ignored. They wanted them left out so that they had something to do to while away the time, and sat contentedly mending on a Saturday afternoon and evening. Not ever on a Sunday though!

Their boats, the *Veronica*, the *Virginia*, the *Wistaria* and the *Watchful*, were immaculate. It would have been a difficult task to

Billy Sloan discharging from *Wistaria* BA208

find a yacht anywhere that was as well maintained as these boats were.

It was a fact that they were as clean after discharging a shot of herring - a dirty job which scattered scales everywhere - as other boats were when lying idle!

Like all successful men they were single-minded, and their pursuit of the herring took priority over almost all else. They were God-fearing men, however, and would not, for example, tolerate any work being done on the Sabbath.

There was a ban on all week-end fishing, self-imposed by the fishermen, a ban which was rigidly enforced everywhere except Whitby. There the governing body was composed of Whitby skippers, and they allowed Sunday fishing as the season there was a very short one.

The Sloans, and indeed I think that I am correct in saying that the same applied to all of the Maidens fishermen, would not take advantage of this extension to their week, and invariably lay in the harbour until midnight by which time, of course, the Sabbath had passed.

One advantage of the care and money lavished on their boats and gear was that they were able to work in weather which sent lesser breeds scurrying for shelter in their less well maintained boats. I remember talking to 'Uncle' Jimmy one day as they were discharging a shot of herring caught when they were the only boats at sea, and he said to me - "Aye boy, I'd raither ha'e fifty cran when there's naebuddy else oot, than the fill o' the boat when aa'body has the same!"

Many hours were spent trying to figure out the 'luck' of the Sloans, but in my opinion if the men so engaged had spent more time at sea, and less in fruitless speculation, they would have been nearer to equalling their successes.

I spoke to Andy Alexander - who sailed with them for many years – not long before he died and we touched briefly on the subject of this 'luck'.

He told me of one occasion when they were as he aptly put it 'ploughing' Loch Striven in the upper reaches of the Clyde estuary. A small fleet of boats had steamed up to the head of the Loch and back down again, without any of them seeing any herring at all.

The Sloan brothers continued this relentless monotonous combing of the Loch, from one side to the other, disregarding the rest of the fleet as they left, having convinced themselves that the Loch was barren.

A tiny mark was spotted on the echo-sounder. Matt shot, and the result was 800 baskets of prime herring.

Luck?

Not in my opinion. Sheer dogged persistence is nearer the truth.

On another occasion, a fleet of boats were working in Loch Scridain in Mull. They sought the small herring for which the Loch was renowned, but were finding only sprats which made a similar trace on the fish-finding devices. This effort had been going on for some time when the Sloans arrived late in the afternoon, shot, and filled their boats with the only herring to be taken that day.

Explain that one to me, please!

Again in one of the Mull Lochs, Andy told me that one day Matt had been frantically trying to correct a fault in the echo-sounder without success. Andy, standing in the bow, reported that he could see a seal playing with a herring, throwing it in the air then retrieving it.

As the boat passed through this area the sounder started to work of its own accord, marking a large concentration of herring, and continued to function only for as long as it took to shoot the net. It then gave up the ghost and did not work again until professional help had been obtained. It had, however, worked long enough for them to fill the two boats with herring!

Matt told me, and his tale was repeated later by Hugh MacPhee who crewed with Billy for over sixteen years, of the tale about Matt's son-in-law, the minister. Matt had rung about 400 baskets, shooting on a gannet, when the pair were on their way into Tarbert early one Friday morning. The shot was split between them and as Billy required to have some electrical work done, he went to Ayr while Matt took his share into Tarbert. Matt asked Billy to take his son-in-law aboard in Ayr, as he had promised to take him out for the night.

They met up at sea in the early evening, and the minister transferred aboard Matt's boat when the pair were lying alongside, yarning and waiting for darkness to fall. Matt took his son-in-law into the wheelhouse and switched on his echo-sounder to demonstrate how it worked. He immediately called out to Billy, who was still lying alongside, "Huv ye got yer sounder on?"

"No," replied Billy. "Why?"

"Jeest gie her a wee kick ahead, there's a guid spot o' herrin' below us here!"

He shot around the place where they had been lying, and filled both boats!

What say you to ministers bringing bad luck, now?

The Sloans, in common with, I believe, the rest of the Maidens fishermen, went home for Christmas but fished over the New Year. They were off Shepherd's Bight, near Loch Skipport, Andy Alexander told me, one Hogmanay night and Matt had tuned his radio to the 'Home Service' to check when midnight, and another year, arrived. Immediately after the midnight bells had heralded a New Year Billy put on his deck lights, a sign that he wanted to talk with his neighbour. He came alongside and called, "A guid New Year tae ye all." Then, without a moment's pause, he continued, "Ah saw a wee mark in at the Duff (a well-known low headland in Shepherd's Bight) – we'll go back an hae anither luk at it."

These were the kind of happenings which fostered the Sloan legend and their total commitment to fishing - and they are not isolated events by any means.

A beautiful model of the *Watchful* BA124, built by Derek Goode

Matt had a keen sense of humour and I laughed out loud when he told me the following tale concerning his daughters – remember, he had five of them!

It was his custom, when at home on a Sunday afternoon, to take the whole family out for an afternoon spin around the countryside. Of course the car was rather crowded with the two parents and five children aboard. One evening, just after they had finished their meal, the oldest girl announced that she had been thinking about cars and had consulted her sisters. "We decided, Dad, that we really need another car. What do you think of that?"

Matt told me that this speech had, in his opinion, been well rehearsed and that he thought that he could well be about to become the victim of a well-thought out plan for the girls to have a car of their own.

"Ah thocht aboot it fur a meenit an' then told her that I thocht that wis a braw idea, an' asked her when she was going to buy one!"

That was the end of that scheme!

Not many years ago I visited Cockenzie on the Firth of Forth seeking to view the site of the Weatherhead boatbuilding yard, the birthplace of so many ringers, but could not identify it.

I asked a man who I later discovered owned the fish-processing building from which he had just emerged - I think his surname was Murdoch - where I might find the remains of the yard.

The resulting conversation is worth recording, and went thus:-

"Weatherhead's yerd, that's it ower there. The last ringer frae there wis the *Watchful*, BA 124, beelt fur a man ca'd Sloan, frae Ayrshire."

He was wrong on that score, I believe, as the last boat to be built there was the *Wistaria*, BA 208, but realising that I had found someone who knew more than I had dared to expect, I asked if he had been at the ring-net fishing.

"No, ah wisna', but ma faither wis. He hid a share o' a ringer ca'ad the *Budding Rose*. Ah drove ma mither daft when Ah wis at the school, Ah was jeest desperate tae get oot o' the school an' away tae the ringing. The year afore Ah left school ma faither bocht anither boat frae Fife, second han', an' he asked me if Ah'd go wi' him tae sail it hame."

"Aye faither, but we'll be aye gaan tae the ring-net wi' this boat, will we?"

"Weel, son," he says, "we will, but whiles we'll ha'e tae gang tae the white fish. This is a bigger boat an' it's costin' a lot o' money, so we'll need tae pey her quick."

"He widna' budge frae that, so Ah nivir pit ma fit abaird her. Ah widna' gang tae onythin' but the ringing!"

He left me then, saying that he had a lot of work to get on with.

I returned a year or two later, hoping to have a yarn with this fellow again, to discover that his processing plant was closed down. I went into a small fish shop nearby and found it empty. There was a bell on the counter and ringing it brought forth an elderly man who had to climb up a steep set of stairs from what appeared to be the filleting area downstairs.

I apologised for having disturbed him and explained that I simply wanted to find the man who had owned the now derelict yard on the pier. I had found him, I explained, to be very knowledgeable on ring-net fishing.

The reaction I got was quite amazing! "He's got a new place jeest a mile or twa doon the road, but he wis nivir at the ring net. Ah wis at the ring-net! We worked it here in the Firth an ah wisny lang at it when we went through the Forth an Clyde canal tae fish in the Clyde. Aye, we wir gaun tae show they Wast Coasters hoo tae catch herrin'. We gaed intae a loch there, Loch Striven ah think it wis called, an shot. Weel, this Ayrshire man – ah think he wis called Sloan - he wis awfy namely fur catchin' herrin' - shot at the back o' oor net. We got hauf-a-dizzen baskets, but he filled their twa boats! Show they men hoo tae catch herrin, wid we? We went intae Greenock the next day an' I gaed awa hame. That wis enough fur me. Ah got a job drivin' a bus in Edinburgh an' jeest a year or so later, war broke oot an' ah wis in a reserved occupation. Jeest shut the door ahint ye when ye go oot."

Billy had a son and two daughters, Matt had five daughters.

Matt came ashore from the fishing whilst still relatively young, to the surprise of many, and started to work in a fish salesman's office, leaving Billy and his son to fish the two boats. It is my belief that Matt reviewed the future of the herring industry, didn't like the conclusions he reached, so chose to leave.

Billy carried on fishing alternatively for herring, then trawling for prawns and white fish, until one day in the Clyde, after he had taken aboard a good haul of coley, a dreadful accident happened.

The weather was bad and a lump of water struck his boat, the *Wistaria*. Two crew men were thrown into the water. Billy instantly went astern to get them back aboard, but unknown to him a part of the net had also been washed overboard. This went into the propeller, disabling the boat, and the two men in the water were drowned.

The two, Cameron Ware and Tom Harvey, had been with Billy for many years and his anguish at seeing such close friends die thus, must have been dreadful.

When the *Wistaria* was towed into Ayr later that day Billy went ashore, never to set foot on the boat again.

She was sold.

It was agreed generally among fishermen that the *Wistaria* had not been a good sea boat at any time in her career. There was something radically wrong with her design. They came very close to losing her off the west end of Canna some years before when they were heading for Mallaig with just 25 crans of herring aboard, on a very wild night. She broached while running off a sea and one of her crew – who never went back to the Minch to fish herring - told me that the only thing that saved them was the wheelhouse, when it slowed and steadied her as she went over far enough to let it hit the sea. She was that far over! The two lights that were fitted on the roof inside the wheelhouse were later discovered to be filled with sea water!

Several years later, after a foray into the full-time prawn trawling business, Billy himself died, probably of a broken heart.

Billy's son, Barry, who had contracted a horrendous fatal illness after an accident at sea, died very shortly after his father. Thus ended the Sloan legend but wherever men talk of herring, their names are spoken of in awe, and without any doubt, they would be wondrous and very welcome guests around Angus's fireside.

At last I come to the man who really started this entire meandering tale, Turner McCrindle.

Turner is now dead, but I visited him some years ago while his wife was still alive, and they were living in their little cottage in Maidens.

As we approached their house I had been telling my wife a little about this legendary man, and as we got closer I spotted an open launch around 18 feet long, lying in the garden. I told Ina to take heed of the condition of this boat, as I was sure that Turner would keep it in the same manner as he had kept all of the ringers he had owned.

It was winter time, and the engine had obviously been taken out of her to be stored safely, but the boat surpassed all my expectations. It was varnished inside and out and was absolutely immaculate. I have eaten from tables which looked less clean than the bilges of this wee boat.

Turner opened the door to my knock, and when he finally recognised me and shook my hand, it was like being gripped by a bunch of tarry ropes. He was a big man and had a tremendous aura about him. When I remember the *Saffron*, the *Sapphire* or the

The McCrindles
(l-r) Alex, Turner, JT, Roy and Bill

earlier *Margarita*, I see the boats dimly, but the oilskin clad figure of Turner still stands out tall, unbent and unblurred by time.

We were taken in and sat down, then I asked him what he was doing with himself. “Ye’ll hae seen the wee boat in the gairden,” said he. “I gang tae the screenge net (a small otter trawl) wi’ her in the summer months, jeest oot here below the hoose. We get a few plaice. This year was guid, we had 645. Last year wisna sae guid, we only had 482, but the year afore that wis grand, we had abune 700.”

Now of course I cannot remember the exact numbers as quoted by him, so have invented them, but if Turner said that he had 482, then you may be certain that was exactly what he had.

When I asked him if this was boxes or stones of fish that he was referring to, he told me that he was talking of the numbers of fish caught! Not boxes. Not stones. Individual fish!

"I keep a list o' all the puir auld folk in the village," he replied when I asked if he sold the fish to the Hotel, "an' they all get their turn o' a fry." Knowing Turner, it would not matter what price anyone offered him for his catch, they would not be able to buy it. It was destined for the "auld folk" of Turner's choice, though probably most of them were younger than he was, and no-one else was going to get them!

He also told me that he wrote a lot of poetry, and opened a cupboard to reveal these compositions which were typed for him by a young lady in the village. There were many themes there for us to look at, but most of them had a religious bent, as befitted a man of Turner's faith. I believe that they have now been published, but I have no idea how to obtain a copy.

When I asked after the health of his brothers, he told me that one brother, Alec, better known as "Sugar", was dead. "He died," said Turner, "because he went tae the sea on the Sabbath. He had moved tae Stranraer, an' had a wee lobster boat. Weel he went oot on the Sabbath day, the boat upset, and that was the end o' Sugar."

When I said that I hadn't heard of this drowning accident, Turner said that Sugar hadn't drowned but had died some six months later, as a result of the accident.

I spoke to Bert Andrews, then skipper of the *Pathfinder*, in Mallaig some time later, and recounted the tales which Turner had related.

Bert, another who later tragically paid the price of fish with his young life, lived in Maidens and of course knew Turner well, but his reaction was a revelation to me. Sugar, he told me had died of cancer, and his death was in no way related to his going to sea on the Sabbath. Turner would not have accepted that!

"Did Turner tell you who his crew is on his current fishing activities?" Bert then asked me.

Turner went to sea with his wife as crew on his small boat!

Bert told me that Turner was convinced that the Fishery Protection patrol was out to get him for his 'poaching', and that when he saw the smoke of this ship leaving Ayr, he immediately hauled his trawl, raced the half mile or so into Maidens harbour, and took trawl, doors and warps up into the store on a barrow!

He and his wife were in their seventies at this time!

Turner was one of six brothers, and he was undisputedly the dominant one. Although he himself did not go into the wheelhouse of any of the boats which they owned, he dictated where they went, and when.

Roy, one of the brothers, often told the tale against himself of the occasion in Oban when they had finished discharging herring late one night and were preparing to go to sea again.

"D'ye think it'd be a guid idea tae get fish an' chips for the supper, Turner?" he queried. The answer being - "Aye, I'd enjoy that," Roy called in his usual peremptory manner to a young lad who had been loafing around the pier watching them work. "Come here small boy. Ye'll gang up tae the chip shop an' get six fish suppers richt awa. Noo they're two an' sixpence each, so here's fifteen shillin's an' a shillin' tae yersel' fur going fur them."

Needless to say, 'small boy' and the money were never seen again!

Turner and his wife were always a team.

I remember being in Maidens one spring when our engine was being overhauled by Andy Marr, the marine engineer, and one evening my uncle Crawford was taken to Turner's house for a meal.

The ringers then all carried old lorry and car tyres on their starboard sides to protect them when they came together at sea, an action which was a necessary part of the ringing operation. When Turner took Crawford into his house, his wife said to him, "I see the *Margarita* is lying port side tae the pier, Turner. Dae ye no' think that's a guid opportunity tae lift in the fenders an' let the air get roon' aboot the wood on the starboard side?"

"That's a guid idea," said Turner, so he and Crawford went back to the pier and did just that.

When my uncle related this tale he was of the opinion that no wife of his would ever be allowed to tell him what to do with his boat, but I fear that he was missing the point totally. Turner's wife was just as much a part of the team as he was and was concerned – rightly so - that the boat should be properly cared for.

When I thought quietly over the short time spent with this wonderful old couple, the idea that gradually became an obsession with me that this man and his wife would die one day in the not-too-distant future, and that no tangible record of their remarkable way of life would remain.

We daily watch so called 'celebrities' being fawned over by television interviewers. These self-styled celebrities are mostly balloons filled with nothing more substantial than their own egos, and it might well be fair comment to say that the vast bulk of them are at best, 'legends in their own minds'.

In fact, I fear that this entire society is built upon a ladder system, where those below support the ones above regardless of worth, in the certainty that they themselves will one day succeed to this artificial grandeur. In my opinion this system is a self-propagating cancer which will one day destroy the host.

What would Turner have to say about today's society in which our elected leaders appear to lie and steal openly and blatantly? A world where, as far as I can ascertain, the only place in Britain in which no one is allowed to accuse another of lying, is in the Houses of Parliament!

Why was there not a film producer somewhere with the vision to capture something of the life this couple were living? They were people worthy of being remembered.

I know that I have neither the abilities nor the facilities to catalogue the story of such a giant as Turner McCrindle but as I thought of it, gradually this book was born in an attempt to pay a tiny tribute to his life, and to the lives of the others I would dearly love to meet around the fireside with Angus.

I can see Turner yet, perched forward on the *Saffron*, his big powerful figure dressed in a yellow oilskin and wearing the 'paddy' hat which always adorned his head. The same figure can be seen again in the dim glow of the *Saffron*'s double stern light at night, as he still stands with the wire in his hand, still feeling for his beloved herring.

The 'Auchies'

I was severely – and understandably - taken to task over my lack of mention of the Avoch fishermen in an earlier book, by a friend of long standing, Ian Jack. Ian, who currently resides in Buckie, has strong Avoch connections and took part in the ring net fishing out of that port for a time. This omission was simply because I did not really have many connections with these men, therefore wasn't able to write of them.

I could of course be criticised regarding the lack of material on the Eriskay and the Scalpay fishermen. The reasons for these omissions are that I simply did not know any of these men well enough to invite them to someone's fireside, or to promote them to the rank of 'Captain'! Some years ago I was asked, on a trip on a car ferry to Arran, why there was no mention of a certain Ayrshire ring net skipper in the original version of this book. The man who posed the question was his son, who was captain of the ferry we were aboard. I explained to him also that I had been aware of his father, but unfortunately did not know him at all well, certainly not well enough to write of him.

My cousin, Angus Martin, wrote a book, 'The Ring-Net Fishermen', published by John Donald in 1981. This will most certainly be the universally accepted reference book on the beginnings and workings of ring-net fishing. In it he states that, "The fishermen of Avoch, on the Moray Firth, began visiting the Minches in the mid-1920s, in the Skaffie as well as the Zulu type (of boat)." This information was gleaned from an interview of George Jack, conducted by Will MacLean.

George Jack seems to me to be the man on whom I should first concentrate my short reminiscences of Avoch.

When I knew him he was skipper/owner of the *Integrity* and was also vice–chairman of the Mallaig and North-West Fishermen's Association. The name of his boat mirrored this man's standing with his fellow-fishermen; his integrity was never questioned.

I was present at one of the Annual General Meetings of this Association, held in Inverness, and witnessed at first hand the common sense that George had in great abundance.

The Chairman, William John Manson and the Treasurer, Robbie Hepburn had – or so hindsight would have me believe – agreed beforehand that the Association should fund the purchase of boxes for use in the summer herring fishing. It was essential that the rich summer herring had to be boxed in an attempt to ensure that they were landed in good condition and at this time the Fish Salesmen supplied these boxes. This was a big drain on the salesmen's finances as the boxes were subjected to a lot of misuse as well as hard work.

Several questions were raised from the floor. What size would the boxes be, should they remain at the four to a cran currently in use, or should they be downsized? How many would be supplied to each boat? Whose responsibility would it be to ensure that the boats did not lose boxes to the buyers?

Eventually, after well over two hours discussion, it was agreed that the new boxes would be six to a cran – it being felt that the smaller size would help keep the herring better than the bigger ones currently in use. This decision in itself spawned a long discussion about pooling. Would the smaller boxes pool with the big ones in use by the Clyde boats that landed into the same markets? They would not, it was eventually decided, but the Clyde boats would have to be informed of this decision, without delay.

Much talking ensued before it was minuted that each boat would be given a number of boxes – I believe it was in the region of 200

– and it was the boat's responsibility to ensure that they got their boxes back from whoever they landed to.

Thus far, the subject of discussion had been really very worthwhile, if rather drawn-out. Incidentally, all of the decisions reached that day would eventually be put in place many years later and would be seen as being for the good of the industry as a whole. On this occasion however, all did not go well.

George Jack, who had been silent for much of the time, eventually got to his feet and asked several pointed questions.

"Each boat gets 200 boxes, and there are 'X' number of boats in the Association. So, if we multiply 200 by the number of boats in the Association, we reach" – and here I am guessing that the number was in the region of 10,000.

"Now, if each box costs £2, we will need £20,000 to buy these boxes. Do we have that amount of money in the Association?"

The answer, admitted after much furtive whispered conferring among those at the top table was 'No!' so George moved that we rescind all the decisions taken thus far, and move on to the next item on the agenda!

A man who is much nearer my age is Donald Patience. Donald, who died a few years ago, was a very successful fisherman and he also, in my experience, displayed many of the qualities of George Jack.

Donald was much better known perhaps as "Donal the Vision". The latter part of the name refers to his last boat, which was named the *Vision*.

He told me the tale - which was really quite hilarious as he told it in his own inimitable way - of his adventure with a broken-down German coaster.

His father was skipper of the *Maureen* at this time and he, with Donald as a part-owner and crew member, was working great lines with her in the Minch. They were hauling these lines off

Dunvegan on a bonny, quiet, late autumn day when Donald became aware that a large coaster, which had been steaming north, had come to a halt some miles west of them. At his prompting, they stopped hauling, loosened an end of their lines, buoyed it and set off to see what ailed this ship.

They discovered that the she was German and the skipper, who spoke good English, told Donald that they had a "small problem" with their engine. His engineer was working on it, and he hoped to be under way shortly. Thanking Donald for his concern, he stepped into his wheelhouse and closed the door, thus ending the dialogue.

The *Vision* returned to the task of hauling the lines but when the last of them was aboard Donald insisted that they remain where they were instead of going to anchor in Dunvegan. He wanted to keep an eye on the coaster, which was still lying stopped.

They got the forecast at 6 p.m. and it was not good at all. The wind was to freshen from the south-west, and was to reach gale force. Off they went back out to where the coaster lay. There was now a light breeze from the airt that the forecaster had warned them of.

"Ow's yer engine doin' now?" queried Donald of the German captain.

"Mine enchineer still vorks at it," was the reply.

"Ah weel, the forecast is verra bad," says Donald. "Ye'd be weel advised tae tak a tow while daylight lasts, an' afore this gale comes. There's a lot o' bad rocks no' far tae the north o ye. We could tow ye tae Stornoway, nae bother."

The German thought about this for a time then asked, "Your ship is small. How large is your enchine?"

"We hiv a five hunder horse-power diesel here, an we could tow ye nae bother at all." (They had, in fact, a one hundred and fourteen horse-power Gardner!)

"Zat iss a very large enchine for such a small craft!" replied the German slowly, looking very doubtfully down on the diminutive *Maureen*.

"Ah weel, jeest you tak' an en' o' this rope, an we'll see 'ow it goes. Did ye feel that wee puff o win' there? It's gaan til freshen fast an we canna bide ere much langer!"

The tow was eventually secured and as soon as the strain was on the rope, Donald disappeared below where he lifted the cold-start button on the Gardner's fuel pump. Black smoke poured from the exhaust but the ploy was successful and the coaster slowly began to move.

"Ah'll tell ye somethin, Tommy," Donald said, with a huge grin on his face, "Ah wis nivver so glad tae get intil a herbour in aal my life as ah wis that night. It wis jeest a pure gale o' win', an I nivver thocht we'd see Stornoway alive! We managed it though, an the salvage we got for that night's work, paid for the *Maureen*!"

I witnessed, by accident, Donald's greeting on the telephone one day when he called a lawyer in London. He was involved in another salvage claim, I think, and had breezed into the fish salesman's office in Mallaig.

"Wid ee get me that number richt away, ma lass? It's 'at lawyer lad in London that ah'm needin tae spik til," he asked the young lady who was then employed as the telephonist, handing her a note as he left her for the main office.

She called through to Donald when she had the correct person on the line, and Donald lifted the 'phone.

"Aye, aye. Noo lissen 'ere. Ye're spikkin til Donal the Vision fae Mallaig!" he roared down the mouthpiece.

I left then, trying to keep a straight face at the thought of this poor fellow sitting in his London office, whose ear was being assailed in such a fashion and in a language he had no hope of understanding.

It was also Donald who told me of the Auchie who had been called up to serve in the Royal Navy at the beginning of the war. After an initial medical, he was seen by the dental officer who told him that his teeth were in very poor condition.

"I'll have to do a fair bit of work on them, to bring them up to scratch," he announced.

"Weel noo my mannie," replied the Auchie. "From what ah've seen o' the grub doon 'ere so far, ah think my teeth'll dae fine. Jeest you lee them be!"

Donald was forced to retire from the sea several years ago through ill health. His spirit was not dulled by his physical suffering, however and he recently compiled a book on his time at sea. I think that this book was eventually published but although I saw the transcript, I have no idea where to get a copy.

Donald's letters to the press, mainly the "Fishing News", have been published on many occasions. Almost all of them display a degree of truth and of common sense that is sadly lacking in those whose aspirations are aimed more at political kudos than at advancing the cause of the fishing industry. His passion for justice and truth, however, caused him to use words that were more suited to the deck of a fishing boat than the whispering parlours of lying machinations that are the domain of our pitiful political aspirants.

Donald's direct approach is alien to these poor people. I recall with delight hearing of him approaching Lord Mansfield during this poor man's thankfully short spell in office.

"Noo look 'ere, Mansfield," Donald roared, by way of introduction!

Not really the way to make friends and to influence people, however.

Sadly, Donald died in July of 2007 in hospital in Inverness, after a long illness that he bore with typical courage and humour.

‘Abie’ or Abraham Skinner was, and still is a man of some substance on the Black Isle. He was skipper of the ringer *Rose* in the 1960’s, having taken her over from his brother, Sandy, when he bought the *Aspire*.

During Abie’s time at the ring net it was the habit of the Avoch men to use a searchlight shone over the bow, as they searched for herring in the rock-strewn lochs north of Skipport. We, for our part, could not understand this – as far as we were concerned, this habit could only frighten herring away and as a consequence, when we passed one of their boats, our usual roar advised them to stick their lights up their arses!

This language did not sit well with Abie and I well remember his opinion, delivered to Hendry Addison and myself that “Mallaig’s the maist lawless place on the West Coast o Scotland!”

Abie was then, and probably still is, a good living man who neither smoked nor drank alcohol. I recall hearing the tale of one of his adventures whilst they were working out of Seahouses. They had been fishing there for a few weeks and the skippers had taken their cars to the port. This enabled them to get home every weekend, a wonderful advance on previous years when they would have been away for weeks on end. One night there was just too much wind for them to work – this resulted in a night in harbour. Some of the *Rose*’s crew spent some time in one of the pubs, and much hilarity ensued!

The following morning, Abie confronted them and advised them of what he perceived as the error of their ways. By way of punishment for their transgressions, they were not allowed home that weekend. Abie kept them in Seahouses where they spent their time picking over the net, repairing all the small holes they found, no doubt contemplating their sins as they did so!

Mallaig Memories

In the early summer of 1956 I left Campbeltown and went to Mallaig, a small West Highland fishing village. My reasons for leaving home were the usual ones, I had met Ina Sutherland, daughter of the well-known and much respected 'Big Willie' Sutherland, and although she was not at that time aware of it I knew, very early, that I wanted to marry her.

Mallaig clings to the rocks at the mouth of Loch Nevis in what was – before Regionalisation - Inverness-Shire. The name of this loch is translated popularly but, as far as I am concerned, rather puzzlingly as 'Heavenly Loch'.

The *Golden Fleece* in Mallaig Harbour, 1953

The late Archie MacLellan, hotelier and local historian, told me that his mother, who had worked in the Post Office in the days when telegraphy was the norm, and who was therefore an expert in Morse - told him that when sending Inverness-Shire in Morse code as she did many times every day, there were a total of 18 successive 'dots' to send. Try it for yourself, from the 'dash' in the 'n', to the next 'dash' in the 'r', there are indeed 18 dots.

It is out of chronological order here, but may possibly be worth recalling a letter which I wrote to Moira Kerr, who was then editor of the Oban Times, as a prank. It went something like this:-

Dear Rona,

Islay odds that Jura very nice girl, so I thought I'd Colonsay that Iona Barra and that if you're too Tireed to walk, I'd Coll and Gigha lift tomorrow. I Shiant be late, for Lewis and Ben Becula are coming too. It is not pie in the Skye, and I Canna Muck about, nor am I Uist to Crowlin, but it would be a Rhum thing if I couldn't do this without anyone having to Eigg me on. It is not Eriskay thing to do, but if you think you Shuna, I'll understand, but I muStaffan answer soon.

Yours aye,

Sanday.

Moving to the West Highlands is a traumatic event for those who do not understand the people who live there, but I was fortunate in that I had worked among them for some time and had learned something of what made them tick.

This understanding - or lack of it - of the people is epitomised by the apocryphal story of the old lady who lived at Ardvasar on the Island of Skye.

This old dear had developed a very sore throat and had called the doctor in to attend to it. This man had only recently arrived on Skye from the Home Counties, and did not yet understand the innate shyness of the people, making the common yet fatal mistake of confusing this shyness with backwardness.

He examined the old lady and wrote out a prescription for a product which he thought would cure the sore throat.

Noting as he did this, that the low seat upon which she sat revealed that she wore long red underwear with elastic around the knees, he decided that he could have a little gentle fun at her expense, so he approached her, looked down her throat again, told her to open her mouth really wide and commented, "Yes, I think that the medicine I have prescribed will do the trick. By the way," - this said peering intently down her throat - "I notice you are wearing long red bloomers."

His lesson was learned the hard way when she replied quietly, "Ah yes, Doctor. Now while you are here, will you have a look up my arse and tell me if my hat is on straight?"

Another story which illustrates the humour of the area concerns the old crofter in Ardvaser who wanted to sell his croft house, and who was approached by the ubiquitous rich American who wanted to buy a piece of his forebear's land. He was shown around the house, and expressed delight with all he had seen, but finally remarked of his reservations on the apparent absence of a toilet. The old crofter then took the prospective buyer down a slope and through an increasingly muddy field, arriving at a very small dilapidated wooden outhouse. "There you are," he announced, pointing proudly at the bucket inside the hut.

"What about security?" demanded the Yank, looking askance at the huge gaps in the planking of the sides and roof, and at the lock-less ramshackle door of this outhouse, which was hanging off one hinge.

"Security?" retorted the old chap. "My grandfather did his business every day here until he died. My father did his business here until he died too, and I have been doing my business here since I was old enough to walk. Now do you know something, we haven't lost a shit out of it yet!"

The other classic – and absolutely true - riposte to an attempt at a smart remark, from a Southerner, was delivered when two young soldiers, newly posted to the Army rocket range at Benbecula, went into their new 'local' to view the opportunities for some highflying nightlife.

The rather limited facilities available in this pub obviously did not meet with their approval, so one of them, having had a good look around, remarked to the other in a loud voice which was obviously meant to impress the 'natives' who were drinking there, "I think this must be the arsehole of the world, mate."

An old chap who was standing at the bar put down his whisky, had a pull at his pipe, looked this young soldier up and down and then, fixing him square in the eye, furthered the lad's education by saying quietly to him, "I wouldn't worry about that if I was you sonny, you're just passing through it!"

Some years ago, a friend and I had, in a misguided moment, become involved in chartering yachts out of Mallaig. During this spell there was an incident which illustrated another facet of the nature of West Highland people, which is often misinterpreted as nosiness A group of young people had chartered one of our yachts, and had anchored one evening in a bay north of Kyle. They had gone ashore to dine in the local hotel, and had met some other yachtsmen there who had invited them aboard their very large blue yacht for a nightcap. Their host was none other than Sir Isaac Woolfson, who was then, I believe, the owner of Great Universal Stores. In the morning they went ashore to the only shop in the village for some food. This shop was self-service, and also doubled as the local Post Office.

When they went in, the owner, a burly old chap who smoked a pipe incessantly and who took no active part in the running of the shop, revealed this facet of nature to which I refer, by quizzing them relentlessly about their background while revealing none of his own. He was the kind of man who, given an hour with anyone, would be able years later to relate not only their history back as far as their great-grandparents, but would be able to give a fairly accurate estimate of their bank balance also!

Sir Isaac then appeared with his wife, so the old chap zeroed in on him, but was instantly struggling because apart from revealing that yes, the blue yacht which was anchored in the bay belonged to him, nothing was going to be revealed.

"What line of business are you in then?" asked the old chap.

"Oh, the same as yourself," was the reply.

"By Jove you must have a big Post Office in your shop, to be able to afford a yacht like that," was the best response the poor old chap could muster.

When I first went to Mallaig as a fisherman, I lodged with David and Rosie McMinn. Rosie is my wife's sister, and I would find it difficult to repay their kindliness to me then.

One weekend, shortly after my arrival there, David developed a severe pain in his abdomen and the doctor was sent for.

This doctor was an extremely clever man whose diagnostic skills were legendary among his peers - indeed I had a doctor in Weymouth not many years ago tell me that we were lucky to have had such a skilled man in our community - but he had a weakness for whisky.

When he arrived in the house, it was obvious to me that he had been indulging in this weakness, but he did examine David and confidently announced that he was suffering from appendicitis, and that this would of course mean a trip to hospital for its removal.

Having made the diagnosis he appeared happy to sit down and drink the tea he had asked for, taking no action to get an ambulance for David, who was now audibly suffering!

Eventually the process was started - the local ambulance was summoned and arrived, and off we went on the fifty or so miles of the single track bumpy road which had then to be suffered before reaching Hospital.

Cars were a rarity in those days, so I did not of course know any of the villages en route to Fort William and Hospital, but I now know that we were close to the rather oddly named Quality Cottages, just a few miles beyond Arisaig when all of the lights in the ambulance went out, the engine stopped, and the driver shouted, “Get out, the engine’s on fire!”

We did as we were told with some haste, patient and all, but it then became evident that the fire was electrical, and although we were now stranded at the side of the road in total darkness, we were safe!

The driver then asked me to carry on up the road for about half a mile, where I would find some cottages. I was to knock at the door of one of them, and ask for a loan of a torch - an item which to my surprise did not appear to be considered a necessary piece of equipment in an ambulance but which was now essential if repairs were to be made.

I followed his instructions, and found myself running and stumbling along this dark and deserted road, with not a light in sight, at around eleven p.m. on a bitterly cold winter night, wondering why I had ever left home and civilisation!

At last I spotted a dim glimmer of light just off the road, and correctly assumed that this was one of the cottages for which I was searching, so I carefully picked my way down the path to the door and knocked.

Eventually, after much bumping and banging from inside, the door opened, and I excitedly demanded the loan of a torch from the elderly man who now stood in the doorway.

I soon realised that the reason for my lack of success in my demands, was due to the fact that I was talking much too fast for this poor man who was later described to me as being a wartime refugee from Belgium, one for whom English was decidedly a second language!

Eventually however I arrived back at the disabled ambulance, and Jackie - the driver - commenced repairs, under instruction from David, the suffering patient, who was fortunately an electrician.

The outcome was a happy one, the operation was successfully carried out, but it was literally a baptism of fire for me, and was not the sort of introduction to the emergency services which inspired confidence!

Mallaig is a community of around one thousand souls, which owes its origins to the fact that the small bay where it stands was chosen as the railhead and steamer connecting port for the West Highland line. Its name it owes to the Vikings - translated it means 'rocky bay'. It has thankfully thus far successfully resisted the efforts of a misguided few incomers to add 'Port of ' as a prefix to this name. Its Gaelic name was Bagh na h'Acarsaidh Mor – Bay of the Big Harbour.

The coming of the railway and the building of a pier in the very early 1900s opened up the markets in the south, and it rapidly grew in size to service the railway, the steamers and the herring boats which used it.

In the early days of Mallaig's growth as a fishing port, the lack of mechanical devices for splitting herring prior to the salting and smoking processes necessary to turn them into the kippers for which the port was rightly famed, meant that girls were imported for the task. These hard-working ladies, mainly from the East Coast of Scotland, were housed in 'huts' built adjacent to the kippering plants which employed them.

Planning controls were conspicuous by their absence, so huts were built higgledy piggledy, with absolutely no thought for their aesthetic values.

The area which housed the kipper yards and the huts was unimaginatively known as the 'Point', simply because it was built upon an area which jutted out into the sea, near the pier. I had heard many cautionary tales of the 'Point' long before I left school, so had looked forward, with some trepidation, to seeing this Soho of the North at first hand, when first I came ashore there as a boy.

My initially cautious exploration of this place revealed only the scrupulously clean wooden homes of hard-working fisher lasses, whose moral values were generally far higher than those of the fools who had sought to mislead me.

My move to Mallaig was primarily to be near to Ina, the girl who was to become my wife, and who lived there. Her maiden name was Sutherland, and her father - "Big Willie" - had been a notable fisherman with the Mallaig fleet as owner and skipper of the *Jessie Alice*. Sadly, he had died before I came to Mallaig, so my great loss was that I never got to know him personally. Her mother was from the famous Mallaig fishing family, the Mansons, and it was with them that I was now about to start work.

Her uncle Jim Manson, 'Black Jim' as he was popularly known, is the first of my Captains there.

He was a big powerful man with a dark, almost swarthy complexion, and he had very piercing black eyes. His hair had been black but, by the time I met him, it was almost white.

At that time the Manson family owned or controlled four boats, and Jim was very much in charge of every move they made. He dictated when they went to sea, where they fished, and when they came back again. He was, like all successful men, the subject of much controversy, and even now, years after his death, the very mention of his name can provoke much discussion.

There was despite all his bluster and bravado, a great deal about him which suggested a deep-felt shyness. For example, on the rare occasions when he went on a shopping expedition with his family to, let's say Inverness, he refused to eat in a restaurant, but preferred to have a sandwich or the like, sitting peacefully in the security of his own car.

His model of justice was a mixture of the Judaic ideal of 'an eye for an eye', with a liberal dose of his own sense of fun. He used to say of anyone who had mortally offended him, "Shooting's too good for that one: he needs a good kick up the arse!"

A typical week then started of course with going to sea early on the Monday morning.

Jim Manson at Canna

The first boat to leave had to be Jim's, simply because he would not tell anyone else just where he proposed that they would all fish that night, so no one else knew where to go. This promoted the theory that he was never sure of which part of the east coast of the Outer Hebrides he would arrive at, in what was the typically bad visibility in the driving rain that is so prevalent in the winter there so wherever they arrived was, they reckoned, the place he would later say he had been aiming at!

This slur upon his navigational abilities was stimulated by some of the theories which he expounded at times. For example, he said that, "If ye're no' sure what side o' a buoy tae go on, keep close tae it. The boat that pit it there draws mair watter than yours does!"

I don't think I would advise anyone to follow that lead, nor his habit of using a match to measure the distance between two points on a chart. "A match is aboot an hour's steam," he would say, taking no heed to the differing scales of the charts that might be in use!

Those statements owed more to his sense of fun than to his ignorance of navigation I am sure, and those who would denigrate his abilities choose to ignore the fact that he never failed to find the 'West End' (of Canna) - a much sought after landmark - on the inkiest black gale-riven of nights en route to market in Mallaig, and this when a barely reliable compass and a battered old alarm clock were the only navigational equipment to which he had access.

On that subject, I recall a conversation I had, quite a few years ago, with the late Archie MacLellan. He had, he told me, been out for a week with Jim and towards the end of this week they had set off from Uishnish Point, headed for Canna. Duncan "Porter" Gillies was on watch and Archie joined him in the wheelhouse. It was a foul night – not much wind, but there was a heavy drizzle which limited their vision considerably. After nearly two hours steaming, Jim stuck his head up from the forecastle hatch, and told Porter to head for the Hyskeir.

Porter, Archie told me, immediately turned the boat's head around 80 degrees to starboard and after nearly an hour's steaming, to Archie's complete amazement, he saw the 3 flashes of Hyskeir Light right ahead of them.

How, Archie asked, did Porter know the course that took them there? This was, remember, well before radar was introduced to fishing boats. The only navigational aids they had were the aforesaid compass and clock.

I thought about this for a moment then asked Archie, whose background had been in the hotel and bar trade all his life whether, if he was given a bottle of whisky and a dozen glasses, he could empty the bottle into these glasses and, without measuring them, could have poured a very similar amount in each?

When he answered that yes, he probably could, I told him that Porter had been across the Minch many more times than he had poured out glasses of whisky!

He accepted this analogy without further question.

Jim's preferred fishing grounds were the rock-infested lochs on the east coasts of South Uist, Benbecula, and North Uist, and over the years he took a vast amount of herring from these areas.

Whilst fishing there, an essential part of the gear kept ready for use was a tow rope, because prudent navigation took a poor second place to the pursuit of his prey, and it was an almost nightly occurrence to have to tow a boat off one of the many rocks.

The result of this single-minded chasing of the herring was that his boat, the *Margaret Ann*, was rarely a pleasing sight to the eye of those who did not understand that he did not seem to mind knocking lumps off his boat, if it meant that he was catching herring!

Another result of fishing on these grounds was that there was a lot of damage done to the nets, and it was rare indeed to see the *Margaret Ann* without her deck swarming with crews repairing this destruction.

It was common for Jim to lift his anchor and set off fishing earlier than normal when he saw a strange boat approaching, and I am sure that this was done because he did not want them to see the battle scarred boat and net, at close quarters.

He was one of the very few men to whom money seemed merely a necessary evil. For example, he rarely appeared to bother about the price obtained for the herring he had caught. Catching them was paramount in his eyes.

He also gave away far more than anyone will ever be able to catalogue. I remember one boat from the Clyde, which had not been enjoying the best of luck, losing her ring-net due to it being washed overboard on a stormy passage across the Minch. This seemed to be the final blow to them, but Jim gave a perfectly good net to this unfortunate man. In today's terms, this gift would be worth well in excess of £20,000!

(l-r) Tommy Mathieson, Tommy Ralston, Jim Manson, Alan Moffat

He paid for a new engine of a small boat whose owner - from one of the islands - had fallen on bad times. Other gifts, of which I am aware, ranged from radio receivers to refrigerators! On another occasion a family in North Bay – who had precious little in the way of luxuries – suffered the loss of their precious cow. The practical difficulties of burying the corpse in countryside that had an extremely thin covering of peaty earth would not be apparent to one who did not live there. The problem was recognised by Jim and so all hands were mustered to get the corpse to the water. Then he towed it out to sea, where, with a degree of difficulty, it was sunk. Jim then bought the family another cow - but very few people knew of this. I was there at the time but it fell to a cousin of my wife, the late Jimmy Coull, to remind me not long before his death, of Jim's kindness.

Two brothers of this family spent a lot of time aboard the Manson boats. Both of them were rather simple lads. One suffered quite badly from asthma. He was christened 'Towrow'- the 'ow' pronounced as in 'how' - because of his habit of sitting quietly in a corner of the forecastle singing a melody using the phrase 'tow row row row'.

'Towrow' is long dead but late in 2004 I was delighted to discover the other brother, Donald Patrick, living in the hospital in Castlebay. Ina and I called to see him, and to my delight he seemed very happy, and was certainly well cared for.

Jim took this pair to Mallaig on one occasion. They were suitably amazed and scared stiff when they were taken to the railway station to see their first steam engine but were very unhappy walking on the wooden pier, as they were afraid that they would fall through the gaps between the planking. This was almost certainly the only 'holiday' the poor souls ever had.

I remember asking Jim why he gave away so much, and will never forget him fixing me with his black eyes and growling, "The giving hand's the receiving hand."

Some people of course, took advantage of this philosophy of his.

I personally was annoyed on more than one occasion, when he took a fry of fish which we had caught, and were now looking forward to eating, and gave them to what he thought was a deserving case. It was my jaundiced opinion that the recipients of these gifts were simply scroungers who were down at the boats to see what was on offer!

During the spring months, there were often line-fishing boats working in the Minches, and Jim took it upon himself to see that they were kept supplied with the herring which they used to bait the hooks. At this time we were usually fishing in daylight on the west coast of Skye, around the Neist Point area. Moonen Bay, to the south of Neist, was the area where we got the good quality herring, but they were thinly scattered, and to get a marketable amount of them meant a lot of work, so as a result it was a relief when darkness came, and it was time to call a halt and go to bed.

Jim had different ideas.

In the shelter of Loch Pooltiel there were usually thin scatters of immature herring, so it was there that we now went, to catch bait for the line-fishers. Having caught the few cran which were needed, one of his boats was then despatched to deliver them to the liners who would be working perhaps two hours steaming away.

Our sole reward for these efforts would be a few ling which the grateful crew of the liner would throw aboard us, and which were subsequently given by Jim to the inhabitants of Pooltiel!

The Mansons' *Jessie-Alice* in Loch Pooltiel

Jim had a dark intense air about him which lent itself to the tales which were told about him and several strange experiences which he had known. I asked him about one of these stories, and he confirmed it to me in that odd off-handed way of his.

This incident had happened when his grandfather, old 'Dodie Bainie', had died and the corpse was being taken back to Buckie in a hearse. Jim told me that he had been sitting in the front seat of this hearse on its journey to the East Coast, when a hand had appeared from the roof and rested on his shoulder.

Now if this had happened to me then I am afraid that I would have probably died of fright, but when I suggested this to Jim he just laughed about it and told me that there was nothing to be afraid of. That is not how I viewed it at all: I would have been petrified!

There was another incident that I have yet to have explained to me. This happened when we were lying at anchor in Canna one summer morning. Three of us were lying alongside and Jim got up at what we considered an extremely early hour, and woke everyone. We had no idea what was going on but thought that we must be setting off on some wild goose chase. To our surprise, Jim went to the pier at Canna where there were already two or three Clyde boats lying. This was most unlike him, as he usually preferred his own company.

We were not long there when one of the local men arrived to tell Jim that Robbie Hepburn had called to ask him to try to get the news to Jim that his father had died.

Jim growled something to the effect that he knew, as he had heard him dropping his anchor!

Years later I asked him about this and he replied that it was perfectly simple; he had heard the chain rattling out over the stem and knew that this was his father dropping his hook!

When the Austin 1100 car was unveiled to the public first, many years ago, everyone was greatly impressed with the then revolutionary new suspension which was its main selling feature. This was of course in the days when it was unusual for working men to own cars. Jim ordered one of these vehicles from his usual supplier, a dealer in Fraserburgh, but stipulated that it had to be red. Of course, everyone was keen to see this amazing new model at first hand. We were at sea all week in these days, so it was agreed, well in advance of the probable delivery date, that when it was eventually available for collection, Jim would drive through to Fraserburgh with his son Jimmy and daughter-in-law Violet - who belonged to the Broch, as Fraserburgh is universally known - in his old car, and trade it in for the new one.

This trip would start in the early hours of a Saturday morning, as soon as the boats docked.

One day Violet received a 'phone call from her brother-in-law Victor, a native of Poland who had settled in the Broch and was a kipperer there, telling her that Jim's new car was in now. "Oh, that's great," says Violet, "fit colour is it?"

"A sort o' maroon shade," replied Victor

Knowing that the *Mary Manson* was in with a shot of herring, Violet sped down the pier to find that the boat was just pulling away from the pier, en route back to the fishing grounds. She shouted to them, "Tell Jim his car is in, and it is maroon."

When we met up with the message bearing boat however, the message was wrongly relayed as, "Your car is in Jim, an' it's broon!"

"Who the Hell ever saw a broon car?" raged Jim. "He can keep it, I ordered a red car an' I'm no' gaan tae accept anythin' else!"

When we got into Mallaig on the Saturday morning at around 4 a.m., Jim's son, young Jimmy went home and was getting ready for bed when Violet got up and started to get dressed, reminding him that they were going to get his father's car. She laughed when her husband said that his father was not going to accept a broon car, and explained the mistake to him.

Jimmy got dressed and went to inform his Dad of the error, to find that he was now in bed, and had no intention of getting up again, so the instruction was given that Jimmy and Violet were to go to the Broch themselves.

When they arrived, they went straight to the dealer's garage, and rushed around excitedly, looking for this car.

Seeing a man polishing a green Austin 1100, they asked to be shown the maroon one they were there to pick up.

"This is the only 1100 we hiv," replied the worker, "an' it's fur a lad in Mallaig." Violet's brother was colour blind!

I am not sure that Jim would be at ease in the crowded room around the fireplace with all the other Captains, but that is certainly where he belongs. Jim had a daughter and two sons. The elder son, Jimmy, lost his wife at a very young age, to cancer. Jimmy himself contracted that dreadful disease, Huntingdon's Chorea and died some years ago. He lived long enough to have to bury his elder son, James. Whilst skippering a large purser that belonged to Ricky Donnan, a prominent figure in the fishing industry, James had taken a shot of mackerel to France and was set upon by a gang of murderous thugs. He died as a result of this cowardly attack.

Jim's second son, Zander, lost his life when his purser was sunk as a result of a collision with a German ship off the coast of Denmark.

William John Manson was a half-brother of Jim's, and he was Chairman of the Mallaig and North-West Fisherman's Association for many years. He remained an active fisherman until he was almost 80, and he epitomised the single-minded pursuit of fish, which is all that such men cared about.

Ina and I visited William John in hospital in Fort William some years back. He had no idea at all that we were coming and when we got to the door of his small ward he was standing with his back to us, being helped round the end of his bed by a nurse.

"Aye, Weelum," I said. "There are plenty of herring in Moonen Bay – d'ye fancy a look there?"

Without hesitation and without turning around he answered, "Aye, Tommy, ye're at the wrang time o' year for Moonen Bay! You should know that!"

I remain confounded that he recognised me so quickly from my voice alone and that he was quick enough to spot the error I had made.

He was dead less than a week after that.

Duncan "Porter" Gillies, who owned the *Mallaig Mhor* was another great worthy in the same era as Jim Manson but unlike Jim, who came to Mallaig from Buckie, Porter was of old Mallaig stock. One of the few who could claim to be a native of the village, he would bring a smile to the faces of the rest of the Captains, and would certainly enjoy a glass of whisky!

It was usual for the ringers in those days to have on board a box of kippers from one of the small kippering yards which abounded in Mallaig at that time. Knowing this, crofters on some of the islands would come aboard quite often, looking for a fry. Sometimes they brought a few fresh eggs, scones, or a can of fresh milk, which they offered in return for the kippers.

On the Island of Canna, one such man, Hugh Steel, often rowed out to the anchored boat and if the crew were not on deck he was notable for his habit of knocking on the side of the boat until invited aboard. Hugh was a regular visitor to the *Mallaig Mhor* and had often been the recipient of a fry of kippers. Arriving back at Canna after landing herring in Mallaig one day toward the end of a week during which they had enjoyed reasonable fishing from around the island, they had hardly got their anchor down when the worthy appeared again, this time carrying a can of milk. After the usual pleasantries had been exchanged Hugh asked about the kippers, and it was only then that Porter realised that they had sailed without getting any. On being told this, the man quietly got up and left - taking the milk with him!

Porter, who really didn't swear much but used the word 'puckin' often, to replace the more commonly used expletive, told me of this occasion more than once, saying, "D'ye know this, when we told him we had nae kippers he jeest sat there for a wee while then he got up an' left. Aye, an' he took his puckin milk wi' him!"

If one of his crew did something slightly wrong Porter used to growl, "If it wasn't Friday, and me a good Catholic, I'd chew the puckin balls off you!" This was of course in the days when Catholics were expected to eat fish instead of meat on a Friday.

Porter was skipper of the *Mallaig Mhor* for many years, and I do not think that he ever did anyone a knowing wrong. If he couldn't do a good turn, he would not do anything.

Hugh Steel of Canna, was a time-served carpenter and Robert Ross, of Tarbert, told me a tale about this man that showed him in a different light to Porter's tale however. During the war Robert was one of the crew on board the ringer, *Little Flower*. They were working around Canna and one Friday night they rolled against their neighbour boat, lifting around ten feet of the top rail. In the morning, both crews went aboard their faster neighbour and set off to Crinan and home, for the weekend. The *Little Flower* was left lying at anchor in Canna and the repairs to the damaged rail were shelved until they returned.

When they got back on the Monday evening, Robert told me, the damage had all been repaired, and the rail had been repainted. Hugh, who had done the work, stoutly refused payment of any kind!

A much younger man, though unfortunately no longer with us, was Jimmy Maclean, better known as "Clainey". He is definitely one of the Captains who sailed from Mallaig.

Clainey fathered seven sons, all of whom were fishermen at some time. Indeed almost all still earn a living the hard way - from the sea. He was a tall, very powerful man who commanded instant respect from all who knew him - respect for the absolute integrity that he displayed in every aspect of his life and his work. He was a nephew of "Black Jim" Manson, and resembled him closely in appearance and in his life style. His physical strength was legendary, and it was said that he was the only man who had ever broken the perfectly sound cork-rope on a ring net which was full of herring, such was his eagerness to get them aboard! John 'G' Henderson, himself a successful skipper of many years standing, told me that in his younger days he had neighboured Clainey, and gave me an instance of the kind of man he was.

They had been anchored one night at the north end of Skye. There was a gale of wind blowing, when another boat dragged her anchor and blew down on top of them, scratching the varnish on Clainey's new boat, the *Minnie McLean*, in the process. This incident caused him to jump up and down in temper, and so off they went to sea. All night they scoured the stormy waters, seeing no sign of any herring. As daylight broke and the wind eased, they were among the Summer Isles at the mouth of Loch Broom, and had gone alongside one another for a discussion of the options available to them. This action usually meant that the night's efforts were over, and that anchor and sleep were imminent. As they lay there close to the shore, the herring - which had obviously been lying extremely close inshore - did what they often did, rose and 'played' off the shore. John said in describing it, "The whole sea rose just inside us." One ring filled the two boats!

The last Mallaig fisherman to be singled out by me as deserving of Captaincy is the late Willie MacDonald, a native of Benbecula. He was a very powerful man, who had hands like the proverbial shovels!

He was a lobster fisherman, skipper of the *Winner* and with his brother, Murdo, in this boat - which was not more than 40 feet long - he used to fish as far away as the west coast of the Hebrides on occasion. When fishing there his wife, who belonged to Cairnbulg on the East Coast, used to say - "Wullie's awa' tae th' Atlantic!"

He was a great Church man, was married but had no children, and his favourite pastime on a Saturday night was to wander round to the village shop where he bought sweets which were dispensed to the children who gathered around him.

Nowadays such largesse would attract the attention of the police, but Willie simply loved children.

There were a great many 'nomadic' fishermen who on occasion worked out of Mallaig, and from this rich field I would choose one whose presence is essential at Angus's fireside, and who certainly attains the rank of Captain – or Admiral.

George Alexander, known better as "Dodie Icey" – as then I thought his nickname was spelled - to all who were privileged to make his acquaintance, hailed from Gamrie, or Gardenstown as it should be called. He was a short round barrel of a man, although the first time I met him after he had retired and asked how he was, he told me that he had lost some weight, "half a hunnerwecht" to use his words! Unmarried, he was a kenspeckle figure everywhere he went, dressed in a grey jersey under his neat grey tweed jacket, with a matching 'fore and aft' hat, dispensing pinches of snuff to all those unwary enough to accept this proffered gift.

Only recently I discovered that his nickname should be 'Ae shee' in Doric, This, of course, translated into English means 'one shoe', and relates to an occasion, long ago, when a forebear lost one of his shoes in snow. Just how this came about, is beyond me, but I feel sure that there is more to this tale than was told to me!

His accent was pure Buchan, similar to what was used on the famous occasion when two old fellows met one morning when out for a stroll. "Did ee hear 'at aul' Peter wiz deed?" asked one. "Na! Fan did 'e dee 'n fit 'id 'e dee o'?" What would someone from the Home Counties make of that? In case translation is required, the first question was, "Did you hear that old Peter died?" The reply was, "No! When did he die, and what did he die of?"

Dod skippered drifters that fished all around Britain, but his last boat - the *Bracoden* - was a steel trawler which he had built for him on the Clyde. I well remember during one sprat fishing season going to him early in the morning on Mallaig pier in order to find out how successful the previous nights fishing had been. In telling of the amounts he thought had been caught, he said, "Aye, yon local boatie, ye ken, the *Bunch o' Wifies* - weel he hid twa or three lifts early on in the nicht, but I dinna ken if he got any mair or no'." I knew full well that there would be sense in what he had just said, but also knew that there was no such craft as the *Bunch o' Wifies*. It was a while before I realised that he was referring to a Mallaig boat, the *Five Sisters*!

Dodie's observations were legend wherever he went. For example, when he retired a few years ago, he amazed everyone by immediately booking on an extended cruise in a liner. Knowing that Dodie had never done anything like this, and no doubt seeking to air his own knowledge on the subject, a contemporary told him that at some time on this voyage he would be invited to dine at the Captain's table. Dodie's retort - "Na na, ah'm no' peyin' a' they bawbees tae eat wi' the crew" - passed instantly into the abundance of tales about the man.

He was a very successful fisherman, who helped many a young lad get started as a boat-owner and was, as I later discovered, as honest as the day is long.

He told me one tale, a true one that is certainly worthy of repetition. During the war he spent some time with the Navy aboard a drifter in Scapa Flow. There, he told me, an older man gave him a piece of very good advice. "It's nae aye best tae tell the truth, Dod," he began. "Noo I'm no advising ye tae tell lies. All I'm sayin is that sometimes it's better tae keep yer mooth shut. The truth's nae aye appreciated!"

How true that is. If only I could keep it in mind!

His home town is renowned for the church-going strengths of its population, and Dodie took delight in poking gentle fun at his fellow townsmen on occasion. He once told a spellbound group, who knew that he dabbled quite a lot on the stock market, that he had suffered greatly the previous weekend. He had, he said, become convinced on the Saturday morning that he had to sell all his shares in Imperial Tobacco, Distillers, and Scottish & Newcastle Brewers, but had been unable to contact his stockbroker until Monday morning. Asked if he thought that they were headed for a fall, he replied deadpan, "Na, but I jeest took the thocht that if I was tae dee, and a' my neighbours found oot that I had shares in booze an' baccy, they widna' come tae the funeral!"

I will never forget my first visit to Gardenstown, many years ago. Ina and I were on the east coast for reasons that I have forgotten and found ourselves, en route back to Mallaig, at one of the junctions that lead down into Gardenstown. We decided, as we were ahead of schedule, to go down into the village and try to find Dod. At that time, we had no idea of his address or of his telephone number.

We followed the steep road down into the village, passing through the higher up, modern villas, then through the older houses, down to the very narrow road that separated the village from the sea. It was a lovely Sunday afternoon.

As we drove very slowly along this road we spotted two men, leaning against the low sea wall. Drawing nearer, I recognised them as fishermen who had landed fish at Mallaig, but I could not recall their names.

They both stared intently at the car and, as we drew closer, we saw them transfer their attention from the number plate – which they obviously did not recognise – to the two occupants.

I drove slowly past them watching their intent scrutiny as they bent to look inside the car, out of the corner of my eye.

We turned at the end of the road and, as we approached the pair again, their attention was still fixed on trying to recognise either the car, or the occupants.

This time I stopped alongside them and wound down the passenger side window.

"It's a fine day," I offered.

After a short pause, one of them replied, "Aye, fairly that."

"I'm looking for a Mr. Alexander, George Alexander," I said.

There was no reply at all, this time so, thinking that there was quite possibly more than one Alexander in the village, I tried to make it easier for them by saying, "You'll maybe know him better as Dodie Icey. Where does he live?"

Again there was a painful pause, accompanied by an even closer inspection of us both before finally one of them replied, "Aye, aye. Faa's speirin?' (Who is asking)

Dod fairly laughed when I told him this. We were both well aware that in this close knit community, no questions posed by a stranger would be answered until the questioner had properly identified himself!

Dodie was a born story teller, and for a time I had a good natured competition going with him, to see who could tell the best yarn. Each time he landed we each had a story to tell, but I always came off second best. This 'competition', carried on however, until one day he told one which beat me hollow, and which I have never heard bettered. It was told in his broadest Buchan accent, one which I cannot hope to capture on paper, but which went as follows.

One Saturday night an old bachelor who lived alone in his big family house, decided to have a good look up in the loft. There he found an old fiddle, covered in dust and cobwebs. He took it downstairs, and when he had cleaned it off, or as Dodie put it, "Dichtit it", was amazed to see that it was a Stradivarius.

First thing on the Monday morning he took this priceless instrument, wrapped in a plastic bag, to the local antique shop and announced - "I've got a fiddle for sale here, and it's worth a lot of money."

"What makes you think that?" replied the dealer.

"Because it was built by Stradivarius", says our man.

The dealer turned round and shouted through to the back shop, "What do you think of Stradivarius fiddles, Tam?"

"They're lying all over the place, canna get movin' for them", says Tam, "They're nae worth nothing."

The dealer then got possession of the fiddle for £20, which offer he made only because, he said, "I've known you for a long time".

The old chap was not at all happy, but after a few drams he cheered up, and on the next Saturday night he again explored the loft, this time unearthing an ancient painting which on investigation and severe "dichtin" was seen to bear the signature of Rembrandt!

Wrapped in the plastic bag, he bore this treasure to the antique shop, first thing on Monday morning, thinking that he'd never be poor again.

"This painting is worth a fearful amount of money," he proclaimed to the eager dealer, "for it was painted by Rembrandt!"

"What do you think of Rembrandt paintings, Tam?" the dealer shouts once again through to the back shop.

"Lying all over the place, canna pit my feet down for them. Worth nothing at all." was the short reply.

"You heard that", says the dealer, "but the frame's quite good an' as you are an old friend, I'll give you £30 for it."

The painting changed hands for this pittance and off went the old chap, feeling decidedly unhappy.

On that Saturday night he went to the local fairground where he won two coconuts at a dart throwing stall, so on the Monday morning he took them, in a plastic bag, to the antique shop.

The dealer, seeing him coming, was out like a shot holding the door open for the old man.

"Now then my friend, what have you got for me today?"

"Have you ever heard of the Wooden Horse of Troy?" began our ancient hero, taking one of the coconuts from the bag. "You see, this is one of his bollocks - and afore ye shout through the back tae Tam, the horse only had twa - and [holding up the plastic bag] I've got the other one here!"

I chanced upon him one Friday on Mallaig pier as he was making his way toward his car preparatory to going home for the weekend. As we chatted, another fisherman called to Dod in passing, "Mind an' keep clear o' ------ on your wey hame noo, nae stoppin' for a dram." I asked Dodie what place this chap had referred to. He told me, then shook his head and advised me to keep clear of it at any cost. In explanation, he told me that he had gone in one day with two of his pals to this remote country Inn for "A wee dram". He was intrigued to see for the first time, one of – "Thae wee things lik a Christmas tree, ye ken fit Ah mean - fan the barmaid pits a gless ower them an' presses doon, they firl roon an' roon, an' watter scoots a' roon aboot the gless, an' washes it. Weel, there wis an aul' lad sittin' in the corner eatin' crisps an' drinkin' a pint o' beer. Fan he hid finished, he squeezed past us an' leant ower the bar, an' then he took oot his falsers an pit them ower this thing tae wash all the bits o' crisps awa'!"

Many of Dodie's stories had a wee sting in the tail as instanced in the following:

A fishing skipper decided that it was time that his son had a boat of his own, so to that end they both went to visit the three banks in their home town, to see which offered the best rate of interest. The son was sworn to keep silence during the times they were doing the negotiating.

Bank number one agreed to loan the money on the father's security, and would charge a rate of 12%, but the father's next question, "Hoo often d'ye ha'e a bath?" puzzled the son as much as the banker, who answered "Every morning of course," in deference to what he obviously thought was an eccentric potential customer.

Bank number two was visited, and offered them the money on exactly the same terms, and this time the question, "Hoo often d'ye ha'e a bath?" brought the reply that the puzzled banker had a bath and a shower on alternative mornings.

The third banker offered similar terms - and in reply to the same question asked of the previous two said, "I bathe every evening before retiring of course."

When the pair had left the third bank, the son's curiosity at last caused him to break his vow of silence and he asked, "Fit wey are ye speirin' at they lads hoo often they ha'e a bath, Da?"

"Weel, ma loon," the father replied, "if ye're gaan' tae ha'e tae kiss they lads erses for the next twenty years, it's as weel tae ken hoo clean they are!"

I personally missed Dodie greatly when he retired, and not just for his stories. It is my considered opinion that any young man - whether fisherman or not - could do a lot worse than model himself on this Captain.

Ina and I went on holiday with Dod on several occasions and we enjoyed his company greatly but his apparent inability to drop his Doric speech led to confusion on several occasions.

Such was the case when we arrived at a hotel in Manchester where we were to spend the night. This hotel allowed us to use their car park whilst we were away. Our flight was to be very early in the following morning so after we had eaten, we sat for a short time in the bar, then Ina announced that she was going to bed. Dod and I elected to go for a stroll before turning in.

There had been a lot of severe flooding in England just before this time and Dod was a wee bit worried about the safety of his car, in which we had travelled from my house. As we neared the hut in which the hotel's security guard sat, Dod hailed him. In Doric!

“Hey min! Foo far abune the high watter mark ur we here?”

“Pardon,” replied the poor man, not understanding a word of what Dod had said.

“Ah’m speerin’. Foo far abune the high watter mark ur we here?”

This question, delivered in a louder voice than before, struck the fellow dumb.

Dod waited for a moment for a reply before roaring, angrily, “Hey, ma loon! Ur ye tryin’ tae mak a feel o’ me?”

I judged it a suitable time to ‘translate’ Dod’s query, and will never forget the look of relief that appeared on the man’s face when he realised that he could understand me, at least!

He also caused a deal of consternation when he approached a young lady at the immigration desk in Kuala Lumpur airport. He was dragging his case with one hand and in the other he bore a sheaf of papers. Holding them out to this lady he asked, “Noo then, ma quine. Fit ist yer seekin frae me?

Her face was a picture!

His brother, David, told me of an incident that occurred when they were much younger. He and the middle brother, Charlie, were sitting at their tea one day when Dod arrived.

He sat down and without any preamble announced that he had bought a car.

“Whit kind o car?” asked Charlie.

“A motor car!” Dod replied.

David told me that he had never seen anything so fast in his life as the slice of mealy pudding that Charlie threw at Dod. After that, whenever Dod made a slightly sharp comment to me, I would tell him to watch out for the mealy pudding!

Since writing the above, Dod has gone from us. He died in early March 2006. He died quietly and quickly on a Sunday afternoon whilst sitting in a chair in the kitchen of the house he had been born in. I know for certain that his passing was just as he would have wished it.

He had his last holiday with us, just a few months before this, on a rented boat on the Canal du Midi, in Southern France. We discovered that we could buy quite drinkable wine for one Euro per litre, so at around 10.30 every morning I would teasingly ask if he wanted coffee, or a glass of wine! I believe that we used a greater volume of wine than of fuel, on that trip.

I asked him, nearing the end of the holiday, if he had enjoyed it. "Michty, aye!" he replied. Then, after thinking for a wee while he added, referring to the muscular problem that is increasingly affecting my mobility, "Ah'd say that if ye iver think o a holiday in a boat again, Tommy, ye should pick somethin aboot thirty thoosan' tons bigger nor this ane".

He was, of course, referring to the lack of mobility from which we both suffered.

He was buried beside the parents he had lost at such an early age, and had his ancient 'fore an' aft' hat on his chest.

My wife and I miss him greatly.

While I was still going to sea, there was a small fleet of seine-netters, most of them from Lossiemouth, which was the Scottish home of this method of catching white fish, working around Coll and Tiree. They chatted almost incessantly on their radios. This was a nuisance to those trying to make contact with someone on the same frequency, but it also was a source of information on fishing generally, and provided entertainment on dull watches crossing the Minch.

I remember hearing one skipper complain that his Decca (an electronic navigational device) had failed. As his radar had also failed the previous day he now asked, "Does anybody ken hoo tae work they compass things!"

Seine-netting consisted of shooting great lengths of rope to which the net was attached, in a triangular pattern. The ropes were bought in 'coils', each coil being 120 fathoms, or 240 yards long, and the skippers measured distances in these 'coils', rather than the more conventional yards, or miles.

This fact was brought home quite comically when idly listening to the long-winded story of how the narrator, a seine-net skipper, had spent the previous week-end. We were treated to a minute by minute description of how he and his wife had spent all their waking hours on the Saturday, then he moved on to the Sunday.

After a nice breakfast, which was carefully itemised, they had gone to the Kirk. A lunch, equally well-documented, followed this and then they had gone for a drive around the countryside near their home.

He then told how he had "cam tae yon little wee roadie, ye ken, the first on the left comin' north oot o' Elgin. We hid nivir been up that way, so I canted the car, an' off we goes. Weel, we hid only got aboot five coil up this roadie, when we cam' tae a dead end …!"

He was not trying to be funny. He lived on the sea and for the sea, and distances - be they on land or sea - were measured in coils, not miles, and Boysie qualifies as Captain in anybody's book, not just mine!

We often saw, when going into Loch Eport at low tide, the remains of an old boiler sticking out of the water on the south side of the loch, not far in from the narrow entrance. This is all that can be seen of a drifter called, I think, the *My Seal*, that had been owned by Boysie's father. She struck a rock there and sank, many years ago.

Without doubt my favourite watch-mates of this period was Jimmy Coull, a cousin of my wife. Jimmy was a well built chap, a very competent fisherman, who had travelled a lot and whose tales of his experiences on these travels lightened many a weary hour on watch.

He and one of his pals had bought a small car - which must have been one of the first in Mallaig - and the ploys which they got up to in this car were legion.

On one occasion, he told me, he and his pal had set out to visit Jimmy's brother who was doing his National Service, and who was then stationed at the airfield near Lossiemouth.

They had visited several hostelries en route - this was, remember, before the advent of the breathalyser - and were eventually granted access to the airfield itself. Jimmy said that he only realised how much alcohol they had consumed when his pal who was now driving down the centre of one of the runways commented to him, "Smashin' roads they've got on the East Coast, eh!"

The pair of them had developed a liking to poultry, and my late mother-in-law, who at that time kept hens, was losing one or two just about every week-end. Her complaint to the police was withdrawn when she discovered that it was two of her nephews who were guilty!

Jimmy took this liking for poultry with him when he joined the Merchant Navy, and was only cured of it after one unfortunate experience in Stranraer.

He had been ashore with some of his mates and had succumbed to temptation when they passed a hen-house on their way back to the ship. They arrived in their mess with the results of the raid, and plucked the unfortunate fowls before cooking and eating them. The feathers were disposed of, by putting them into the fire.

They were visited in the morning before they were awake, by the police, who asked where they had been on the previous night. This question answered, the next one was an enquiry as to when they had last eaten chicken?

"Chicken?" was the reply. "Ye're lucky tae get corned beef on this ship. We haven't seen chicken for years."

Jimmy Coull

They were then invited to accompany the police on to the deck.

Their case was completely destroyed when they did this. It had snowed after they had come aboard, and the ship was covered from stem to stern with the feathers which had blown – unburned - up the chimney, and which were now sticking in the snow all over the ship!

As I wrote earlier, Jimmy was a great lad to be on watch with, but it didn't end there. He never seemed to be in anything but a good humour. He had a fund of wonderful stories, but they were almost all about himself – Jimmy did not ever speak ill of anyone. Nothing ever seemed to faze him and if I had to choose someone to be the best shipmate I ever sailed with, without question Jimmy would come top of the list.

Jimmy died just a year or so ago, after living very happily in Buckie with his wife, Kitty and their family. I visited them on occasion and he once reminded me of a man I knew only as "Mr. Petersport", after the name of the tiny harbour where he kept his small fishing boat. His real name, Jimmy told me, was Johnston. This man was one of the hardest working fellows you could imagine.

It was quite a commonplace occurrence to see, when we were creeping into one of the lochs in the cold early hours of a January morning, a dim light. This was his boat lying to a few drift nets he had shot earlier. We always went alongside him to ask for news on what herring he had seen. Gaelic was his first language, and his English left a bit to be desired on occasion. I recall him replying to us one night: "Ah Jeemy – you should have been here yesterday. It came in wis the flood and went out wis the ebb and it didn't come back again!" He was, of course, referring to a shoal of herring. They seemed to always be referred to as 'it' by Gaelic speakers.

Jimmy Coull told me that they had approached his boat in Loch Carnan one very rainy night and Jimmy hailed him, asking if he had seen any signs of herring.

"No, nossing at all," came the reply then, immediately after this he cried – "Who is that?"

"The *Margaret Ann*," answered Jimmy, wondering why the boat had not been recognised.

"Ah, eet's you, Jeemy. It's seeck (thick) up at the top of the hole – there's plenty of it!"

Mr. Johnston, I guess, had been sheltering from the rain, if not asleep, when he was first hailed, and was not about to divulge any information to a stranger.

He went over to Mallaig with Jim Manson once, to negotiate for a new engine and stayed for the weekend with Dan Cameron and his wife. Dan was an islander like himself. On the Monday, he travelled back with the *Margaret Ann* and old Jim Manson teased him, saying that he thought that he was after Dan's wife.

Unloading herring at Mallaig, about 1960

"Oh no, Jeemy," he replied, covered in confusion, "I'll get it when it dies!"

He meant, of course, that he would wait until Dan had died before making any move on his wife.

Jimmy Coull was one of this world's gentlemen, a man who left a much better world than he entered, and he would contribute much more than his share of stories to the company around the fire in Angus's home. I would dearly love to meet him there.

During one of our trips to the north-east I took Ina to Portsoy to visit a relation of her late father. He was a very old man at that time, but was still very alert, and had a wonderful memory. While we were there his wife called her daughter to come round and meet Ina. She arrived shortly afterwards with her husband. He and I sat together and while the others talked of family history, we blethered about boats and fishing. He had, he told me, a small boat that he went to the creels with in the summer months. He caught some partans (crabs) and an occasional lobster but he stressed that it was just a hobby, not a money-making exercise. When winter weather arrived, the boat and creels came ashore and he passed the time away making and repairing creels in a small store that he shared with like-minded men, close to the harbour.

In spring, when the boat had been cleaned and got ready for the coming season, the creels and ropes were tarred. Then, when they had dried and it was deemed time to go to sea, they were taken down on to the pier, baited and were taken aboard the boat. There was only one man on each boat so he was responsible for seeing that his creels were stored in the correct order. He would coil the ropes and place the creels – which were handed down to him by a friend – in the proper order, ready for shooting. Then it was his turn to hand down the creels to the friend who had helped him.

One old chap set off out for his first day of the new season. Reaching the favoured area, he dropped the creel anchor over the side and as the boat, with no-one at the helm, steamed ahead, he lifted the creels and threw them overboard in turn. To his horror he saw, as he grabbed one of the creels, that a cat had obviously gone in after the bait, and had been unable to get out. There was nothing he could do - creel and cat went overboard!

He wasn't able to get out for a couple of days as the weather was not good but on the third day he felt that he had to go. In the interest of safety, his son insisted on going with him.

They hauled away for a time, getting a gey sparse fishing when the son, who was at the rail lifting the creels aboard, let out a great roar of delight as a creel surfaced. It was just full of crabs! He shook them out and then stuck his hand into the creel.

"Look at this, Dad!" he said, holding out the bedraggled corpse of the cat.

"Aye, jeest pit it back intae the creel again," said his father, a practical fisherman if ever there was one. "It'll dee fur anither day or twa!"

Just recently I met an acquaintance here, out for a walk with his lady friend. He told me that he now had a small boat, and was working a few creels locally. I started to tell him the tale of the cat and had just reached the part where the old fellow discovered the animal as he was shooting his creels, when his friend stopped me.

"I don't find this story amusing at all," she said angrily. "I happen to love cats."

I was rather surprised by this attack but then, she is a cat lover!

Someone, I cannot remember who, told me the lovely tale of the lady, married to a drifter skipper, who had long pleaded with her husband to take her on a holiday. Eventually, he ran out of excuses and reluctantly booked a cruise. They arrived in Southampton and boarded the great ship by climbing up a gangway. The fisherman's wifie was close behind an extremely elegant lady and the wifie, in great excitement exclaimed to this lady, "Eh me, is this no jeest a braw big shippie. Hiv ye ivver been aboard een o this shippies afore?" When she had deciphered what this obviously lower class person had said, the lady snootily replied – in a very cultured accent - "Oh yes, I take several trips each year. My husband's a Captain, don't you see, and he works for Cunard!"

"Is that richt? That's a rare coincidence, my man's a Captain, an' he works fuckin hard as weel!"

Sandy Scally was another favourite shipmate of this era, and was one who confounded all of the medical theories about longevity. A thin man of medium height, he ate sparingly, drank unbelievable amounts of strong tea, and smoked 'Woodbine' cigarettes almost incessantly - yet he lived into his eighties. He also had a great love for Guinness.

Sandy's stories about himself were unique in that they almost all ended in personal disaster. He was a very accomplished goalkeeper in his youth whilst still living in his native Campbeltown. Sandy told us that after one cup game played in a blizzard in Glasgow, he was approached by a scout for Third Lanark who promised him a trial, and prophesied that he had a good future as a professional. This scout - who had been soaked and frozen whilst watching the game - promptly caught influenza and died before taking the matter of poor Sandy's new career any further! It might be worth noting that the team for which Sandy kept goal so well was one of the most accomplished ever produced in Campbeltown, and that it rejoiced in the name, 'The Currant Buns'!

Sandy Scally

He had come to Mallaig initially to work for a kipperer best known by the nickname of 'Waldy', who was married to a lady called Mary-Ann, a diminutive lady whose strength of character more than compensated for her lack of stature. Mary-Ann ran a small grocery shop then, and kept a very firm grasp of the purse strings of their combined enterprises. Their one luxury was a car which neither of them could drive, this task being entrusted to Sandy. Waldy was fond of a dram, but usually could only indulge in this passion when he was able to 'skin' some cash somehow - one method being to get the salesman to charge his poor wife more for the herring than the boat actually required to be paid, the difference being given to Waldy in cash!

One Sunday Waldy appeared at Sandy's door in a state of great agitation. Mary-Ann had fallen asleep in front of the fire. Waldy had removed the key of the shop from its place of safe-keeping around her neck without disturbing her, and was now hell-bent on getting drink!

"It was like one of these bank raids you see in films," said Sandy. "I stopped outside the shop keeping the engine running, while Waldy in a fearful rush, unlocked the door, dashed in, and grabbed one of the paper bag, that contained Saturday's takings from the counter, where his wife had left it ready for paying into the bank on Monday morning. He stuffed it into his coat pocket, dived into the back of the car, hardly taking time to close the door, and we took off."

"We made straight for Lochailort Inn for a dram, went into the bar and Waldy took out the bag of cash. It was a pounds worth of pennies he had grabbed, just about enough to buy the petrol we needed to get us back home!"

Like so many of his contemporaries, Sandy was in the Royal Navy during the '39-'45 war, and was in the engineering branch of that service. He told me that for part of his initial training as a stoker, he was taken to a field where stood a steel mock-up of the doors to a ship's furnace. In front of each door there was a large pile of small stones. He and his companions were instructed to choose a pile, and then to shovel the stones through the door. When the pile was levelled, they were to go around to the other side and shovel them back again!

Apart from breakfast the two main meals of the day in the Navy were dinner, served around midday, and supper, which event took place around six p.m.. Between these two meals, 'tea' was served at around four p.m., and usually bread or cake of some kind was issued then. Sandy woefully told me that one day he was given three winkles for his 'tea'. That there was not a pin issued to eat this feast with, was of no consequence - he didn't like them anyway!

He had also been aboard a mine sweeper berthed on the lower reaches of the Seine after hostilities with Germany had ceased. They were engaged in 'mopping up' operations there. One day a draw was held aboard to decide which one of the crew was to be the lucky recipient of the free room gifted by the management of a Parisian hotel. The prize consisted of the room and food only. Sandy's name was drawn out of the hat, but he was unable to accept this once in a lifetime prize, as he was stony broke and was unable to raise the fare to Paris!

Life ashore

In 1964, I left the fishing and came ashore to work.

This decision was prompted by several reasons, but the main one was that the whole fishing scene was changing, and I did not like much of what I saw. Large powerful trawlers were taking over from the ringers, and I simply did not want to be part of what was now going on.

I became the mechanic on the local Lifeboat, and took up part-time work on the fish market. In my new job as a lifeboat man, I was introduced to a new circle of men.

One lifeboat man, whose visits to Mallaig were always enjoyed, was Tam Beattie. Although of average height, he was powerfully built and had a craggy face. He had been a professional fisherman before joining the Lifeboat Institution.

Tam hailed from Arbroath and he was, when I met him first, a Staff Coxswain, a job that meant that he was almost constantly on the move around the coast, delivering lifeboats and relieving on stations where perhaps a station coxswain's illness demanded it.

Tam was a born story-teller, and it is a pity that no-one, myself included, ever thought to get some of his tales on tape. That he was well respected by his employers, is borne out by the fact that I was told that he was sent immediately to Penlee as cover after the tragic loss of the Penlee Lifeboat and all of her crew, a few years ago. When he arrived there, he sat down in the boathouse and began working with ropes – splicing here, whipping there.

Within a very few hours he had enrolled enough men to give the station a full crew again.

When he went home to Arbroath, he told me, very often the then Coxswain of the Arbroath Lifeboat would telephone and ask Tam to cover for him, while he went off somewhere for a day or two. On one such occasion, they were launched with Tam in command, to search for 'a craft and one man', which had gone missing from a beach, just north of Arbroath.

"The weather was great, jeest a flat calm." Tam told me. "But the fog was terrible. You could not see the stemheid frae the wheel hoose. Noo this was afore the days o radar, ye ken, an we were searchin up an doon, up an doon, for oors on end. Saw naethin at aal. We got tae the stage where we would start tae imagine things, so I stopped the engine, got the lads aft, an telt them tae get a cup o somethin hot inside them, an relax for ten meenits. My legs wis sair wi stannin at the wheel, so gaed up forrad an lay doon on the foredeck, jeest relaxin, gazin at naethin in parteeclar."

"Then I saw a man on a bike, cyclin past oor stem! I pinched masel an looked away, but whenever I looked back, there he wis, disappearin intae the fog. I got up, an went strecht aft."

'Start her up, lads, we're awa hame,' I says. They didna ken whit wis gaun on, an I nivir telt them. We gets intae Arbroath herbour, an there's the Hon. Sec. – ye ken, he's the lad that's in charge o the Lifeboat on the shore side - stannin on the quay.

'Did ye find him, Tam?' says he.

I never answered him, jeest got the boat alongside, an then went up the pier an says tae him, "I'm feenished, I'm no gaun back tae the sea nae mair this day, nor any ither."

He asked me whit wis wrang, but I widna tell him. He pleaded wi me, but aa I wid say wis that there hadna been any bother abaird the boat, an that I wid tell the Doctor whit wis wrang in due course. Off I goes hame.

Weel I wisna richt in the door, when in comes the Hon. Sec. efter me.

"Tam" says he, "Tam we're auld freens, an' I think ye owe it tae me tae tell me whit heppened abaird the boat this day."

Weel, when he pit it lik that, whit could I dae. "I'm hallucinatin," says I.

"Whit dae ye mean?" says he.

"We were lyin stoppit aboot three mile aff o the shore, in aboot fifteen faddom o watter, an I saw a man on a bicycle gaun richt across oor stem. Noo awa ye go. I want tae rest afore I see the Doctor."

"That's the man ye were lukkin fur, Tam!" roars the Hon Sec. "He pit a bicycle atween twa floats, an' wee paddle things on the back wheel an' gaed awa tae the sea on it afore the fog cam doon!"

He swore that the following was also true. If so, and I have no reason to doubt that it is, then it epitomises a part of the West Highland character which revolves around the fact that they hate to 'lose face', by being unable to help if so requested. Tam was in Ullapool aboard the seventy-foot Clyde class Lifeboat, *Grace Paterson Ritchie*, when he was instructed to leave the boat with the second-in-command, and go to Lerwick with all despatch. It was Saturday afternoon when he got the message, and he couldn't get away immediately, so he went to one of the local shops which had rather grandly designated itself as a 'Travel Agent' - this on top of its usual newspapers, general merchandise, groceries, and Post Office duties. There Tam asked if the shopkeeper could tell him at what hour the ferry sailed from Aberdeen en route to Lerwick, on the coming Monday morning.

The man proceeded to haul out drawer after drawer of timetables throwing them, after a perfunctory glance, on to a rapidly growing pile on the floor - a floor which was already littered with papers of various descriptions - muttering to himself quietly in Gaelic as he did so.

Reaching the bottom of what was the obviously the last drawer, the man scratched his head in puzzlement, looked unhappily at the heap on the floor, and then with a squeak of glee he pounced on a previously discarded piece of paper.

“The first ferry from Stranraer to Larne, sails at precisely seffen o’clock on Monday morning!” he announced joyously.

There then ensued a long pause.

“But I’m no gaun tae Larne,” replied the totally baffled Tam. “I want tae gang tae Lerwick.”

“Ah well now,” said the shopkeeper in a regretful manner, “I cannot find that timetable, but I don’t want to send you off empty-handed from my shop now, do I!”

Sadly, Tam died around six years ago. Ina and I had visited him during his last illness and had made friends with his lovely wife, Ruth. We saw her just recently, and I asked her about one of Tam’s stories, thinking that she would tell me that it was all a figment of his imagination.

Not so. To my surprise she related the tale almost exactly as Tam had told it, so long ago.

When they were married, Ruth told me, they rented the upstairs flat of a building near the harbour in Arbroath. The owner of the building lived in the flat directly below them. Tam was then a fisherman.

There was a black cast-iron cooking range in the kitchen, which Ruth soon decided would have to be replaced by an electric cooker – as soon as they had electricity installed. The wall between them and the house next door was of extremely flimsy construction, so flimsy, Ruth told me, that they could not help but hear all that went on next door. Their neighbour, an elderly single man, appears to have been somewhat eccentric. Every night, Ruth said, she could hear him prepare for bed. His last words, before he climbed into bed, were always, "Poor old Russia!" She could not suggest any reason for this "prayer"!

Anyway, electricity was installed into the flat, with the owner's blessing, and the electrician called Ruth into the bedroom.

"Would ye like a switch on the wall here, beside the bed?"

"Whit fur?" queried Ruth.

"Weel, when Tam gets up in the middle o the nicht tae gang awa tae the sea, he could switch on the licht afore he gets up."
Ruth agreed to this, and the electrician got busy with his brace and bit, boring a hole where the light switch was to go.

All hell broke loose next door shortly after, when their neighbour saw the bit appearing from the headboard of his bed.

The walls certainly were thin!

When Ruth had her electric cooker installed and the old coal-fired range taken out and replaced by a modern fireplace there was a hole left in the wall, which had to be filled before the final plastering was done. To this end, Tam was despatched to the beach to fetch a large stone. This, the builder in charge of the project explained, was the easiest and cheapest way of filling the gap.

Tam eventually staggered up the stairs with a large stone that would, they all agreed, suit admirably.

The builder eased it into position and then asked Tam to lie on the floor and apply a bit of pressure on the stone, in order to get it in flush with the wall. This Tam duly did but he must have put a bit more weight behind it than was necessary. It disappeared downward, a loud crashing noise was heard, and a great cloud of soot came gushing from the hole.

They all galloped downstairs just in time to see the owner of the building emerge from his flat, covered in soot. Looking into the room he had just vacated, they saw the stone lying in the middle of the floor, surrounded by the remains of the poor man's completely shattered cast-iron stove.

"Whit happened?" asked Tam.

"Whit happened! That great muckle stone cam doon an smashed ma stove, that's whit happened. Whaur did it come frae?"

Tam thought for a moment before he replied – "A gull must hae drapped it doon the lum!"

I was told by Tam, of a lovely incident concerning a mechanic who was with him on a trip south in a lifeboat. This boat, for reasons I cannot recall, was required urgently at Cowes, on the Isle of Wight.

They called in at Whitby for fuel and food, on their way south and the mechanic, who had a relative living there, thought that they were going to stay the night. He was not at all amused when Tam explained to him that they would be leaving as soon as they had refuelled.

"This lad took it rale bad," Tam told me. "In fact, he niver spoke wan word aal the wey frae Whitby, tae the Isle of Wight. It was on the Sabbath efternoon that we arrived at Cowes, a rale beauty o' a day – no' an air o' win', an' the sun jeest bakin' doon. It was Cowes Week, an' the sea wis jeest covered in yachts. They wir lyin there becalmed so I eased her doon so that oor wake widna' cause their boats tae roll a bit an spill their gin an' tonics. We jeest crawled oor wey in fur the last twa or three miles."

"Noo, as we got near the quay, I saw that there wis a fair crowd hid gathered tae see this lifeboat arrivin' so ah thocht ah'd gie them a wee show – ye ken, full aheed an' full astern – it fairly pleases them tae see this! Hooiver, ah hid forgotten that this boat hid auld, oot o' date engines that tended tae soot up in their exhausts if they were run slow fur any length o' time.

"Weel, we hid jeest got the ropes ashore when this big buxom wifie spoke up. She hid on a blue scoopit bunnet wi gold braid all roon the brim an' an anchor abeen it, a white blouse wi' an anchor on it, a jecket wi' braid aal doon the sleeves an' blue breeks. She hid they blue kind o' sandshoes on her feet – ah think she wis aff a yacht."

"I say … yes, you, you stupid man – look at the mess you have just created. That filth you have deposited on the water will be carried on to the waterlines of all these yachts!"

"Noo, when ah looked in the direction she wis pointin' at, ah saw the clouds o' soot an' black reek that hid come oot o' oor exhausts hid landed, an' the watter wis jeest fair clartit wi soot."

"This mechanic, the man that hidna spoken wan word frae we left Whitby, wis stannin' up forrit an he roars up tae this wifie – 'Weel, Mrs Wumman, if you hid been runnin full bit aa the way frae Whitby tae here, there wid be smoke comin' oot o' your arse as weel!'"

"Aye," he finished. "That wis anither letter frae heed office!"

Tam is gone, but how I'd love to have him at the fireside with all the other Captains.

I met a very nice chap on Mallaig pier one day who had, with his wife, sailed from somewhere in Ireland but who had found it necessary to return home for a few days. He was looking for someone to keep a friendly eye on his yacht, *Gunna* (which was to lie at anchor in the Bay) during his absence, so I volunteered. When I first went aboard I saw a framed letter from the Minister of Post and Telecommunications, hanging on the bulkhead. It warned him that any repetition of bad language on his medium frequency radio, would mean the forfeiture of his licence to transmit. My curiosity got the better of me so on his return, I asked him about it.

He told me that one night he had been trying to make a link call through Oban Radio, a Coast Radio Station that was notoriously difficult to contact. They heard him – faintly – and replied: "Yacht *Canna*…"

"This is the yacht *Gunna*, I repeat, *Gunna*..."

"Yacht *Canna*, please spell your name," said the operator in Oban Radio.

"This is yacht *Gunna*. I spell: G – Gonnorrhea; U – Urine; N – Nackers; N – Nackers; A – Arsehole ..."

Of course, Oban Radio got this loud and clear, hence the letter – of which he was inordinately proud!

Working on the pier in Mallaig was being at the hub of the entire life of the village, and that meant that I was now in a position to meet, and to get to know more men who were involved not only in the catching of fish, but in the marketing of it also.

When a boat came in with a shot of herring in these days, a random sample of around fifty herring was taken ashore in a basket. A ticket was placed in the basket giving the boat's registration number, and an estimate of the amount of herring in crans. The herring were auctioned by the salesmen, and were bought by buyers who wanted the kind of herring that the sample indicated was available.

There were of course malpractices on each side. Sometimes a boat would discard small herring from the sample, making them look better than they in fact were. Again, if a boat had only a few cran aboard, it was not economic sense to run to market so they might keep them aboard, and hope to get more herring on the coming night. If this was the case, they should declare that they had some 'overdays' herring aboard but as these herring were generally worth less, the temptation was there to mix the overdays with the fresh. The same was done on occasion, when the boat had two different kinds of herring aboard. A sample of the larger ones was sent up, and when discharging, the small were mixed with the large.

In order to regulate the industry and to resolve disputes the samples were kept until the boat had finished discharging, and in the event of a dispute, this sample was compared - by an independent source - with the herring actually being delivered.

At the Isle of Man fishing, the great bulk of the market on the Island was for the kippering trade, and when this demand had been satisfied the remainder very often was disposed of for fishmeal. This meant that the boats so affected had to steam the five hours or so to Portpatrick on the Scottish mainland and before leaving Peel, they were issued with a 'redirection chit', which entitled them to the princely sum of something like 25 pence or so per cran for their trouble There were at this time two or three quite small local boats who were still fishing with drift nets and they, because they were probably still hauling at daybreak, unlike the ringers, were usually last into their home port of Peel. It was felt that 'first come, first sold' system then in use was unfair to them, so a scheme was evolved whereby when the sample was taken to the sales ring, the skipper of the selling boat put his hand into a box and withdrew a numbered disc. This fixed the selling order. The lowest numbers were sold first and of course were less likely to suffer the time-wasting nuisance of being redirected.

Of course this system was abused in that if a low number was drawn, then instead of returning it to the box when the sale was over as was expected, the unscrupulous ones would palm their low number for use again the following morning.

There were continual rows and accusations over this, but it took everyone a wee while to discover that three boats who were working together had evolved a different system. If they had enough herring to warrant having some in each boat, then two set off direct to Portpatrick. The third went into Peel, took three deliberately poor samples up, produced the three high numbers which they had acquired, and so obtained the redirection chits for the other two which by now had probably started discharging in Portpatrick. This strategy gained them quite a few precious hours, but I think I remember it resulted in their being fined by their fellow fisherman when their antics were discovered.

On the buying side, the buyer often made a mistake, and paid more for the herring than they were worth, or - more commonly - discovered after he had bought them that there was a good fishing coming, which meant that the price would probably drop. Then he would 'chuck' or 'cast' the herring, which meant that he stopped the boat discharging, saying that the herring were not up to the sample, and the independent arbiter mentioned earlier, was called in to sort out the dispute.

There were many tricks employed to ensure that the unscrupulous buyer won the 'chuck'. He might gain access to the sample and remove from it the percentage of smalls, making them seem to be better than they were. The ticket might be swapped with one from a boat which had an honest sample of large herring, and it was not unknown for samples to 'disappear' on occasion!

If the 'chuck' was upheld - and this seemed to be the case more often than not - then the herring were offered for re-sale, often being bought by the same buyer for a lesser price. It was said to me on more than one occasion by many different fishermen, "When the good Lord appointed his disciples there were a lot of fishermen, but there wisny wan buyer amang them!"

A cran was a liquid measure, and so the baskets - made of wicker and stamped with a Crown to show that they were an approved size - had to be properly filled. The cry from the buyer was ever, "Keep them baskets full noo!" Now the measure is one of weight, and a set of scales has replaced the native skill and wit which was required then.

This move of mine ashore was made at a time when the herring fishing methods were changing - a change which led to Mallaig becoming for a time the premier herring port in Europe, but which also led to the destruction of the fishing industry as I knew it.

As pair trawling was perfected, it started to oust the ringers gradually, and the few remaining drift-net fishermen seemed to disappear overnight. Purse-seining, when it got under way, was such an efficient way of killing herring that there was no longer any room for less competent methods.

A huge catch of herring alongside the Fraserburgh purser *Andra Tait*

The drifters were larger and more powerfully engined than the ringers, and were therefore more able to be adapted to continue fishing herring using the mid water trawl - thereby delaying their demise - but the ringers were quickly to be relegated to fishing for prawns.

On the shore side of the industry, with the onset of the pursers and trawlers, changes had to be made rapidly in order to keep pace with the greatly increased volume of fish being landed. The pier which was used by fishermen, was made of wood, and was owned by British Rail. Not enough money was being spent on its upkeep, and it was an almost daily occurrence for a lorry which had been loaded with herring, to break through the wooden surface of the pier with one of its wheels and as a result, shed part of the load. This was good for the seagull population, but was not acceptable to anyone else.

It soon became obvious that a new harbour facility had to be built, and its existence today is largely thanks to one man, Gordon Jackson, better known as 'G.G.', who had not only the foresight, but the energy, ability and the courage to take the required action in forming what is now Mallaig Harbour Authority.

He succeeded, under the auspices of this Authority, not only in raising the necessary finances to take over responsibility for the running of the pier as it was, but also - despite fierce opposition from some of the locals whose eyes were firmly fixed on the past - was instrumental in having the harbour rebuilt so that the shore facilities could cope with the vast increase in landings. The pier could now support the weight of the biggest lorries which flooded into Mallaig from all over Europe, and the harbour was able to cope with the influx of large steel purse seiners.

The Buyers

When I came ashore I needed to find another source of income as at that time the pay I earned on the Lifeboat was nowhere near enough to live on. I was naturally drawn to the pier, and managed to get enough odd jobs to keep my family going.

The buyers then were almost all incomers to Mallaig. In the main, they worked for themselves, buying white fish and herring with their own money selling it on to clients as far away as London. Buying on a commission basis for larger firms was mainly confined to the herring scene.

Most of the buyers originated in the East Coast, and they were a very mixed lot indeed.

Andrew Duncan, known locally, for reasons that are beyond me as 'Horsey', became my main source of odd job income. Andrew had run a small kippering business in Mallaig but with the onset of prawn fishing and the resultant increase in by-catches of fish he had given up on the kippering trade, and concentrated on fish and prawns, buying herring on commission for Claben, a big Aberdeen based firm.

The white fish, bought at auction, had to be re-selected, weighed, packed and iced in boxes and taken to the Railway station for onward delivery to their destinations. Roker, or skate, had to be processed so that only the edible part, the 'wings' were sent off. The offal from this work was stored in old forty gallon drums and was sent off, at the first opportunity, to a fishmeal factory on the East Coast. The money earned from this was generally viewed as being the labourers' perks. We were also allowed to cut the 'skate knobs' from the bones of the roker. These were small pockets of flesh, and they are a real delicacy. We sent them off to Billingsgate, and so earned a few pounds for ourselves.

Dogfish, if there were just a few boxes on the market, were skinned and sent to London by rail but if there was a heavy landing of them, they were sent, without any processing, by road to either Grimsby or Hull. There they were skinned and distributed throughout the U.K.

Off the road at Kinsadel

Manchester was the main market for the hake and cod, closely followed by Birmingham. Roker, otherwise known as skate, went to Billingsgate in London, as did conger eels and of course, lobsters. Flat fish, witches and megrims had yet to be introduced to their eventual markets, meeting the excellent demand on the Continent, and were mainly bought by people like Sandy Reid who ran the local fish shop, and who also supplied several of the hotels locally with the fillets.

Monkfish made their appearance along with the prawns, and they were snapped up by Bill Henderson who monopolised the trade in this variety, supplying Allen and Dey, a firm in Aberdeen. Bill's son, George, worked with his father in this very successful business and continued running it after his father died. George and Bill were also pioneers in the prawn marketing trade. They became commission agents for Young's Seafoods, who led the way in processing the prawn tails into scampi, and continued to be the main buyers of this species for many years.

George Aitchison, who had hailed from Eyemouth originally, was another stalwart of these early days. George, who was a gentleman indeed, died of a heart attack at a very early age, whilst working on the pier. He had married a 'local lass', Ina MacLellan, whose father owned the West Highland Hotel. Together they had two daughters and one son. We still remain friends with his widow, Ina, and enjoy meeting her in Perth, her new home, whenever we can.

Alec Henderson, better known as 'Splitpin', was a brother of the aforementioned Bill. Alec was one of the real characters of that time, being very fond of relating many tales of his adventures. Now although the veracity of these tales could certainly be doubted, never once did any of them harm anyone in any way!

One of his favourite tales could be drawn from him very easily when, in really cold weather, he would appear wearing a lovely, long sheepskin jacket.

If things were quiet, someone would ask where he had got the braw jacket.

"I was lookout on the bridge one very cold day – we were on the Russian convoys at the time - and Louis – that is Lord Louis Mountbatten, he was our Captain – came up and asked: 'Are you not frozen, Alec?'"

"Aye, Louis," I replied, "it is a bit parky."

"He went down below to his cabin and came back up with this jacket. 'Just you keep this, Alec,' he said."

"I never put it on without thinking of Louis, and of his kindness to me!"

I think that Lord Louis was also the alleged donor of the binoculars with which, Alec boasted, he could quite clearly see the hens scratching around the crofts on Skye. This was around six miles away!

Alec had also been one of the first men in Mallaig to have owned a car and he told me the tale, several times, of the occasion when a fishing boat had broken its mast. John Henderson, who built and owned the slipway where the boats were repaired, couldn't lay his hands on a suitable piece of wood any nearer than Oban and so Alec, who was one of the few who boasted a driving licence, volunteered to go and collect this 'tree-trunk', driving a small lorry that belonged to the Johnstone family, one of the local oil merchants.

He set off for Oban to collect this new mast, but it was so long that it overhung the tail of the lorry by a fair few feet. The other end stuck out quite a long way beyond the front of the cab. It was dark, and while Alec was driving over what was then the rough road between Oban and Ballachulish, it suddenly came to a halt! He shifted down several gears, but still the lorry remained stationary.

"I jumped out to see what was wrong," continued Alec, "and fell on my backside. The wheels were about two feet off the ground, you see! What had happened was that I had driven into a sharp dip on the road, and the front of the mast was grounded ahead of the cab whilst the back of it had grounded behind us. The lorry was suspended on the mast! I had to slack off the ropes until I got her wheels back on the ground again, before I could carry on!"

Baron Munchausen wouldn't have had a look-in with Alec but I repeat, no-one ever heard him speak ill of anyone.

'Jaffy' Lawrie was another kenspeckle figure on the buying scene. He had, for a time, kippered herring in his own right but when I first came ashore, he had given up this side of his business, concentrating mainly on sending white fish to the various inland markets. Jaffy was succeeded by his two sons, George and Archie. Following their father's death, they took over the business and soon built a successful modern kippering facility which is still used by his grandson, Jeff Lawrie. For reasons that are beyond me, neither George nor Archie took a very active part in marketing the vast amounts of herring that were landed in Mallaig with the onset of the pursing and pair-trawling fleet.

Mallaig's main source of income in the early days prior to the onset of the prawn fishing was herring. At that time the vast bulk of the landings were from the ring-net fleets, although drifters also maintained a presence from the beginning right up until the coming of the herring trawl.

The buyers mentioned above were all involved in marketing the silver darlings, mainly acting as commission agents on behalf of the big processing companies. As agents they kept in constant touch with their bosses and took buying instructions from them. They were paid a fixed commission for whatever they bought but were not, of course, responsible for payment of the catches they bought. D.A.Macrae had a fairly big kippering yard in Mallaig as did National and Mac Fisheries. The above named kippering yards had full-time employees as managers, men who were either domiciled in Mallaig or who lodged there on a temporary basis. Hendry Young ran National Fishcuring, Johnny Wood ran MacFisheries and Pat Bruce was in charge of D.A. MacRae's although Roddy MacKenzie, his second-in-command, who had been in at the very beginning of MacRae's, was a man to be reckoned with.

Johnny Wood died just a year or so ago and his death left me as the only buyer remaining from those heady days. Woody was always thought of as having a really good head for figures but was renowned for keeping a record of his daily buying on the back of his Gold Flake cigarette packet. This habit resulted, on many occasions, in search parties wandering all over the pier looking for the empty packet he had thoughtlessly discarded!

A group of fishbuyers at Mallaig, 1973
(l-r) George Henderson, Sid Grainger, Jackie White, Johnny Wood, Jimmy Sutherland
(front) Tommy Ralston, Alex. Macleod

Sid Grainger, an employee of Claben, immediately springs to mind, epitomising the type of men who replaced the long established buyers. He was a native of Hull and was employed as a buyer for Claben, one of the biggest herring processing firms in Scotland. The work he was doing meant that he spent most of his time in lodgings, away from the restraining influence of a wife - which influence is necessary to us all - and as a result, his marriage suffered badly and eventually, ended.

He could well be described as the 'life and soul of the party', and his fun-loving nature helped to lighten what was often a very stressful time.

Sid was in demand at parties and in pubs, accompanying himself on the guitar, while singing his favourite modern songs. This led to a confrontation with another buyer one night.

While Sid was belting out his usual favourites, he was constantly being interrupted by Bruce Cordiner, a colleague from the North-East of Scotland, who was demanding to hear 'The Northern

Lights o' old Aberdeen'. Sid suffered these interruptions for a time, then stopped playing and spoke.

"Did I ever tell you about the time I accidentally stood on a leprechaun, and killed him, Bruce?"

The reply being in the negative, Sid continued: "Well, the King of the leprechauns put a curse on me. Yes, the curse was that every time I started playing, some idiot would interrupt me and ask me to play 'The Northern Lights'!" Bruce was renowned for having a 'short fuse', so instant war followed this remark!

One day in the month of July - normally a quiet month as far as herring fishing went - Sid appeared driving a new car which had been supplied to him by 'the firm'. Two days later he came to me very early in the morning and asked me to take him round the bay to his car to collect some of his gear, as he had, he explained, "A bit of bother with it last night." I drove him to the bottom of a hill in the middle of the village, and was amazed to see this sparkling example of automotive excellence lying upside down among the rocks beside the road, with the broken glass sparkling in the bright July sun.

We got out of my car, and while I was still trying to fathom just what had happened, the local sergeant of police arrived on the scene.

"What happened here, Sid?" began the sergeant.

"Fog and black ice, Willie," – remember, this was in July - was the instant response from the intrepid Sid!

Such was the charisma of the man that Willie just shook his head, and having made sure that no one had been injured in the incident, he went on his way, leaving us to look in the wreckage of the car for any bottles that remained unbroken!

Sid was engaged in a very highly competitive and cut throat business, but he never stooped to underhanded tactics in order to gain advantage over any of his fellow-buyers, to my knowledge, which cannot be said for many of the rest of us.

He once said to me, "I was invited to a reunion party for kamikaze pilots at the weekend but I left early - there was no-one else there."

Sid was head-hunted from Claben by a firm in North Shields, a firm that – with hindsight – was run by a man who turned out to be quite an unsavoury character. Sid's marriage had broken up by this time, but he met a lass there who struck me as being a very nice girl. His time in North Shields was not destined to be long; the firm went bust and Sid then discovered that the flat he had been 'given' by the firm's owner was in fact, rented. Sid had several jobs after this heart-breaking experience and finally died during what should have been a relatively simple operation on his leg.

If we could bend the rules of this book slightly, Sid, his guitar, and his ready quip, would soon charm our Captains round to his way of thinking.

Old Robbie Hepburn was the manager of the local branch of George Walker & Sons. Robbie, who was close to retiring age when I came ashore, was very highly regarded by all, buyers as well as fishermen, and he was very fortunate – as was the firm he worked for – in having his son, James, to follow him. When the great boom in herring landings from the Minches took place in the early seventies, one man did much more than most to ensure that the many and divers needs of the fleet were met, and he must therefore instantly qualify as a Captain.

James Hepburn was - and still is - a short rotund man with a beaming round red face below a shining bald head. Everyone, regardless of their station in life, was greeted with a ready smile and the usual call, "How's it going, me old fruit?" He was the manager of the main fish salesman's office.

This task was a very demanding one - not for him was there a 'nine to five' time limit. Herring sales started at eight a.m. on a

Monday morning, and continued as necessary until eight p.m. This went on until the Saturday, when the last sale was at midday. No landings were permitted on Sundays at that time, but still any demands from skippers for James's services on the Sabbath, were met ungrudgingly.

The hours listed above were times for sales; the landing of the herring continued for as long as it took to finish the job, so James was in demand for 24 hours, 7 days per week. He not only had to cope with trying to satisfy the many demands of fishermen, but had to make the difficult decisions of who among the many buyers were in a sound financial state, and were therefore credit-worthy.

The pressure on him must have been immense, so on more than one occasion he took off with his beloved accordion and found relief in a ceilidh somewhere.

His brother once told me that he and his wife had gone for a drive down toward the Ardnamurchan peninsula one Sunday, and en route had pulled into a hotel seeking lunch. There, in the middle of an otherwise empty car park, lay James's accordion! It was rescued and returned to its rightful owner, who expressed no surprise at the event, saying only that he knew that he had left it somewhere, but had been certain that someone would return it!

James bought a very expensive car on one occasion, and it was only a few weeks old when a friend asked me if I had seen the damage around the boot lock on this beautiful vehicle. I hadn't, but soon after this remark James himself appeared, so we asked what had happened.

"Well, me old fruits," he explained, "I was out for the night, and invited some skippers home for a dram. When we got there I couldn't get the boot open to get at the 'carry-out', so I had to take a pick to it, otherwise we'd all have gone thirsty!"

He was in a much less expensive car which went off the road one Hallowe'en. Draped in a white sheet which had peepholes cut into it, he had made his ghostly visitations to a friend in Morar, about three miles from Mallaig. Whilst negotiating one of the many bends in the road on his way home, the sheet which he was still wearing, slipped around his head. This meant that his eyes were no longer aligned with the holes, and the resultant loss of vision sent the car off the road!

Hallowe'en was celebrated in Mallaig by many grown ups as well as children then, and the Chlachain bar was a favourite meeting place for guisers. It was very often impossible to guess the sex of some of the people who had dressed up – many times guisers who eventually revealed themselves as men, sported 'bosoms' that were very large indeed.

One Hallowe'en night James and Jessie were hosting two Norwegian fish processors in the Chlachain and they, having consumed a fair few drams, were enjoying the spectacle. They must have spotted some of the 'ladies' having their 'bosoms' felt – as their real gender had been discovered – and when one of the Norwegians left the room to go to the toilet, he decided that he quite liked this local custom and grabbed a handful of a perfectly respectable lady's breast! Oh dear!

James's behaviour, which to the less understanding reader might seem crazy, was perhaps not condoned but was almost certainly accepted as necessary by his long-suffering wife, Jessie, who I am sure knew better than any just how much stress his job could generate, and knew that he needed to let off steam somehow. Many people have had their efforts recognised publicly by being awarded some 'honour' or other. James, who contributed more to Mallaig's success than anyone else I know of, never got this recognition. Kissing arses springs to mind instantly once more – that is one thing James did not do!

Prior to the herring boom there was only one other fish salesman in the port, Ian MacLennan. Ian, whose family roots lay in Scarp, a small island off the West Coast of Harris, plied his trade from a small wooden office - not much bigger than a telephone kiosk - on the approach to the pier. He was the only man I ever heard of who could add up three columns of figures while running his pen down them once. This, remember, was in the days, long before decimalisation, of pounds, shillings and pence. Twelve pennies made one shilling, twenty shillings made one pound. Ian would certainly, in my opinion, have beaten a man with a calculator, at the addition of columns of cash figures.

Ian, in the days when the Loch Seaforth arrived every morning – except Sunday – from Stornoway, would occasionally get a few boxes of flat fish consigned to be sold locally. This was an extraordinary affair as the men who consigned them used to 'hide' expensive fish below the inexpensive witches or plaice. It was not at all unusual to discover a halibut, or a turbot, in the bottom of one of the boxes. Ian didn't want to know about these finds!

Of the older breed, two men stood out, in my opinion. Hendry Young and Roddy MacKenzie had both perfected the art of making kippers the like of which we will never taste again. Of the two, I believe that Hendry had the edge on Roddy in making kippers, but Roddy was without doubt the most skilful buyer I have ever met anywhere. Hendry latterly would not leave the yard while his beloved kippers were being smoked, and slept beside the kilns more often than he slept beside his wife! When eventually he retired, he got a gold watch and thanks - a miserly reward, in my opinion, from a firm to which he had devoted most of his life. Roddy was in semi-retirement when he occasionally deputized for the then regular buyer for MacRae's, and it was on one of these occasions that I witnessed him completely destroy the inflated self-esteem of one of the major buyers of the day, with one stroke of sheer brilliance.

When herring were being sold at auction in Mallaig, the smaller kippering firms would usually be keen to get a start to their day's work by buying early. Their requirements would range from 5 to 20 cran, depending on the size of the yard. Occasionally they would also, if they thought that there might not be supplies on the following day, buy a few cran late on in the day. This was to ensure that they had work on the following morning.

One day a purse seiner arrived late and unannounced, with a good shot. Roddy had been left in charge of the herring buying for the day. I cannot remember exactly what the prices were, of course, but when they were put up for auction, Roddy was in there bidding. 'Woody', the other buyer concerned in the story, was trying to assert his power by forcing Roddy to pay dearly for what everyone thought was a few cran for the following morning's work at the local yard. No-one else was really interested; everyone's orders had been filled. Macrae's requirements for other places, which could be considerable, had, we all thought, also been met.

Roddy started the bidding at £4 a cran, but he was driven up to £7, a far higher price than the last few shots had been sold at. He took three crans – confirming our thoughts that he only wanted a few for the following day - and started to walk away from the auction ring, muttering curses under his breath at the man who had made him pay so dearly.

His opponent then started the bidding again at £4.

At this, Roddy started back saying, "Ye'll no get them for that, ya bugger!" and ran the price up again to £6. When they were knocked down to him, his face showed despair, and he took just two crans. He walked away again, looking like a beaten man.

"£4 again," cried the other man, sensing that Roddy was crushed.

"£4 and two shillings," called Roddy, in a despairing voice.

"Take them!" his opponent shouted.

"Aye, ah'll take them all right. Ah'll take them ALL!" roared Roddy, glee plain on his face. "Ah needed them all – an' so did you, ya bugger, but ye're no getting them noo."

Roddy had indeed wanted the entire shot, and so did 'Woody'. That bit of buying required an enormous amount of nerve, but it left his opponent with egg all over his face.

Johnnie Geddes, who had worked for a time in Mallaig for the Herring Industry Board, became the buyer for the Edinburgh firm of R. Croan. Johnnie's marriage also failed because of the separation endured whilst he was working so far from home. Stress played a major part in the large number of buyers who became martyrs to the demon drink. I know one who was taken in and cared for by the local banker's wife when he collapsed – totally stressed out. He, and two others I know of, were eventually taking Valium to help them to keep going.

Where was the stress in buying herring, I hear you say? Well here is a small example. One of the firms I bought for was W. Donnan, of Whitehaven. The man who ran it, Ricky Donnan, was an extremely hard taskmaster and he made my life a misery, for a time. One part of his business was supplying a number of small kippering firms in the North-East of England and for this, I had to load a lorry with, say 100 crans. This lorry would set off and when the driver arrived at his first stop, Grimsby, he had to telephone Ricky to see where he was to deliver them. I was finding it increasingly difficult to cope with the constant barrage of complaints about short measure, relayed at full volume by Rick. It really was getting me down, big style. Eventually, purely by accident, I discovered what was going on.

The driver would perhaps go to X's yard to deliver 25 cran, a quarter of his load. The yard manager 'very kindly' sent the driver into the yard's canteen for breakfast and then took 100 boxes (25 cran) off the lorry. The driver, when he came back out checked his load and agreed that only 100 boxes had been removed. What he didn't know was that the unscrupulous manager was taking a small shovel of herring out of some of the other boxes, adding the extra herring to the boxes he was unloading. Hence, when the lorry arrived at its last drop, the boxes that were left aboard were all half empty! Didn't I enjoy telling Ricky where the problem lay?

People dealt with stress in many different ways. I remember arriving on the pier one morning at around 5.30 a.m. and – this was before the new pier and fish market was built – when I was wending my way through the stacks of wooden boxes toward the wooden hut that served as my office I was pounced upon by two of my fellow buyers. One of them grabbed me by the lapels and roared, "Did you steal our shite?"

They were both obviously still under the influence of the previous night's libations, but I asked what was going on. They told me that they had set out to smear shite on the office door handle of a competitor who had annoyed them during the previous day's work. They had found one and had scraped it on to a piece of wood, when they heard someone coming. They ran off to hide and when they returned, they couldn't find it so they decided that someone had stolen it!

Now for certain, they would never have done such a horrible thing, so the whole episode had been invented by them but they spent a large part of the coming day accosting astonished skippers of boats that had just arrived in the harbour, accusing them of 'stealing our shite'!

Crazy? Well yes, as I sit here quietly I would be inclined to agree, it was crazy – but they were crazy times!

Having experienced at close hand the trail of havoc and sadness that followed the misuse of alcohol I decided that I would not ever resort to it whilst I was working. I remembered my old friend, Cecil Finn, mentioned earlier, relating to me the problems that skippers of seine-net boats in Campbeltown experienced when they developed the habit of stopping off at the pub for a 'wee dram' on the way home for a few hours sleep following a hard day at sea. This, he said, soon became a necessity for them, and the 'wee dram' soon became several.

"I never take a dram when I think I need one, I only have one when I don't need it," he said. That rule made sense to me, and I still try to keep to it!

I kept to my self-imposed rule until one day after the skipper of a Dutch 'klondyker' gave me a present of two bottles of Genever gin. I left these bottles lying on the floor of the wee shed that served as my office, untouched, until one morning when I was waiting for one of my clients to return my 'phone call. As I sat there my eye lit on these bottles. I idly wondered if this stuff tasted anything like the gin I had drank on occasion, in Campbeltown, so I unscrewed the cap from one and smelled it. To confirm my thought that it was different, I then drank the capful of neat gin – which I found to be quite pleasant. The immediate effect from this small dose of alcohol, taken on an empty stomach at 7 a.m., was that it banished the 'butterflies in the stomach' that, - certainly in my case - was the overpowering feeling as we waited for the sales to begin. It also didn't smell as strongly as whisky so no-one, I figured, would suspect anything!

The following morning as I began my round of calls, I gave no immediate thought to this stuff but when my eye lit on it again, I scoffed another capful which of course, had the same calming effect.

On the third morning I went into my office and the first thing I did was pick up the bottle. Thank God, reason prevailed. I took both bottles to the edge of the pier and smashed them into the harbour!

I used to visit George Henderson as often as I could on my rare visits back to Mallaig, until he died not so long ago. One day George, whose health had by then failed very badly, asked me during one visit, in a rather agitated tone, how I had got away in the busy days. I wasn't sure just what he meant, so I asked him to elaborate. How did I get a day off if I needed to go somewhere, he asked. Still rather puzzled, I replied, "Well I just asked one of you guys to look after things for me. We looked after one another that way."

"Aye, and did any of us ever take advantage of someone who was away?" When I replied that this had never happened he said, vehemently, “Well you couldn’t do it now. You would get stabbed in the back. Times have changed!”

Sadly, I had to agree with him. He and I both realised that while we were buying, we were deadly enemies, we hated one another, but as soon as the sales were over, we bought one another cups of tea, and were the best of pals again – until the next sale started! I do not believe that any one of us harboured a grudge against another.

In the height of the herring season, we buyers had to be about very early indeed. A quick look around the village, to see how many lorries our competitors had lying ready; down the pier to see what boats were already lying alongside, and what loads they had on board; try to find a fisherman who might have some idea of what other herring were still to arrive – it was a mad dash to glean as much information as possible to convey to our buying bosses, before the sale started.

A telephone was certainly the most important - in fact probably the only piece of equipment that a buyer needed in the boom days of the herring fishing, and we were very lucky that we had a team of telephonists in Mallaig who understood how important it was to get through as quickly as possible to the processors we served. To make a call then, you simply lifted the telephone and waited until one of the girls answered, and then told her the number you required. This seemingly antiquated technology had advantages which are not readily obvious to anyone who has not used it. More often than not, you simply asked for the required person, by name. It was not necessary to remember all the numbers - the girls willingly did it for you. It was common too for an incoming call to your number to be diverted to the place where perhaps the operator knew you were to be found, or if she couldn’t find you, she would call around all the likely places until she was successful.

Calls to numbers outside Mallaig required that you ask the local operator for “Trunks, please.” This got you through to an operator in Fort William exchange, who would dial the number you wanted. Quite often the number would be engaged and, if you were on good terms with the lady you were talking to, she would ask if it was urgent. If it was – and we didn't cheat on this – she would simply keep re-dialling it until the number answered, chatting the while!

Eventually, however, progress took the place of common sense - new machinery was installed, and our girls - often referred to by us with affection as our 'call-girls' - were made redundant. They had a going away party for all the staff, past and present, in the exchange one night just before it closed down finally. This 'do' was going full blast when James Hepburn passed on his way home from a session in the Chlachain Bar. He had with him a man who was in Mallaig from the East Coast on business, a man who lacked the sense to know that he should not try to keep up with James on the drinking scene, and who was now "carrying more canvas than keel".

"Ah!" said James when he heard the noise coming from the exchange, "The 'call-girls' are having a wee party, we'd better see how it is going, me old fruit." In went the happy pair, and all went well until James's inebriated friend - having scanned what he thought was on offer - invited one of the perfectly respectable girls to go upstairs with him, proffering a handful of notes as he did so. She, not knowing of James's remark to the poor chap on the way in, took umbrage at this, and threw the foolish fellow out on his neck!

I remember one girl, Annette Banks, who worked part-time in the exchange telling of an occasion that today, will seem a complete fabrication. I can assure you that I am repeating it as she told it to me, that I believe it and that it was, in those crazy days, totally feasible.

Annette's father, Sergeant Willie Banks, lived with his family in the Police Station. At this time, if anyone had to report a fire, they did so to the exchange and the girl on duty switched on the siren that was mounted above the exchange building. This alerted the local volunteer fire brigade.

One night Annette got a call from a local man who lived alone in quite a large house, not very far from the Police Station. His house, he told her, was on fire, and she should set off the siren 'right away'. Her hand, she told me, was on the switch when she stopped. There was something wrong! The complainant was far too unconcerned, she thought, so instead of triggering the siren she called her father, and asked him to quickly check it out and call her back.

Willie found the man who had made the call seated alone at the table in the kitchen of his house.

"Hello, Willie," he said. "Just sit down and have a dram. The Fire Brigade will be here soon, and we'll have a wee ceilidh!"

He was lonely! Try that nowadays, when policemen are not allowed to think for themselves, and you'll end up in the clink!

When the new fish market was built it housed offices for the buyers, upstairs. To cope with the telephone calls, a klaxon was installed along with a system of lights. If you were down the pier and the klaxon went off, a quick look at the coloured lights on this board indicated whose phone was ringing.

Of course it always seemed that one's phone never rang until one was down near the bottom of the pier or aboard one of the boats and this meant a really quick dash up the pier, through the market and up the stairs to the office – by which time there was no breath left to talk, so something had to be done. Someone, I have no recollection of who it was, unearthed a supplier of what was the forerunner of the cell phone. It consisted of a base radio set into which the telephone line was plugged and a battery driven portable telephone which we could carry with us. There was a long aerial that had to be extended when making or receiving a call and the 'radio telephone' – for that is what it was, was very bulky in comparison with its modern counterpart. Its range varied, but was not really more than half a mile, but it very soon became an absolutely irreplaceable tool.

We knew that it was not 'type approved' and that if an employee of British Telecom found us using it, our line would possibly be cut off. The telephones would, we were told, interfere with radio-controlled model aircraft. We'd never seen any of these around Mallaig, but these were the rules!

Strangely, although we often heard of 'investigators' having been seen in the area, no-one was ever caught. Our espionage system was good!

There were, on the processing side of the industry, almost as many 'characters' as there were on the catching side. I was privileged to have close dealings with one of the more notable of these characters, Sans Unkles.

Sans was a very powerfully built young man who had been a keen rugby player until a bad neck injury put paid to that side of his life. He became the biggest processor of queen scallops in Scotland, working from his factory in Glasgow, and then made what was with hindsight, the mistake of becoming involved in exporting herring. He rapidly expanded this venture until he was one of the biggest in that scene also and he was to the forefront of changing from open lorries, to the use of refrigerated lorries to carry the herring from the port to the factory. In fact, I think that the very first refrigerated articulated lorries to load in Mallaig, was one of his. He had it driven to the low railway bridge near Fort William that had barred the high trailers, let down the tyres, drove it through and the had the tyres re-inflated by the breakdown truck he had accompany them from Fort William. When it had been loaded and was bound for Glasgow, it sat down enough to allow the truck under the bridge without having to resort to deflating the tyres.

I then had a task on my hands trying to talk him out of his next idea – he wanted to hire a digger, to dig out and so lower the road under the bridge!

In later years I became concerned that he was putting too much faith in the herring boom - which could not possibly continue, in my opinion - and took myself to Glasgow to see if I could possibly talk him into slimming down his operation somewhat.

When I arrived, he told Ross Osborne, his financial director, to take me to see his latest factory at Bellshill. The existence of this place was a revelation to me, and was news which filled me with foreboding. I could not see how he could continue to get the raw material to keep his existing operation going - to increase his processing capacity at this time was nothing short of lunacy. I was completely mortified when eventually I was told that in fact the new place was for processing mackerel!

Where on earth was he going to get all the mackerel, I needed to be told? There were not enough of these fish landed in Scotland in a year to keep this factory going for one day, in my opinion.

Everyone now knows that he was correct. There was a total ban introduced on herring landings, and history tells us that the pursers found shoals of mackerel in undreamt-of quantities. Sans however, had acted just six months too early. The financial strain of this new undertaking was too much, the bank pulled the plug on him, and the fishing industry lost the most far-sighted man it had possessed in years.

Strange organisations, banks. They call to mind a business which will loan out umbrellas on bonny days, but as soon as they see a cloud on the horizon, they want the brollies back again!

Sans played as hard as he worked, and I have always regretted not accepting the invitation to attend a Hallowe'en party in his house on the southern outskirts of Glasgow. This beautiful house was very old, and had been bought by him almost as a ruin. Maggie, his beautiful wife, told me that when she first saw inside it - prior to it being renovated - she sat down in the hall and cried because she could see the sky through the roof!

I was told later of some of the events of the night of the party.

A bus had been organised to pick up his guests, and to take them home at the end of the night. This transport solved two potential problems. Firstly, no one had to worry about drinking and driving. Just as importantly, everyone left at the same time!

He had also hired a piper clad in full Highland dress to welcome the guisers when they arrived. As soon as the bus was in sight, Sans ushered this musician up a ladder so that he could stand on the battlements to play. He then removed the ladder so not to spoil the splendid visual effect of this magnificently clad piper, who was of course illuminated by floodlight.

The guests - all in fancy dress - were ushered into the house amidst great jollification, the door was closed, and the outside lights switched off.

Some considerable time had passed before someone fortunately heard the plaintive calls for help which emanated from this poor frozen piper who was stranded on the roof!

While having a cup of tea together one day Jimmy, one of his drivers, told me that he had arrived back from a trip to the Continent, some time before. He was, he told me, dead beat, and was relishing getting home to bed. Sans, seeing him draw up in the yard, rushed over and asked him to set off north immediately.

"I'm dead beat, Mr Unkles. No way could I drive any distance!"

"Jimmy, I am desperate! I need you for this. I'll tell you what, get yourself to Ballachulish and call me from there. When you do, I'll tell you whether I want you to go to Oban or Mallaig. You'll get a good bonus for doing it."

Jimmy, very reluctantly, set off up the road although he needed – in his own words – matchsticks to prop his eyes open. He got to Ballachulish at 4 a.m., stopped at the telephone kiosk and, exhausted, called Sans. "That's me at Ballachulish, Mr. Unkles. What do I do now?"

"You are a champion, Jimmy – you must be knackered. Just you go back into your cab and get yourself a good sleep – you deserve it. Oh and Jimmy, call me back in an hours time!"

I was reliably told of his first connection with the Highland cattle which he loved, and which grazed the grounds around this house.

Sans had been at a cattle auction in Oban with a pal one day when perhaps he should have kept a clear head, and had wakened up with a hangover on the following morning, the proud but puzzled owner of a cow! It was in calf, and in due course the birth was announced in the Glasgow Herald - "To Bella, a son Rory. Both well."

He was the biggest independent shellfish producer in the U.K. at a very early age indeed, and was also the first in the country to have a shrimp-shucking machine, an achievement which he likened to being a pheasant plucker to trade!

⚓

I have known Fred Buchan for more years than I care to think about. Originally from Pitullie, in the North-East of Scotland, Fred chose to make his home in Ayr where he worked for Ricky Donnan - a well-known figure on the herring scene, Fred then moved on, as take-over succeeded take-over among the marketing and processing high-flyers, eventually becoming the managing director of Scotprime Seafoods. Fred always looked to be far younger than his years and he still, as I write, retains an enviable shock of wiry hair. He opened a shellfish production branch of Scotprime that still survives and for a time, took Sans under his wing, managing the financial side of Sans's business. Now retired, Fred maintains an interest in the industry he grew up in through his financial interests in several fishing boats. He was never one to panic, retaining his cool where others despaired. I still cherish his friendship!

⚓

The final man in this category to be invited to the fireside in Angus's house is James Burgon of Eyemouth. A big man, who became very stout in his later years, he was a lobster, crab, herring and whitefish processor. It is generally agreed among all who were privileged to have known him, that he was one of the most honest and upright men ever to have taken part in the fishing industry, and I certainly consider it an honour to have known, and to have dealt with him.

I remember taking him to task on one occasion early in our dealings together. When a lorry load of herring was despatched, the driver was always given a delivery line which would simply read, for example '100 cran herring @ £15'. This was purely a delivery line, and was not an account. James, however, paid on this line, which meant him issuing perhaps ten cheques to me in a week, and also meant difficulties for me when I tried to reconcile what he had paid, with the account sent out to him at the end of the week. James's reply was that his last action every day of business was to sign and send out cheques for all that he had received that day. It had always been thus, and he was not going to change it for me! I wonder what he would think of business practice today, which seems to dictate that firms hold on to monies owed to others for as long as is possible.

He told me one day that he had once had a dispute with the skipper of a boat, and that this man had, in a temper, told James that he would never sell him anything else again for as long as he lived. I never forgot the reply.

"Well," said James, "I am fifty four years old now, and for forty of these years, I never knew that you existed. I got on fine without you, and I am sure that I'll continue that way if I never hear of you again!"

Billy Buchan, one of his trusted managers and a shareholder in the firm, told me that one day many years ago, James took some fifty boxes of haddock from the skipper of a boat who just could not sell them, gave him £5 a box for them, and told Billy to send them to Granton market. Two days later, he sent for the skipper of this boat, and proffered an envelope of cash. "What's this for?" queried the man.

"It's the balance of what I owe you for these haddock, you see I got more for them than I expected," replied James.

I may be cynical, but I just cannot see this happening now, anywhere.

In his fish processing yard, you would find old men who had worked for James or for his father John, all their lives. When it came time for them to retire, or if through illness they became unfit for heavy work, they all knew that there would be some kind of job for them, repairing wooden boxes or painting something, among the men with whom they had toiled for so long.

When the boom days were in their infancy I made contact with a Dutch buyer, who sent his own lorries to Mallaig to collect the herring I had bought for them. These lorries were light years ahead of those used by British firms! They had sleeper cabs that were literally the drivers' homes, and these cabs were kept immaculately clean. They had much more powerful engines than any of their British competitors and when loaded, they simply sailed up the steep hill that, at that time, led out of Mallaig – a climb that had been the downfall of many less powerful units.

I paid for these herring myself, and resold them to the Dutch firm. I had reckoned, earlier in my career, that the Dutch, Norwegian and German firms were very honest, as a rule. Sadly, the same could not be said of some of the other nationalities who flooded into the port, a port that was now the biggest herring port in Europe.

A Jac Hulst lorry lies at the side of the road east of Arisaig, after a mishap

Everything went well with this firm. They sent a man to Mallaig to oversee the loading and icing of the herring and he usually left Mallaig on a Friday night, drove to Aberdeen and caught a flight on Saturday morning, to Amsterdam. On Monday night, he was back in Mallaig, so I started to give him the weekly account before he left. He gave it to his boss on Saturday and to my complete amazement, he re-appeared on the Monday – with a cheque for me, made out in sterling on a bank in Hull. Brilliant, I thought, I had the money in my bank before I needed to pay the salesman!

Everything was going swimmingly until one day, the bank manager called, asking me to come to his office. One of the Dutchman's cheques had bounced. I had another one in my office and we were almost at the end of the 3rd week. The combined total was going to put me out of the door, without question!

I called Jac, the owner of the Dutch firm, immediately. He told me not to worry – the sterling account was funded by fish that he had exported from Holland, into Hull, and he had bought more value of herring than he had sold of fish. "Re-present the cheque and I assure you, it will be paid at once."

I sent both of the cheques off for special presentation and, believe me, I almost chewed my fingernails up to the elbow until they were cleared.

Characters also abounded on the railway, which was then a powerful force in the area.

The railway tracks at this time ran all the way down the pier, and there were two steam cranes engaged nearly all the time, lifting loads of herring boxes into wagons, and helping discharge the heavy cargo from the *Loch Seaforth*, when she arrived early in the morning from Stornoway. It was the duty of one of the drivers of the steam cranes to use it to shunt goods wagons down the pier to clear the way for passengers, from the steamer to the railway station. This done, he was then expected to unshackle his crane from the wagons so that they could be pulled, by a steam engine, back into their position of readiness beyond the station buildings.

One morning, a stalwart by the name of Angus Cameron - better known as 'Angus the cran man' (yes cran, crane does not rhyme with man) - had done his duty and, wagons in tow, had stopped his crane abreast of the *Loch Seaforth*. One of her crew on seeing Angus's red face deduced - correctly - that he was suffering from a severe hangover, and invited him aboard for the traditional cure.

Angus was enjoying the second half of this cure when he heard the whistle of the engine as it started to pull the wagons back up the pier, and he suddenly realised that in his hurry to partake of the golden libation, he had neglected to uncouple his crane.

The sight of the diminutive Angus running full tilt up the pier after his crane, screaming Gaelic oaths as he did so, and of his despairing wails as the jib of the towed crane demolished a goodly part of the glass station roof, will live for ever in the memory of those lucky enough to have witnessed it.

The driver, fireman, and guard of a fish special seeing that - at seven a.m. on New Year's morning - there was still life in the rail-side house where 'Woody' lived, stopped and went in to wish the inhabitants all a “Happy New Year!” Another train was stopped as it left Fort William on a very warm day, so that the fireman could get an ice cream from a nearby shop for the signalman a mile or so ahead.

I do not think that we shall see such happenings in the squeaky clean days of the super efficient, squealing-wheeled Sprinters. Perhaps it is just as well, but I for one am glad that I lived in these days!

⚓

Of course, there were also on the pier at this time men who - although not buyers themselves - were if anything, more indispensable than anyone in the day to day running of the shore side of the operations.

One of them, Donnie ‘Hector’ MacLellan, was a driver with British Rail, but every spare moment he had was spent in working - and working very hard - on the pier. We often used to speculate just when Donnie got any sleep.

He was of average height, of a very wiry build and stuttered slightly, except when he sang. He was a fanatical Celtic supporter. I think he celebrated for months after they had won the European Cup.

Perhaps his worst moment occurred one day when he had ‘fallen heir’ to a couple of boxes of haddock. Donnie managed to get them - unseen - on to the engine which he had to drive to Fort William, and spent a good part of the journey filleting them. His mistake was to dump all the offal at the side of the track, in the fish boxes which had contained the haddock.

This offal was of course discovered by the track maintenance squad, and the resulting inquiry as to the origins of these fishy remains concluded with poor Donnie being given two weeks suspension!

He once asked for, and was given, a boil of expensive prawns by me. He said that they were to be a present for “A priest who is on holiday before going to a foreign mission in Africa, and who is

A fish auction on Mallaig Pier
Seated: Donnie 'Hector' MacLellan; seated in boiler suit: Sandy Reid; rolled up shirt sleeves: Tommy Ralston

staying with my mother." I discovered weeks later that they were in fact given to the owner of a local public house in return for a dram!

Probably as a result of Donnie's slight stutter, he tended to talk in a form of shorthand, never using two words where one would do. One night the diesel engine which he was driving broke down just short of Morar. Donny went to summon help from - well, where else but the bar of Morar Hotel? "What brings you here at this time of night?" asked the barman after he had served Donny with a dram.

"Power – nowt," was the short reply!

He, with his bosom pal Charlie MacPherson, was just about the hardest workers anyone could hope to meet anywhere. Charlie had been dux of Broadford School, and would have gone far were it not for the love of whisky which he shared with Donnie, whom he resembled closely in build.

The pair of them used to spend any leisure time they had repairing wooden fish boxes, and always had a stock of liquid refreshments hidden close at hand in case a sudden attack of thirst came over them. One Christmas we were all amazed to see among the usual 'Seasonal Greetings' to customers printed in the 'Oban Times', one from - 'Donnie and Charlie, proprietors of the Pier Bar, wishing all their customers a Happy Christmas.'

It was not unusual for this pair to spend all night working aboard one of the 'klondykers', helping to load and ice the herring bought to be exported in this ship, and then come ashore in the morning to help load some of the lorries which carted the fresh catches off to the Continent. This was very heavy work, and they must have longed at times for a gale to put paid to the fishing effort, and give them some rest.

I am sure that Charlie would forgive me if I told one more story about him, he and I laughed about it several times, over a dram!

Shortly before the ban was placed on herring landings, I had a contract to salt ungutted herring into barrels for a Dutch customer. This work was labour intensive and also required the use of a fork truck.

Charlie at this time was driving a fork truck for a local fish salesman, and he offered not only to supply 'his' fork truck, but also undertook to ensure that the labour demands, which varied from day to day, were met as required.I gratefully accepted these offers, and Charlie was hired!

There were at this time a few mackerel mixed among the herring, which had to be kept out of the barrels, and which were, I thought, being dumped.

Some months later, long after this salting episode was over, Charlie furtively asked if he could talk to me privately. He had, he told me, a potentially lucrative contract to supply a lobster fisherman on the Island of Mull with bait for his creels, but lacked the cash to transport the bait to the customer. If I would pay the transport costs, I could have half of the profit.

Now this sounded like a good deal to me, but I later discovered that the bait was in fact the mackerel - I thought they had been dumped - which had been paid for by me. They had been preserved in my salt, and the containers were the barrels belonging to the Dutchman! Charlie's sole contributions were his labour, his foresight, and his native wit - a formidable combination indeed.

I can see this pair sitting quietly by Angus's fire, glass in hand, listening to the yarns!

Of course there was a large infrastructure ashore that had to adjust, very quickly, to the increase in the number of boats that used Mallaig's facilities and also had to adjust to the growing complexity of the electronic equipment they carried. Gone were the days of the old Kelvin Hughes MS24 echo sounder and the Coastal and Marconi radios; the new pursers and trawlers had fish-finding equipment, including sonar – which I believe was miles ahead of the equipment carried by the anti-submarine ships of the Royal Navy!

David McMinn, who traded under the banner of Western Battery Service, was the right man, in the right place at the right time. Largely self-taught, David very soon mastered the complexities of the latest equipment and also was willing to turn out at all sorts of ungodly hours to fix someone's problems.

It is telling that on the rare occasion that I meet with one of the pioneers of this fishery, David's name crops up and someone has a tale to tell of his expertise. I recall talking with a young man from Sri Lanka, I think his name was Chris Coorie – at least, that is what it sounded like! This chap was in Mallaig for a time, taking part in some sort of training programme that would enable him to service the marine equipment that was being fitted in his homeland. He spent a lot of time looking over David's shoulder and declared to me that David had "lucky hands." I deduced from this that David had somehow fixed something in a manner that was totally beyond Chris's understanding!

When he first came to Mallaig from Fort William David, having met his wife-to-be, Rosie, settled there and went to sea as a fisherman for a few years. He then gave up fishing, came ashore and became mechanic, and then Second Coxswain of the Mallaig Lifeboat and in time succeeded Charlie Henderson as Coxswain.

I well remember David's attempts at getting a television signal that would serve Mallaig. He eventually succeeded and a photograph appeared in the National Press of a group of boxing fans grouped around an old black and white television set at around 3 a.m. one cold winter morning on a hill above Mallaig Vaig. In the background, a small generator powered their viewing of a fight involving this new boxing sensation, Cassius Clay or as he was later known, Mohammed Ali!

David's efforts bore fruit and eventually he embarked on the massive task of connecting every home in Mallaig to the aerial he had erected on the only spot where a signal could be found! He did it, and I do not think I am out of order in revealing that quite a number of residents received their connections free if David and his wife, Rosie thought their financial situations merited it.

The only time I saw David stuck for a suitable reply was on the Island of Eigg. We had been out on a search for quite some time and we were hungry. This was on the old Barnett class Lifeboat which was capable of only about 8 knots and because of this, and thinking of the area we had to cover then, we always carried some tinned and dried food which we heated in an old pot, on a small Calor gas single ring cooker. Having this appliance aboard was completely against regulations, so we had to whip it ashore whenever an Inspector was in the offing!

When hunger got the better of us on a service we would empty something like three tins of soup into the pot followed by three tins of corned meat, which we had chopped up and topped it off by adding a couple of tins of peas and carrots. All of these contents, we bought ourselves, by the way. When this mix had heated, we then poured in powdered potatoes until the whole had thickened into a sort of thick stew.

It may sound terrible, but a dollop of that on a paper plate when you are really hungry, is just the bee's knees!

David, however, stated very firmly that he did not like dried potatoes, so he had to get his ration, in a much more liquid form, before they were added.

Back to the Eigg tale. The Coastguard decided that we should take a break from the search at nightfall, and resume at daylight. As it was summer, and this break would only last as long as we would take to steam to Mallaig and back, we went to the wee pier at Eigg. One of the local lads came to greet us and said that we were to come home with him, to where his wife had a meal waiting for us. This kindness was typical of the Islanders of that era!

Off we went in the trailer towed by his tractor and soon we were seated round a table in this lady's kitchen, on which she put two enormous, steaming bowls – one with stewed meat, carrot, onion and turnip in a lovely thick gravy, the other piled high with mashed potatoes.

We helped ourselves to this feast and after tasting it David stated, "Ye jeest cannot beat these Island tattics – it's the seaweed they use as manure that gives them that flavour!"

The lady of the house then said, in an apologetic tone, "Sorry, the steamer didn't call last week with the stores. That's dried tatties, I'm afraid!"

That ruined David's reputation as a gourmet, I fear, and we never let him forget it.

David retired some time ago, but the name, and the reputation within the fishing industry for service beyond self is continued by his sons Billy and Bertie, and by his grandsons.

Native wit was exemplified in a story told to me by the late Charles Simpson, an oil merchant in Mallaig.

The incident had taken place many years before, when coal was king, and Charles had a lorry which was kept in a garage attached to a local hotel, and which was used to make deliveries of this coal to local houses. One morning, Charles went up to get the lorry out for the day's deliveries, and noticed that there was a freshly killed hind hanging up to mature in the garage.

His companion who must, for reasons which will become obvious, remain nameless, commented on this hind and made much of the delights of a feed of venison.

The following day, the local bobby sought out Charles and his companion, and ascertained from them that yes, they had seen this beast, and that when they last saw it, it still had four legs! Someone, the bobby told them, had stolen a haunch from this hind, which belonged to the proprietor of the hotel, but if it was returned, no more questions would be asked.

It was by now obvious from the expressions on his face that Charles's companion was guilty, but despite repeated requests he refused to admit guilt nor, of course, would he return the haunch. The bobby asked him for a look at his knife, and when it was guilelessly handed over, he pocketed it and announced that this knife would be sent now for police laboratory tests which would show if it had been used to cut the venison, and that our (clearly guilty) man had one more chance to repent.

When this offer was spurned, the bobby strode off, raging that the knife would now definitely be sent for analysis and that a jail sentence was likely as a result if, as he thought likely, the tests were positive.

When he had gone, Charles said, "Did you take the venison?"

"Oh yes!" was the reply.

"Then you'd better go after the bobby and tell him, because the test will show up traces of blood, no matter how well you have washed it," said Charles.

"No it won't," said the guilty party. "This is the knife I used to cut it." Yes, he had two knives in his pocket, and had handed over the 'innocent' one!

This same man was a native Gaelic speaker, and was never entirely at ease when perforce he had to use English. He obviously thought in his native tongue, and when he was under any kind of pressure, he made mistakes in translating his thoughts into this alien language. On being served with a plate of very thin soup one day on a boat where he was a crew man, he cried, "Two peas and a barley, and you call that a soup!" Questioned one day by a holiday-maker as to how long the fishing boats remained at sea, he replied, "Ah well, some weeks they stay out for a fortnight!" His most notable error, as far as I am aware, was when he made the heartfelt cry one day, "If you came through what came through me, you'd know all about it," but this mistake must be closely pursued by another made whilst attempting to forecast the weather, when he said, "The sky's away to the north, there'll be more weather tomorrow!"

Anyway, the people of whom I write had all, without exception, a far better grasp of English than I had of Gaelic!

One of the nicest tales I ever heard was narrated by the writer and raconteur extraordinaire, the late Finlay J. MacDonald. He was a native of the south of Harris and until he went to school he, and all his contemporaries, spoke no English at all. At school, the steep learning curve began with having to master the language in which all of the lessons were conducted, English.

A new young lady teacher arrived from somewhere north, in 'Wee Free' territory, to take over the class that Finlay was in and, in order to help with the language difficulties, she announced that she was going to start a competition. Each pupil had to introduce a 'new' word, explain its meaning, and spell it. Whoever had the best word each morning would get a star, and at the end of the term, the pupil with most stars, would get a prize. There was great competition among the pupils!

One morning Finlay greeted his pal, a boy named Gillespie, who called each day for Finlay, on his way to school. Finlay was greatly excited because he had found, late the previous night, a word that he just knew was going to be a winner. To his disappointment, Gillespie was even more excited because, as he explained to Finlay, he had a word that was a sure fire winner!

After morning prayers the young teacher called for the new words. “You now, Master Gillespie, what is your word?”

“Please Miss, pennies!” announced Gillespie, face beaming with pride.

“Pennies? Well, plurals are not really permitted but anyway, what does it mean?”

“Please Miss, it is an organ. I have never seen one but my father saw one once when he was away in the Navy during the war.”

The teacher had now a puzzled frown on her face. “Can you spell it for us, please?”

“Yes Miss, it is p-e-n-i-s!” Gillespie said triumphantly, beaming round at his classmates.

The teacher raised the lid of her desk, hiding her face while the class, seeing that the lid was shaking somewhat, sat bemused. Eventually the lid was lowered and Miss proclaimed that the competition was null and void for the day and that they should now break – a little early – for the play period.

Outside, Gillespie was instantly surrounded by a group of aggressive peers who asked him just what he thought he was doing. “You should have known that the teacher would not know what an organ is. She is a Wee Free, and they don’t have organs or pianos in their Church!”

Another tale of the Islands, that I loved, was the one of the old fellow from Lewis who had emigrated to America in his youth. He never married and in his old age he lived alone, save for his faithful old dog, in a small flat in New York. He decided that his remaining time on Earth was now getting short and, thinking back to his youth in Lewis, he remembered a favourite food that had been often prepared for him by his loving mother – the boiled guga. The guga was a young gannet that had been killed, plucked and salted down, mainly by the people who lived in the Port of Ness, way up in the north of Lewis. It was, I am assured, very much an acquired taste!

He wrote to a nephew in Lewis, describing his longing and very soon afterward a parcel arrived that contained three guga. He sat for a long time looking at them, relishing the smell that took him back to what he now tearfully perceived as his happy youth, then washed them and put them on to boil. The smell of them cooking did nothing to raise his melancholy memories but eventually, he sat down to feast on them. As he ate, he threw the scraps to his old dog who sat below his chair.

When he had finished, he looked down to see that the dog was licking its arse to try to put the taste of guga out of its mouth!

There are a great many tales that might be told of some of the characters in and around Mallaig concerning what might well have been described as the local pastime of poaching. This poaching was not the kind of work which is popularly described today as being carried out by "gangs of criminals in high powered vehicles", but was claimed with a degree of justification, as being the right of the locals to take "one for the pot".

Indeed I have often wondered how a Sheriff would deal with the claim from an accused poacher, borrowed from Para Handy, that they would instantly return to the sea any salmon which bore a label declaring that it was the property of the Laird!

During one such poaching escapade, which was led by a Mallaig man who was renowned for his coolness, a stag was shot whilst they were high up on a ridge on one of the islands. As he and his companion approached, this poor beast was seen to stagger to its knees. They ran up to it, to discover that it had been stunned by the bullet, so the companion of our hero prepared to finish it off.

“No, don’t shoot him just now,” says our man calmly. “We’ll walk him down to where the boat is and then you can shoot him. That’ll save a lot of carrying!”

The same man came home one day to discover that the local police sergeant (who had heard that another poaching expedition had taken place) had visited his home and had been allowed access by the wife of the suspected poacher. This sergeant had taken away a haunch of venison which would, he told the wife, be the evidence against her husband, and had also confiscated the (properly licensed) rifle which belonged to him.

When he heard of this from his wife he decided that the information necessitated a prolonged visit to a local hostelry where the ‘poacher’ would get a lot of sympathy - and whisky - which might help the thought process!

Returning home late that night, he noticed the sergeant’s car parked at the rear of the police station. Investigation revealed that the ‘evidence’ was still in the unlocked boot of this car, so he quietly liberated it, throwing the venison as far as he could into the sea. The following morning he went to the police station, and quietly asked for his rifle back. This politely phrased request was granted in a less than friendly manner by the hopelessly outwitted sergeant!

There was another episode where a ‘poacher’ - not the same man - displayed a remarkable degree of calmness in adversity. He, with two companions, had made the long trip by boat to the head of a sea loch near Mallaig to try for a few salmon. When they arrived and had carried the net up the shore toward the first of the pools where their prey might be lying, they were horrified to spot three men approaching from landward, obviously with the same objective in mind. They had come to the spot by land, which had involved them in several miles of hard walking. A ‘Mexican standoff’ might be the result of this confrontation, you would be excused for thinking, but our subject was made of sterner stuff than that.

Telling his two companions to lie low, our friend donned his 'fore and aft' hat, an adornment which was favoured by all ghillies - adopted a very pugnacious attitude and a cultured accent, and told the competition in no uncertain terms to - "Clear off my land immediately!"

As soon as the hapless trio had hurriedly complied with this demand, and he had succeeded in stopping his friends' laughter, our intrepid lads set about the work in hand.

⚓

Another episode which had a rather less happy ending as far as the poaching fraternity was concerned occurred when a pair of heroes set out to 'do' a river some distance from Mallaig. They made their way there via half of the public houses in Lochaber, and as a result, on the final leg through the heather toward the targeted pool, they felt obliged to rest for a while among the bracken which lined the rivers edge, and promptly fell asleep.

Their snooze was disturbed when a man fell over their recumbent bodies in the half light of the summer night, and when he had recovered from the shock, he demanded to know who the pair were, and what they were doing.

They, in turn, thinking that this man was on the same mission as themselves, and being fully conversant with the ploy used by the gentleman in the last story, told him to "go forth and multiply," in Anglo Saxon, questioning him as to just who he thought he was anyway!

When this angler (for such he was) told them that he was a Chief Inspector in the Strathclyde Police, the only reply in their books for such atrocious lies was for one of them to take a successful swing at him for daring to think that they were stupid enough to believe such a tall story.

Unfortunately for them, his description of his profession was absolutely correct, and the only omission he was guilty of was in not telling them that his two companions - hitherto unseen - were also policemen!

Fortunately for our two poachers, when they had been duly summoned to appear and to explain their actions to the relevant body, the court seemed to see the funny side of the charge, so I am sure that everyone would agree that they got off lightly in the end.

The marketing of herring had come a long way from the old days when the ladies carried fish from the ports to sell them in the towns and also in the surrounding hinterland, a practise remembered in the song, 'Caller Herrin'. The late Pat Croan, owner of the well known Edinburgh fish processing firm, proudly boasted that his mother made a living by selling a creel load of fish that she had carried into residential Edinburgh. What is perhaps not so well known is that farmers' wives carried out the same task, travelling in the opposite direction with farm produce, carrying the butter and cheese they had made, along with eggs from the hens that were their responsibility.

I heard a lovely tale concerning this era, which almost certainly is at least partly true. A farmer's wife had secured the 'contract' to supply the three shops in a small fishing village on the east coast. She was paid sixpence a dozen for them. One day she made her call on the first of these shops, carrying her basket of eggs. The shopkeeper greeted her with a mournful expression and began: "Ah, my dear, things are aawfu' bad wi' the fishin jeest noo. There's jeest naethin' daein at aa, an money's verra scarce. The three o' us shopkeepers hiv had a meeetin' and we've decided that the best we can pey fur eggs is threepence the dozen. Ah'm awfu' sorry, but ye see, we've had oor meetin', an' that's the best we can dae."

The poor lady was mortified at this drastic cut in her income, but there was nothing at all that she could do about it, so she sold her eggs for the proffered pittance.

Next week, she visited the surrounding farms, collecting all the tiny pullets eggs she could get her hands on. These she took into the village. When she went into the first shop the owner approached her once more but when he saw the tiny eggs she was carrying, his face fell.

“Far did ye get they eggs? They’re gey small!” he began

“Weel ye see, it’s like this,” said the lady. “You shopkeepers had a meetin’ an’ drapped the price, so the hens decided tae ha’e wan as weel, an they’ve decided that they’re no’ gaan tae rax their erses fur threepence the dozen!”

Captains Ashore

There were of course several men in and around Mallaig who were not directly connected with the fishing industry but who would certainly qualify as Captains, and who would be welcome at many a fireside apart from Angus's.

Foremost of these in my opinion has got to be Charlie Henderson, who died just a year or so ago. Charlie worked all of his life in the boatyard in Mallaig which he owned and ran successfully. He also served with distinction as coxswain of the local Lifeboat, for many years.

Of medium height, he was sparsely built, and had a disconcertingly quizzical way of looking at the person he was addressing. He was very well known and respected in many places. I was aboard the Lifeboat with him on one occasion when we called at Tobermory to get something to eat, hungry after a particularly long service. We went into the Mishnish Hotel, only to be told by the young receptionist that we were too late for lunch and too early for dinner, but we agreed to wait till she could get some sandwiches made up for us. While we waited Bobby MacLeod, the owner of the hotel appeared, and hailed our hero like a long-lost brother. "What brings you here, Charlie?" he asked. When Charlie told him we were waiting for sandwiches to be made up, Bobby's roars had to be heard to be believed. An hour later we sat down to a three course meal in the dining room of the Mishnish. We were then given the sandwiches that had been made - "In case you get hungry on the way home" - on our way out, having been subjected first of all to a real West Highland scolding for daring to attempt to pay for the meal!

I was the victim of Charlie's wit on more than one occasion. A friend and I called on him one New Year to be welcomed with a dram and the comment, "Aye, come in and make yourself at home. That's where you should be anyway!"

Later that night another caller was asked if he would care for a plate of yesterday's soup. When he said that he would love it, Charlie replied, "Well, away ye go home and come back tomorrow!"

I was in a bar one afternoon, having a pint with a couple of the Lifeboat crew when Charlie joined us. He had a wee dram in him, and he announced that he had enjoyed a plateful of fried herring for his lunch, earlier. Being well aware that no herring had been landed in Mallaig for some time I asked him where he had got them.

"Off the plate!" he answered.

Charlie is gone from us now. He left this sad old World a happier – and wiser – place than when he entered it.

Whilst writing of the Lifeboat, I am reminded of a story told to me as true, some time ago, by one of the fund-raising staff of the Royal National Lifeboat Institution.

He had gone one morning to visit a man who had been of great help to the R.N.L.I. in the past. When he arrived at what could best be described as 'The Manor', which was situated on its own estate somewhere in central Scotland, he was taken into the kitchen where his host made tea for them both. As they sat there discussing their business, the aged mother of the host came tottering into the kitchen, made a beeline for a cabinet which stood in a corner and, opening the door of this cabinet, poured a glassful of some amber liquid, then tottered out again without a word being spoken.

Some ten minutes later, this process was repeated, but this time, the son exclaimed: "Mother! That's your second, and it is only ten o'clock in the morning."

The old dear turned round and replied in her beautiful aristocratic accent, "Would you have me walk on one leg all day then?"

As she turned round to make this statement, my informant noticed with horror that the bottle from which she had poured her drink was clearly labelled, 'Parazone' in large red felt-tip pen applied letters. Seeing his horrified look, she nonchalantly offered, by way of explanation: "Take no heed of this. I put that label on to keep my housekeeper away from it. She's an alcoholic, don't you know!"

There are one or two tales – true ones – which I would like to relate, but I would wish the main characters to remain anonymous. The first one took place here on the East Coast and relates, in a way, to the murder of John Lennon, who was shot dead in a cowardly attack in New York.

There was a whole gale of south-easterly wind blowing and the crews of the local prawn trawlers were sheltering behind buildings around the harbour in Arbroath. It was dark and cold. There was no sense in going to sea: no boat would shoot a net in the prevailing weather but still they hung around, waiting for their skippers to tell them to go back home to bed. The skippers, for their part, were unwilling to go home while any of their counterparts remained – just in case one of them went to sea and got a few prawns ahead of them! The stalemate continued. Then someone started the engine on one of the boats, probably to charge the batteries.

That was enough to start everyone off. If one was going to sea, they would all go!

Once clear of the land, the fleet dodged slowly up through the weather. It was certainly not a morning for being at sea, never mind shooting a net. One of the skippers tuned his radio to get the latest world news, and heard of the shooting of John Lennon.

Switching to his VHF radio he called his pal.

"Eh 'Bill', did ye hear that? That's John Lennon shot!"

“Weel he wants his fuckin’ heid looked fur shootin a net on a mornin’ lik’ this!” came the reply from ‘Bill’ – who was obviously not a music fan.

The other tale concerns a young Mallaig skipper – who will also remain anonymous. Alex – let’s call him that – was persuaded quite suddenly to take religion very seriously, and became quite evangelical about it. He wanted everyone to share his enthusiasm and, as he had never had any real grounding in his faith, he was prone to become quite radical and violent in his opinions if anyone disagreed with him. He was also a very powerful young man, in a physical sense.

One Friday, not very long after his ‘conversion’ his only crewman had to stay ashore to keep a medical appointment, so ‘Alex’ had to recruit the assistance of a young cousin, a lad who was still at school. Let’s call him Jamie. This fellow told me the tale years later.

‘Jamie’ got one of his pals to come with him. Not much coaxing was needed to make either of them to take the day off school. They left Mallaig at about three in the morning and shot down about Arisaig Sound. When they heaved up the cod-end, it was just full of prawns. They filled the whole aft deck!

‘Alex’ came out of the wheelhouse.

“On yer knees”, he shouts. “We’ll give thanks to the good Lord for the bountiful harvest he has given us this morning”.The two youngsters did as they were told right away because, as ‘Jamie’ explained, they were well aware that ‘Alex’ was quite likely to clout them if they didn’t do as they were told – at once!.

“You know what he is like,” ‘Jamie’ said. “If we hadn’t done just exactly what he said, he could quite easily have thrown us into the water! He went into the wheelhouse, came out with a New Testament and started to read from it. Me an’ my pal were on our knees among the prawns. We were too scared to even look at him. He must have read nearly half a chapter when one of the other boats called him on the VHF radio.”

"I see you've hauled up there, 'Alex'. How'd ye get on?"

'Alex' stuck his hand into the wheelhouse and brought out the VHF handset.

"Fuck all," he called into it. "Jeest fuck all!"

Obviously his new found religion had not yet overcome the overwhelming need for secrecy - at the expense of truth - that the fishing had instilled in him.

Still on a religious theme, Billy Hughes of Anstruther, who is manager of the Pittenweem Fishermen's Association and who works in Pittenweem, told me the following lovely tale.

He had formed the habit of going every night to his mother's house in Pittenweem after he had finished work for the day. There he shared a cup of tea with his widowed mother, and they exchanged gossip, a ritual that they both enjoyed and looked forward to.

One day, he told me, his work had started off badly, and got worse as the day progressed. By finishing time that evening he had just about reached the end of his tether. When he arrived at his mother's house, she immediately saw that he was not 'in good form'.

"Eh Billy, whit's a dee wi ye? Ye're awfy worrit lookin," she asked.

"Ye don't want tae ken, mither. It's been a bad day!"

"Weel Billy, if it's been as bad as ye say, jeest as soon as ye get hame tae Ainster ye'll get up the stairs tae yer bedroom an ye'll get doon on yer knees. Pour all yer worries oot tae the Lord. He'll tak them aa on his ain shooders."

"Aye right, mither, ah'll dae that."

His tone must have been unconvincing, because she repeated the instruction again, stressing that the Lord would willingly take all Billy's cares on his able shoulders.

When it came time to leave Billy stood and went to the door.

"Mind noo, Billy. On yer knees as soon as ye get hame. The Lord is a willing listener an he'll shooder aa yer burdens."

"Aye mither, ah'll dae that," replied Billy, a little testily.

His hand was on the doorknob when she spoke again. "Billy!"

"Whit is't noo, mither?" – his voice revealing that his patience was growing thin.

"Mind, son - when mornin comes ye're on yer ain again!"

There are many, many tales that could – and should – be told from and of the fishing communities of the East Neuk of Fife but I am not really able to do this fully here. I do recall, with great glee, the beautiful tale told to me by Ian Murray, a very successful fishing skipper. His wife, Sybil comes, on her mother's side, from another eminent fishing family, the Watsons of Pittenweem.

A relation of Sybil's, he said - and I will go no further in identifying him than that - owned a wooden fishing boat and decided that although she was getting a wee bit past her best, she really needed a new wheelhouse. In due course the boat was put on the slip and whilst she was being painted from truck to keel, the old wooden wheelhouse was removed and was replaced by a magnificent new one, which was fitted with all the latest state-of-the-art equipment. When the work had been completed our hero strode up the pier, chest sticking out with pride at his bonny newly-painted boat and her crowning glory, the new wheelhouse, and approached a group of old worthies who were seated on fish boxes at the head of the pier, enjoying the sun.

"Weel, fit dae ye think o ma boatie wi her braw new wheelhouse?" he asked.

After a short pause one grizzled old fisherman replied, "She's lyin' there lukkin' jeest lik an aul hoor wi' a new hat!"

Police tales

We took policemen to sea on the Lifeboat on several occasions while I was Coxswain, landing them at places that were only accessible by sea

One of the first times we had them aboard was when we were asked to convey them to Tarbert, in Loch Nevis. They had been told that a man had, after having had a row with his lady friend, barricaded himself in his house, announcing that he would shoot anyone that tried to enter it. It had been ascertained that this man had access to quite a high powered rifle.

It was around 2 a.m. on a lovely summer morning when we set off. I instructed the crew that we would stop the boat in the middle of the bay at Tarbert and ferry the two young policemen ashore in the small outboard-powered rubber dinghy that we carried. Derek Fowler, who was in charge of this dinghy, was told that he was to return to the Lifeboat immediately, whereupon we would retire to what I considered to be a safe distance.

This was all done and I then attempted to make the policemen's job easier by lighting their way with our powerful searchlight. We could now see them scrambling over the weed covered rocks, headed for the house – which was totally unlit. We watched with baited breath until they disappeared into the house.

They reappeared quite soon, with a handcuffed man and waved for us to come in and get them. When they got aboard they secured this poor fellow, who seemed quite harmless, and then as the tension drained from them, they started chatting, first of all explaining that the bruising on the fellow's face was not of their doing!

On their way up the beach, they said, it became apparent to them that they were being beautifully illuminated from behind by our searchlight and one of them said to the other, "I don't think that this is how the S.A.S. would do it!"

It later transpired that the man was completely innocent. He had been with his female friend, at the pub across the loch at Inverie. They had a dispute and had left to go home. When he started down the ladder to where their dinghy was moored, his 'friend' had waited until his head was level with the pier and then she kicked him in the face!

He fell into the dinghy and, as soon as he had recovered his senses, he had started the engine and set off home, leaving her to her own devices. She dialled 999 from a telephone kiosk at Inverie and related the concocted tale about the rifle, to the police. Thankfully, justice prevailed on this occasion and it was the woman who later appeared in court!

As we made our way back home that morning, the two young policemen, tongues loosened by the release of the tension they must have been suffering, started telling some stories of their adventures.

One of them had been in the Yorkshire Constabulary before coming north and one of his jobs was crewing a police car on motorway patrol. "You might think that this would be an exciting job," he started. "In fact it was really boring. I was driving one afternoon and my mate was a rather garrulous Yorkshire man. We were cruising along at around seventy when a Rolls Royce hissed past us. The driver was a black man who was smoking a big cigar and he was really travelling!"

"We'll have that bastard!" said his mate so off they went in pursuit, lights flashing and siren screaming.

The Rolls pulled over and stopped and the Yorkshire man walked up to the near-side window.

"Now then, Sambo – where's the fucking fire?' he said.

It turned out that this man was the Ghanaian Ambassador and that they hadn't spotted the C.D. plates on his car!

The Embassy's letter to the Chief Constable politely informed him that the Ambassador's name was not Sambo, and that he was not rushing to a fire. It was, he told us, a long time until their Chief Constable managed to appease the Ambassador and even longer before he forgot who had caused all the fuss.

Not to be outdone, his mate told us of an event that had occurred when he was a young Probationer in Glasgow.

A lady had come in to the Station one evening whilst the desk sergeant was having a cup of tea. She proffered a scraggy dog that she had on the end of a piece of string and told the youngster that it was a stray.When his sergeant returned he almost had a fit when he saw the dog and learned how it had got there.

"There'll be a pile of paperwork to do – don't ever do anything like this again!"

Some time later that night two patrolmen brought in a well-dressed man, who was very obviously under the influence of alcohol. He had not, they said, been doing anything wrong, but they had taken him in for his own safety. They went through all the usual procedures, and put him to bed in the best cell they had.

In the morning they woke him up with a cup of tea and when he had finished took him, obviously suffering badly from a hangover, to the desk where they returned his property. During this time the well-spoken man was extremely remorseful, explaining that he was not in the habit of taking alcohol and expressing his heartfelt hopes that he not been of any trouble.

"Not at all, sir, not at all," said the sergeant. "We had you here for your own benefit and safety. You will not face any charges at all.

Now just sign here for your belongings - and take your dog with you when you leave."

"My dog?" asked the man. "I don't have a dog."

"Well sir, you had this one with you when you were brought in and you will have to take it away with you now!"

When the puzzled man had left holding the string and pulling the mutt with him the sergeant turned to the probationer, saying: "That's two lessons you've learned this shift. Don't forget either of them!"

Bob MacLeod was the police sergeant when I first arrived in Mallaig, and he could well be used as a role model of what being a policeman was all about. Bob was a burly man who knew just about everything that was going on in and around the village. His favourite perch was standing with his back against the railings at the head of the pier, a position from which he could see almost all of the centre of his charge. He deserted this post for the railway station when the midday train came in – there he could greet, in Gaelic, all his many acquaintances who were travelling home to the islands.

I fell foul of Bob, just once! I had bought my first car in 1956, before I had a licence and, although I had absolutely no driving experience, the first thing I did when I got it home, was to apply for a driving test. I was still a fisherman then and the only practice I got was a very few hours on each of the three weekends before sitting this test. I had no chance, but I was young, and knew it all!

The day arrived and I drove the examiner around the village, carrying out the manoeuvres he demanded, to the best of my abilities. When we had got back to our starting place, he sat silent while he wrote out what I was certain would be a pass slip, then he handed it to me and got out to greet his next client.

I looked at it and quickly became aware that it was a 'fail' slip. I couldn't believe this, and in a fit of temper I shot off through the village, past the police station and around the bay to seek comfort from Rosie, sister of Ina, the girl who was soon to become my wife. I was alone in the car, without a licence holder who should, by law, have been sitting beside me.

The next morning I walked past Bob, who was in his accustomed position. He called me over and in his best 'official' voice asked me if I thought I was smart. I knew that I was potentially in a lot of trouble, so I told him that I was very sorry for having been stupid enough to drive off without a co-driver. Bob looked at me intently for a time and then told me, in no uncertain terms just where he was going to put his boot if I ever did anything of the like again.

I certainly didn't cross Bob again but now, I suppose, any policeman saying that would be guilty of something or other!

Incidentally, my car was sold just a year or so later when I got married and we needed the money to buy furniture for the single room we had rented.

Over the years I heard a number of police tales from various sources. Allan Macinnes had been a sergeant in Strathclyde Police and when he retired to Mallaig, took on the job of night-time operator in Mallaig telephone exchange. He often told the tale of his young days as a beat constable – this was when policemen actually walked the streets. He was in the company of his sergeant one day when they were confronted by an extremely irate citizen – he was fairly spitting with rage, said Allan. He called them to his van, which was parked at the pavement, and explained that he had left it there for fifteen minutes while he went on an errand.

"Look what I found when I came back!" he spluttered, opening the back door of the van, gesturing toward a deposit of human excreta. Obviously someone, probably in a moment of extreme need, had used the poor fellow's vehicle as a toilet.

"What are you going to do about this?"

"Ah well," answered the sergeant – a native of Skye, and obviously very experienced in city ways – "Just you take it to your local police station and hand it in. If no-one has claimed it in six months, you can keep it!"

At another station a young man who had spent the night in the cells having been charged with being drunk and disorderly, was being released on the following morning. He had been the source of much trouble while he was in custody and was almost at the door on his way out when the desk sergeant called him back.

"This was in your possession when you came here, sir," he said, proffering a can of strong lager.

The man took it without a word of thanks and left.

"Why on earth did you give him that back – I'd have thrown it in the bin!" said one of the on looking policemen.

"Come here, quickly!" said the sergeant by way of an answer, as he dashed to the window overlooking the front entrance to the station.

They were all just in time to see the released man as he sat down on the steps, open the can of lager – which spurted its contents heavenward in a great cascade – soaking the fellow as it did so.

"Always make sure you give these things a good shake before you hand them over," said the sergeant as soon as the roars of laughter had subsided.

Another very experienced sergeant – again from the Western Isles – was on foot patrol in the east end of Glasgow around mid day one New Year's Day when he and his constable companion were accosted by roars of abuse from a man who was leaning from the fourth floor window of a tenement across the road. They listened to a stream of absolutely vitriolic abuse from this idiot until he was yanked forcefully backwards into the room. His place was taken by a woman who called: - "Take nae heed o that drunken bastard, he's full o drink!"

“No problem missus,” answered the sergeant. “If he was a man at all, he would bring us down a can of beer. We’re dying of thirst.”

“Ye’ll get that aa right. Ah’ll send him right doon wi it. A guid New Year tae baith o’ yis!”

They wandered across the road and a few minutes later the fellow appeared at the close mouth, with a couple of cans of beer. As soon as he emerged, he was nicked!

“Ye see, son,” said the sergeant later. “There are two ways of handling something like that. The hard way would have been to have climbed up all these stairs and then have had a barney at the top. I took the easy way.”

Now, of course, vans are used to convey drunks to the stations. These vans have a window that allows the driver’s companion to monitor the state of their rowdy cargos. This window has a heavy wire mesh fitted over it that was designed to stop the unruly breaking the glass.

Another youngster learned one lesson as he was driven by his older companion, from the scene of a near riot. They had four drunken idiots in the back and the young constable was horrified at the abuse these guys were hurling at him through this window.

“As soon as I shout, brace yourself!” said the driver.

The youngster didn’t have time to question this remark when the call, “Brace!” came, as the driver saw that the road behind them was clear.

The driver then stood on the brakes.

When they arrived at the station and opened the door, the youngster was amazed at how quietly their charges accompanied them inside. The reason was revealed when they got into the well-lit station and he saw the lovely diamond-shaped patterns that adorned the faces of the two who had been snarling at them through the wire mesh protected glass!

Through a friend of mine, Roddy Ferguson, I met a lady who was a court lawyer in Glasgow and as you might expect, she had some lovely tales of the people she met in the course of her work. She told us of the time when a policeman in a Panda car stopped a car that had been weaving its way along a road in Glasgow. When the driver got out of the car it was immediately obvious that he was way over the limit, drink wise. A couple of beat constables appeared and when they spotted this incident, they wandered over. The errant driver grabbed one of the microphones that the beat bobbies wore on his tunic and roared into it: "For fuck's sake beam me up, Spock!"

I suppose that some well meaning idiot would take offence at some of the events I have chronicled above if they took place now, alleging the breaching of civil liberties, or some such nonsense.

Some time ago I was privileged to hear an after-dinner speech given by a prominent retired Sheriff who told us of some of his experiences whilst on the bench.

He had before him one day a character who had a long list of previous convictions for theft. On this occasion he had been apprehended on the roof of a church in Glasgow at around 3a.m.. Nearby was a stash of lead that had been removed from this roof and on his person was found several tools that could conceivably have been used in the removal of this lead.When asked by the arresting policeman just what he was doing he replied, "Ah wis takin' ma dug fur a walk!"

"Now," continued the Sheriff, "I have met some liars in my day, but this fellow was a master. Some of them convince their mothers that they are innocent, some convince themselves and a few, very few, almost convince me, but this chap had even convinced his lawyer that he was totally innocent of the charge!"

"At the end of the day, however, I found him guilty and before I announced his punishment, asked if he had anything to say. He declined and I sentenced him to three months in prison. Before doing so I told him that he was without doubt the most fecund liar I had ever heard." (Fecund, as you no doubt know, means fruitful, of course).

"His face was a picture after my use of this word. His brain was struggling to come to terms with the fact that I – who had after all had the benefit of a greatly superior education to his – had pronounced one of his favourite words, differently! It now appeared to him that he had been mispronouncing a word that had been used several times in every sentence that he had ever uttered."

"As he was led below to begin his sentence he was heard, quite clearly, to say to his escorting officer, 'That's the first fecund time ah've iver been in a fecund coort where the fecund sheriff used the same fecund langwidge as whit ah dae!'"

Another policeman with whom I became friendly in Mallaig told me of one of his experiences with a sergeant - this time in Inverness - who would certainly have qualified as a 'character'.

This sergeant was in the passenger seat of a police car that was parked in a lay-bye just south of Inverness, the young constable was in the driving seat. It was around 3 a.m. on a cold winter morning and it came as a relief to the constable when his sergeant instructed him to chase and stop a heavy laden fish lorry that had just passed them, heading south.

When they caught and stopped the lorry the sergeant walked to the front of the lorry and asked the driver where he had come from.

"Kinlochbervie, sergeant," replied the driver.

"And what are you carrying?" was the next question – a strange one, the constable thought as the smell told him that the load was obviously fish.

"Fish, sergeant," replied the driver, who was then asked to produce his log book.

"Have a good look at the tyres and check the security of the load, constable" said the sergeant as he scanned the log book carefully.

Then the driver, convinced that he was going to be charged with some offence or other, asked the sergeant if he would like a fry of fish.

"I wouldn't say no to that offer," came the reply, so the driver jumped down from his cab and scrambled up on to the back of the lorry. He undid some of the ropes and lifted the tarpaulin then asked, "Haddock all right, sergeant?"

"That would be lovely, driver."

"Have you got something to put them in, sergeant?"

"What is wrong with the box they are in?" was the reply!

The last guests

Another of my Captains arrived in Mallaig shortly before I left and has since then died suddenly, at a very young age. I first met Father John MacNeill when he was the priest at Inverie in Knoydart. He was sent from there to Eriskay where he tended to the needs of his flock for a few years before being posted to Fort William, and becoming a Canon. Eventually he got the posting to Morar which was, I think, his greatest desire, although he sadly did not get very long to enjoy it. Brought up in a seafaring community in Barra, he loved nothing more than to be in the company of fishermen.

Whilst he was at Inverie, it would be fair to say that he developed a habit of drinking far too much for his own good, which habit followed him to Eriskay.

When John went to Fort William he called me several times and asked if I was going to Fort William soon, as he had run out of fish, his favourite food! One Saturday I went up but when I went to the door of his house, which adjoined the church, the door was locked and I could get no reply when I rang the bell. I didn't think it was sensible to leave the bag of fish on his door in case cats smelt it, so I left it in the car boot and walked round to the door of the church. Inside the entrance, I was confronted by three doors that obviously led into the body of the church. Not knowing which one to go through I paused, and then decided on the middle one. As I made for it, a Mallaig lady came out of one of the others and walked past me, giving me a quizzical look as she did so.

Inside the church, I saw that there was no sign of John but there were several people sitting at their prayers. As I stood there, uncertain of what to do, an old lady rose and asked me if I was looking for someone. When I told that that I wanted to talk with Canon MacNeil she replied, "Oh, he's taking confession just now, but he'll be finished soon."

I waited a few minutes until he came out but while I was waiting, I had the mischievous thought that the Mallaig lady would soon be spreading the news that I had been in St Mary's in Fort William to make my confession!

I assumed that John was still fond of a dram when he arrived at Morar, so when he visited us one day in Mallaig I offered him one which, to my surprise, he refused. When I asked if he had stopped drinking, he told me that he still took a little wine, or if he was feeling cold on arriving home late on a winter evening, he would have a brandy. He then told me a remarkable story which I will repeat, changing it only slightly to protect the feelings of a few friends.

In another parish, he told me, he had become concerned for the well-being of two of his parishioners' marriage, and it came as no shock to him when the wife concerned telephoned him late one evening, and asked for his counsel. He told her to come round right away with her husband, and when they were all seated around the table, Father John poured a large glass of sherry for the wife, and produced a bottle of whisky and glasses for himself and the man.

It took a long time for them to drag the root of the problem out into the open, but eventually all agreed that too much alcohol was the prime cause. This accomplished, Father John filled the last remaining drams from the bottle and after some considerable thought challenged the husband - "I will toast you with this dram on the condition that we toast one another with the next dram we take!" In other words, he was saying that he would stop drinking if the man before him would do the same. This agreed, they downed the drinks, and the couple went home.

"This took place just before Christmas," Canon John told me. "I watched and worried all the time, especially over the New Year period, but he never put a foot wrong. He went back to sea shortly after the Festive time was finished, and was lost overboard one dark night, so you see I won't take a dram again until he is there for me to toast with it. I think that if I put a glass of whisky to my lips, I would be physically sick."

I was ill for a time when Canon MacNeill was in Mallaig and when I had recovered and was out and about again I met Allan Anderson, a friend and co-worker, who happened to be a Catholic. "What have you got that I don't have?" he asked. When I told him that I had no idea of what he was getting at he told me that there had been a bit in the local church magazine where John MacNeill asked for prayers for my good health.

"I've been sick before now, but he never asked for prayers for me – and I am a Catholic!"

I do not share Canon MacNeil's faith, but his life was an example to me of what religious tolerance really means, and his humanity guarantees him as good a reception at Angus's fireside as he ever got from his many friends in this life.

His predecessor was Canon Macinnes, who was also well loved in the area, and who was the prime mover in a hilarious incident which would not be out of place in one of the many tales about Para Handy. This concerned the scattering of ashes on Loch Morar. These ashes were of a man known to me only as Watty, a very gentle man who had moved to the area from around Glasgow, and whose love of Loch Morar eventually led to his death by drowning, in it. His body was cremated and, as he did not appear to have any close relatives the Canon decided that the ashes should be scattered on the waters which he had loved so much. The story of this ceremony involves several other characters who must be introduced to the reader who is not fortunate enough to know them personally.

Donny MacLellan is better known as "Donny by Gosh", which nickname originated from his habitual response as a child to the question - "What's your name?"

"Donny, by gosh!" would be the unfailing reply.

He owned the boat which was used by the burial party, and his inborn reluctance to waste hard-earned cash on the upkeep of this boat is central to the tale. He is a stocky, well built man - weight is also an important part of the story!

His bosom pal and constant angling companion was the late John MacVarish. This wiry character had been born at the head of Loch Morar, spent his formative years there and fished it as often as he could, so his knowledge of the Loch in all its moods was unsurpassed. They also, just on an odd occasion, shared a wee dram together.

Ronnie MacLellan - "Ronnie Seaview" as he was always called - was recruited by the Canon as official piper for the event, and was instructed to play a lament as the cortege left the river. Ronnie was as heavily built as the Canon.

The final member of Donny's crew that day was Jimmy MacDonald – another big lad as his nickname, Jimmy Bull, testifies.

On the afternoon of the day appointed for the ceremony Donny and John, having spent some time in the bar of Morar Hotel putting the finishing touches to the plans for the event, went down to the river where they saw the Canon, who was in his eighties, Jimmy MacDonald and Ronnie Seaview, safely aboard the boat, and set off out of the river at the head of the convoy which bore all who had come to pay their last respects. Ronnie struck up his lament, and John - under instruction from the Canon - held fast to the casket of ashes which he was to scatter reverently on the waters, on the word of command from the Canon.

Donny had noticed several months earlier that his boat had a slight leak, and had intended repairing this defect whenever he could borrow a little drop of the necessary fibre glass repair compound from someone but now, on the way out of the river, he realised that the extra weight of the burial party was causing the boat to sit lower in the water, and that therefore the leak - previously a trickle - was now somewhat more serious. His reaction to this observation was that of any true Highland gentleman - ignore it and hope that it goes away - so he became very interested in the sky, studying the cloud formations and studiously ignoring the furtive but increasingly frantic attempts of John to bring this rapidly increasing flood to his attention!

John, seeing that he was failing to get Donnie's attention, then concentrated his thoughts on whether or not this casket was buoyant enough to keep him afloat, and was measuring the relative distances to the shore and the nearest boat in the cortege.

The Canon had his eyes closed, thinking no doubt on higher things, and was oblivious to the waters gathering around his feet. Ronnie's attention was only drawn to this life threatening phenomenon when his foot - previously banging in time to the music - started splashing instead!

The water running over the top of the Canon's ankle boot, finally brought to him realisation of why Ronnie's pibroch was now being played at jig time, so his frantic nudge brought immediate silence from the relieved Ronnie, and he quickly launched into the short service.

"In the name of the Father, Son …" This was blurted out at great speed - and John, whose reactions were by now honed to razor sharpness, threw the ashes instinctively.

To windward!

It took a fair bit of scrubbing to make the boat ash free, and I am certain that Wattie was rolling around laughing somewhere.

I sat with the late Canon Macinnes in Morar Hotel for a time one evening during the reception for one of Archie and Barbara MacLellan's children. Also in the company was Dr. Mayhew, who was a frequent locum for Dr. Duck and who was well known in the district. I had taken a few drams – just enough to make me think that I was quite a smart fellow and so accosted the Canon, telling him that 'his Boss' had designed the World all wrong. He should, I told him, have organised it in such a way that man made his entrance at the time of his allotted span – 70 years. This would mean that he would, if he was born with a few bob, be able to use his money for his greater enjoyment. When I was young, for example, I could have eaten my way all through the restaurant menu but shortage of cash meant that I had to look for the cheapest item there. Now that I had a wee bit of money, I still couldn't eat what I wanted – I had to look for the items that were least fattening!

But how, the Canon countered, would man then prepare to meet his Maker? When I suggested that my way he would leave this mortal coil as an infant – and what could be more innocent than that – he took my part, saying that he would have a word with his Boss about this, when he got home.

At that, Dr. Mayhew – whose sense of fun didn't extend that far – told me that I was talking pure nonsense! When I replied to this by telling him – he was unmarried – that I had been watching him eyeing up the young ladies and obviously wishing that he was 20 years younger. "If I had my way, you would be thinking – oh boy, in 20 years time … !"

Donnie-by-Gosh some time ago surprised everyone by taking his wife on a holiday to the West Indies. I met him when he returned and knowing that this was generally felt to be an expensive part of the World in which to holiday, I asked him what the cost of living was like there. He showed that he had his priorities right when he replied after due consideration, "Well, rum is cheap, but whisky is a hellova price!"

Donnie was also involved, albeit indirectly, in another of the fishing tales about Loch Morar – a true story that would not be out of place in one of Para Handy's tales.

An angling competition was organised to start at 9 a.m. one Saturday on Loch Morar, the first ever such competition, as far as I can remember. There was to be a fly fishing section based on fishing from the banks, and another for the boats who trolled lures. My wife and I decided to enter with our boat and I decided that we should leave the river at 8 a.m. so that we would be at the head of the loch in time to start fishing to the west, back toward the river. That way, I reckoned, we would not get mixed up in what I thought would be a melee at the west end of the loch at 9 a.m.

It was not a very nice day when we left; there was a heavy drizzle, but when we got up to the head, it had eased a little. Out went the rods – Ina had one on the starboard side and I had mine on the port side but I also rigged a fly rod which was mounted vertically right on the stern.

After we had taken a few fish aboard, I began to wonder if we had to keep our catches separate, or if both our catches were to be pooled? Were we correct in having 3 rods out, or should we only have two, was another puzzler?

As we went down the south side of the loch I caught sight, through the drizzle that was now growing heavier, of a boat coming towards us. My binoculars showed me that it was Donnie and John – and that they too had a rod mounted on the stern! I lost them as they turned into a bay but when they reappeared ten minutes or so later, the stern rod had disappeared.

Hmm!

The wind and rain increased as the day wore on and around 4pm, we were soaked and cold and had had enough, so off we went for the river. When we berthed, I took Ina back into Mallaig and we agreed that we should eat in the Chlachain Bar that night when I got back from the weighing of the fish, an event that was to take place in the bar of Morar Hotel.

When I went in to the bar I stood beside John McNeil, who had been fly fishing from the banks and who was therefore in a different category than I was. I told John of my doubts about whether or not I should have kept my fish apart from Ina's but John – infinitely more experienced in the angling art than I would ever be said: "You are in the land of the Infidels here, keep quiet!"

John and Donnie came in, but went to the far end of the bar without really speaking, which struck me as being odd. They were followed by a young Irish lad, Terry Byrnes, who had recently appeared in Mallaig and who had a small open boat on the loch. He stood beside us and showed us the three fish he had caught – giving us a graphic and detailed description of where and how he had caught them, explaining that he had only been out for an hour or two.

Returning from a trip to the toilet I stopped by Donnie and John, spotting as I did that their bag seemed smaller than mine. "Well, you see," explained Donnie: "John had on a big Toby lure all day, trying for a salmon. These are all mine, John never touched a thing at all!"

Back I went to join John McNeil who laughed knowingly and said, "I told you!" when I repeated Donnie's tale.

When the weigh-in was concluded, I was pronounced the winner of the trolling section and immediately afterwards, I made for the door to go home for a shower before going out to eat. Terry asked me for a lift but, when I let him off at the door of the Chlachain Bar, he also asked me what I was going to do with the fish I had. The people with whom he lodged, he told me, loved brown trout. I hadn't thought about this but I did then, and gave them to him, as neither Ina nor I cared for them.

When Ina and I went into the Chlachain that evening for our meal Eleanor McVarish, John's daughter, who was then the chef there, (and she made the best haddock and chips I ever tasted!) asked me if I had been on the loch that day. "Didn't young Terry do well," she continued, "getting first prize for having the biggest bag, and him only a learner?"

"No, Terry had only three fish for his day," I replied.

"Indeed he didn't," she said. "He showed me his fish and he had a lot more than three fish, I can assure you!"

Terry had put his catch with mine, and claimed them all for himself!

That wasn't the end of the story. On the Monday Taff Coull, skipper of a local trawler, told me that he had gone out on Saturday with his son for an hour or so and when the rain increased, had given up and made back for the river. "On the way in I passed wee Terry, and threw him the three fish we had – I wasn't going to wait for any weighing ceremony."

Terry hadn't caught any of his fish at all. That episode completed my education on the ethics of angling!

The possibility of Willie Kirk being promoted to Captain may well surprise many people but, remember, these are my Captains.

Willie comes from a family with strong Mallaig connections, and he first came to my notice when he returned from a long sojourn in America to assist his uncle in the running of the grocery and hardware shop at the head of the pier in Mallaig. He presents an unkempt kenspeckle figure, and to those who do not know him, his shyness, retiring nature and very slow speech suggests that he is inward-looking, and rather forbidding. His balding pate is usually fringed by long strands of fair hair, but on the rare occasion when Willie dresses up, the transformation to the epitome of a smart business man is completed by the brushing of this hair over the bald patches, and has to be seen to be believed.

His stay in America was mainly in San Francisco, where he worked with another uncle who owned the Edinburgh Castle, a bar in that city. My first real meeting with him was when I casually mentioned to him that my wife and I were shortly going to visit San Francisco, whereupon Willie produced a scrap piece of paper and drew - purely from memory - a map of the city including street names and numbers, and indicated on it just where his uncle's pub was to be found. When we arrived there, I found that scrap of paper to be so amazingly accurate, that I used it to find my way around! I have since become convinced that Willie's idiosyncrasy is a deliberate cover for a very highly intelligent man, a conviction which is shared by many who have come to know him better than I.

I met him one night in the Chlachain Bar when he was in the company of a man from San Francisco, a nodding acquaintance of his, who had just arrived on his doorstep.

Willie asked me if I had eaten fish and chips during my visit to the Edinburgh Castle bar. When I said that I had, he told me that his uncle had opened this fish and chip shop many years before, and hazarded a guess that it might well have been the first in the United States.

He had sold it several years earlier and Willie told me that he had been warned by his uncle, against going there. "You don't want to meet Big Liz, she's a terrible woman," he said.Willie obeyed his uncle until one evening, returning to the pub hungry after a long walk, he smelt the irresistible smell of fish and chips coming from the open door of the shop.

He went in to be confronted – over the counter – by a veritable monster of a woman. She was very tall and muscular with long, black, greasy hair. Her blouse sleeves had been rolled up revealing muscular arms that sported many varied tattoos.

"What the Hell do you want?" she roared at Willie.

"Fish and chips, please," answered Willie nervously when he eventually recovered his power of speech.

"Get your fucking money on the counter first, you Scottish bastard," said this fearsome lady.

Willie paid his money, grabbed the proffered parcel and made off at once. When he arrived at the Edinburgh Castle his uncle, seeing the container of fish and chips asked, rather superfluously I thought, if Willie had got them in the prohibited shop.

"Aye," answered Willie. "There was this woman in there, six foot if she was an inch. Long, black, greasy hair, sleeves rolled up, arms full of tattoos …"

"Oh yes," interrupted his uncle. "That's Mary. She's a lovely lassie!"

That tale took two or three drams to tell, and his American friend and I listened intently to every word!

Willie had not long arrived back in Mallaig from America, when I discovered the joys of fishing on Loch Morar, a fresh water loch not far from our home, which is famed for being the deepest fresh water loch in Europe, and which is joined to the sea by what is reputed to be the shortest river in the U.K. Fishing there consisted mainly of trolling, towing various sizes and colours of lures behind one's boat in the fond and often futile hope that a trout - or even a salmon - might find it attractive. Willie's Uncle Bertie, who owned the shop where Willie had started to work, sold rods and lures, and Bertie had himself fished the loch for many years, so I allowed myself to be guided by him in my choice of gear. Now I did not expect to become an expert at once, but I was certainly not prepared to accept that for every trout I caught, others caught six or eight, so I pestered the life out of poor Bertie, telling him that this failure of mine must be directly attributable to the poor quality of the lures he sold!

One day I came into the river on Morar where we kept our boats, having been fishing for about three hours with a total lack of success, to find another fisherman - who had berthed just before me - standing on the road. Noticing that he did not have his car there I offered him a lift into Mallaig, which he refused, saying that he was just waiting for his wife to arrive with his son, who had been working, and intended going back out onto the loch again. He asked me if I had caught anything and when I replied that I had none, he completed my discomfiture by saying that he had about a dozen trout.

However, when I jokingly asked him for a couple for my tea, he refused. Smelling a rat, I offered Jackie a fiver for one trout. His refusal confirmed the suspicion which had been slowly dawning on me. He had none! The enormous relief at finding out that my lowly position in the catching stakes was due to the fact that the others were telling lies, was something to relish.

My first call at Mallaig was Bertie's shop, where I wanted to tell him of my new-found knowledge, but instead I found Willie there alone.

"Aye," said he when I had blurted out my tale. "Tell me, do you subscribe to the Monte Carlo theory?"

Seeing my puzzled look, he continued in his usual slow drawl : "Aye, the Monte Carlo theory is that if you toss a coin ten times, and it comes down heads every time, then it is odds on that it'll fall heads on the eleventh time too." Pausing for a moment to allow me to digest this offering, he slowly resumed, "The anti-Monte Carlo theory, however, is that having come down heads ten times, it is odds on that it will change - so it will be tails the eleventh time."

"What has this got to do with fishing on the Loch, Willie?" I questioned him.

"Aye," said Willie at his usual slow pace, "I was just coming to that. You see, one man catches a trout in bay 'X' on Morar, and when you meet him and see this braw fish, you ask him where he got it, he'll tell you it was in bay 'Y', because he thinks that bay 'X' is a good place for trout, and he wants to keep it for himself."

"Now another man catches a trout in bay 'A' on the loch, but he thinks that he has chased all the trout out of that bay, so when you ask him where he caught it, he'll tell you correctly that he got it in bay 'A', for he is sure that there are no more left there."

By now I was completely flummoxed, so Willie, sensing this, said, “Do you not see what I mean?”

“No,” was the best I could muster.

“Aye, well it’s easy, I’m just trying to say that you canna believe a bloody word anyone tells you!”

Willie is fond of playing bridge, and was one of a group which played every week at a friend’s house. Some years ago they had gathered for their game, but before it started, the conversation turned to the topic which was currently headline news - as it still so often sadly is - the sex attack on a young girl. They were all vociferous in their condemnation of this revolting crime, and were discussing the various punishments which should be dished out to the perpetrators when, during a lull, Willie announced that he personally had once attempted to have sex with a five year old girl. There was a stunned silence and then one of the ladies present turned her full armament on him, sparing nothing in her attack. Willie eventually managed to stem the flow of vituperation and quietly said, “Wait a minute Molly, I was only six years old myself at the time!”

Some time ago, Willie became a member of the local Community Council. One night the meeting of this Council was dominated by certain members bewailing the dearth of tourists in the season just past, which had cut their income drastically. Various suggestions were being put forward as being possibly of help in promoting the natural attractions of the area, and it was generally agreed that more publicity should be sought. Willie had taken no active part in the discussion, but then he got the natural pause for which he had been waiting.

“Aye, we’ll buy some baby palm trees,” he announced.

Silence continued while the others attempted to make sense of this mouthful.

"Aye, we'll need to get the roads department to agree to their workmen planting the trees, and we'll wait until we get a good long spell of really hard frost - you know the kind of weather I mean, when the transport system has collapsed, the roads are icy and the signals and points are all frozen on the railway. Permafrost three feet deep into the ground. Aye. Then we'll tell the roadmen to plant the trees. They'll refuse of course, saying that it is crazy to try to plant any kind of trees - never mind palm trees - in this kind of weather. We'll make an issue of it, and insist that they do it right away, so they'll go on strike. This strike will spread all over the country, and of course it will make national news. Now people shivering all over Britain will see this, and they are bound to say - 'What kind of place is this that can plant palm trees while we are all in the grip of a freeze?' and just you wait and see, they'll flock here in their thousands next year!"

This idea of his would probably have worked!

Willie carried his lack of urgency into his shop, where he was happy to chat to a customer after a sale - completely ignoring the growing queue of increasingly impatient people waiting for him to attend to them. One day a colleague of mine, the late George Henderson, a man who was not renowned for his patience, went in to see if Willie stocked any of the patent cat deterrents with which he hoped to rid himself of the growing nuisance of stray cats in his garden. He found Willie head down in a tea chest full of new stock for the hardware department, busily unpacking and checking the contents. Having been studiously ignored for about five minutes, he blurted out impatiently, "Willie, have you anything to chase cats away from my garden?" Without even looking up, Willie in his usual slow laconic drawl replied, "Aye, George, have you tried a dog?"

One great regret concerning Willie is that I was not present in Colin Thom's house one evening when Willie performed the dance of the dying swan to the music of Swan Lake, dressed in a pair of pink tights belonging to Colin's daughter!

Yes indeed, Willie would fit in very well with the Captains by the fireside.

Another Captain is one of the few of my guests who really did wear the four gold rings of a captain on his sleeves. He was skipper of the famous original *Loch Mor*, one of David MacBrayne's steamers. This was in the days before Caledonian MacBrayne took over.

Captain Robertson was a short stocky man with a ruddy seaman's complexion, who spoke in a very high pitched voice. This led to his being better known as "Squeaky" Robertson.

I first encountered Squeaky in the bar of the Imperial Hotel in Fort William many years ago, when he was entertaining four English gentlemen who were in turn, buying him whisky. I was waiting for a train to Mallaig and had bought a book to help pass the time away, but I'm afraid that I did precious little reading, becoming as engrossed as his friends were in the tales he had to tell. He was a born story teller, and once again, it is a great pity that no one had the foresight to record these tales of his for posterity.

I have heard many times of the occasion when he was caught in a severe gale on passage from Mallaig to Lochboisdale in South Uist. They had an extremely bad passage across the wild waters of the Minch on the dark winter night, and great was the relief of all aboard when at last they reached the safety of the pier. As soon as the ship was safely tied up, Squeaky took his place as usual at the head of the gangplank to see his passengers ashore, but on this occasion two dear old ladies - who had suffered badly from seasickness and from fear on the passage - grasped his hands and with great emotion exclaimed: "That was a dreadful night Captain - we know that our safe arrival is due to the grace of God and to your skill!"

"Aye," was the instant reply from Squeaky. "Two good men!"

On a similarly wild morning Captain Robertson decided to delay the ship's departure from Lochboisdale until the weather had eased a bit, and had related his decision to the passengers. One lady who, for reasons of her own, was very keen to be away, on hearing this disputed that the weather was that bad, and indignantly pointed out a blue patch in the sky to Squeaky to strengthen her argument.

"Aye, aye madam, but we're not going up there though, we're going to Mallaig," was the reply!

Another oft-related tale also concerned two genteel old ladies - not the same pair as in the previous tale. This time the duo had booked a passage on the trip which took them around Skye and, as one of them had some clout with David MacBrayne himself, Captain Robertson had been instructed by his seniors in Glasgow to afford them every courtesy including allowing them free access to the bridge - which went sore against the grain with him. Just south of Dunvegan on the west coast of Skye stands 'Macleod's Maidens', three most impressive pillars of rock, similar to the Old Man of Hoy, jutting vertically from the sea below the very high cliffs. The old dears were on the bridge as the *Loch Mor* passed this landmark, and one of them asked if they had a name. "They are called MacLeod's Maidens," was the reply from Squeaky, who was by now thoroughly fed up with the pair's continuing presence on the bridge of his ship.

"Is there a story behind this name, Captain?" was the next question from one of the ladies who hoped no doubt to be regaled with some gem of historical allusion, perhaps like the tale of Lot's wife.

"Well yes, madam, you see there has never been a man on top of them!" A veil has rightly been drawn over the response from the 'Head Office', when this remark was later related – suitably edited - to them by the indignant ladies.

Archie MacLellan told me that when his father - also named Archie - built the Chlachain bar, he opened it in 1939 after the war had started, and one of the immediate problems which confronted him was the introduction of a whisky ration which was based upon the previous years consumption. In his case, of course, this was nil!

The problem was overcome with the help of the Gaelic-speaking head of a whisky-blending and bottling company in Glasgow, who hailed originally from Skye, and who had known old Archie in his younger days. The connection re-established, the Skye man then over a period of years sent several bottles of whisky to Mallaig at Christmas time, with a note of the people to whom old Archie had to present them. Squeaky always benefited to the tune of two bottles of what during the war years, was liquid gold, but one year his name was not on the list. This omission greatly surprised Archie, and he was faced with the diplomatically difficult decision of whether or not he should bring this state of affairs to the attention of the benefactor.

Eventually, however, he telephoned the blending company in Glasgow on another pretext, and spoke to the gentleman himself. Pleasantries concluded, he brought up the case of the missing bottles. All was revealed in the story which followed. Squeaky, he was told, had arrived in the blender's office in person just a week or so previously. He sat down and made himself at home, having placed at his feet a small case. The yarns showed no sign of abating and eventually, in order to get on with his work, the now reluctant host suggested that he give Squeaky the whisky in person, thinking that he might then be left in peace.

This of course met with instant approval, and a girl was despatched to fetch two bottles of the best. When she returned and handed them to our Captain, he promptly retrieved the case from the floor, opened it (in so doing revealing that it was completely empty), and put the two bottles into it. He then quizzically regarded the still open case quietly for a few moments and eventually remarked thoughtfully - almost speaking to himself –

"If I only had a half bottle to jam between them, it would keep them from rattling together!"

Another guest, one who also did wear the four gold rings of a Captain, is the late Hugh Swanson, possibly better known as 'Hurricane Hugh'. He was Captain of a later version of Squeaky's *Loch Mor*. Born and raised on the Clyde, Hugh was well versed in the coastal trade that has been so well preserved through the incomparable books on Para Handy, written by Neil Munro. Hurricane Hugh, in his own way, continued the legends that abound among the seafaring men of those days.

He sailed from Mallaig for several years as Master of the *Lochmor* and that is where I got to know him. I remember late one night when I was waiting with my helper for one fishing boat to arrive with a consignment of prawns. It was a very cold winter night and, more to generate some heat in our bodies than for any other reason, I suggested that we walk down the pier to see if there was any sign of this latecomer.

The *Lochmor* had arrived late from Canna, and was berthed at the far end of the pier where she was discharging a cargo of sheep. These frightened beasts were huddled together right aft on lower deck of the *Lochmor* – just above the waterline - and were being manhandled and urged up the flights of stairs that led eventually to the highest point on the ship, on top of the bridge. It was dead low water, with spring tides. A lorry was parked in a position where the driver and his helper could usher the sheep down the gangway and into the lorry.

Hugh had positioned himself at the foot of the last flight of steps and was doing his level best to help complete the task that required all hands. It is not in the nature of sheep to climb steps, so they required a lot of encouragement! Hugh would much rather have been sitting at his ease on the 'high stools' in the cocktail bar of the Marine Hotel, relaxing from his day's labour. Helping reluctant sheep up a flight of stairs was definitely not high on his agenda.

My friend and I stopped, watching the antics of the men below when Hugh – who was certainly not aware of our presence – encountered a particularly stubborn sheep. He struggled with it for a bit and then roared what was obviously the worst threat he could envisage.

He pushed the reluctant beast up a few steps and then roared after it the ultimate threat - "Mint sauce, you bastard!"

A year or so after Hugh died Ina and I visited Dorothy, his widow, in Largs. She told me a story that Hugh had often, she said, related against himself.

While working out of Oban he had fallen out rather badly with one of his crew. This man had been removed from Hugh's ship and, awaiting a berth on another ship, had been delegated to a pier job. This meant that he was losing money, as the shore job was not so well paid as his normal seagoing one.

A day or so later Hugh was in his usual position, leaning on the rail of the bridge, observing and socialising with the passing populace on the pier. His erstwhile crew member arrived and took up his position beside the gangway, just about 20 feet from where Hugh stood. His task was to count the number of passengers going aboard. He had not been there long when his replacement arrived, a man he of course knew well.

They stood for a time, chatting about maritime matters then the newcomer announced that he would have to go, as he needed to visit the toilet.

"You want the toilet, eh?" asked the man he was replacing, in a loud voice. "Well, if it is a shite you want, there's wan up there, hingin' ower the wing o' the bridge!"

I just recently visited the North East of Scotland and was delighted to have been able to spend some time with a few of the stalwarts from the early days of the purse net fishing.

Willie Tait of Fraserburgh must go down as one of the most unforgettable, and amazing guys I have ever met. He was the extremely successful skipper of one of the first ever Scottish pursers and with his brothers, Andrew and Robert and their combined families he continues today to be a power to be reckoned with in the fishing industry. Many years ago Willie suffered a horrific injury when he had his left arm caught up in the net as it was being hauled up through the power block. He was unable to free it but somehow he braced himself until his arm and shoulder were hauled away from his body. He was then able, while he was lying bleeding on the deck, to instruct his crew how to treat his injury until he was helicoptered to a hospital!

Willie has achieved infinitely more with one arm than the vast majority of people have accomplished with two. He should be held up as an example to those we see and hear whining on television, every day in life!

I also met Willie Whyte, lately skipper of the *Forever Grateful*. Willie now spends much of his time ashore, and he was kind enough to show Ina and me around his net store, on Fraserburgh pier. This was indeed an amazing experience, and we have been unable to think of much else since then!

He now spends much of his life in this store preparing and packing the nylon nets and rope that he has been given, being surplus to requirements, by the other boats in the Scottish fishing fleets. These nets are shipped off, mainly to Russia, to be recycled and the money earned from this is in turn recycled by Willie. Before sending the nets off, Willie does a lot of preliminary work involving the removal of all the ropes so that the lead weights on the bottom and the floats on the top can be removed. He told us that the nylon netting goes in at one end of the factory and that small granules, like lead shot, come out at the other. This end product goes into the making of plastic mouldings, so your car's dashboard might be made from material that once caught herring and mackerel in the North Sea!

Around 30 fishing boats have been bought for fishermen in Indonesia, India and Burma to replace the boats that were destroyed by the dreadful tsunami a few years ago and by a cyclone in Burma last year. Most, if not all of these small boats bear the names of the Fraserburgh, Peterhead, Castlebay, Orkney and Shetland boats – boats from all over the country whose owners have donated the unwanted nets that made it all possible. Homes, schools and hospitals in several countries have all been funded from the same source. He showed us many, many photographs of the grateful recipients of some of this cash, and the letters of thanks they have sent him.

He told us about, and then showed us a photograph of what looked like an unkempt, rough and stony patch of ground. This, he said, was where an estimated 26,000 unidentified bodies, victims of the tsunami, had their last resting places.

Another photograph showed a young couple who had with them a very young child. Willie's guide, one of the few English speaking Christian contacts he had in a predominantly Moslem area, told him that this couple had lost their 10 month old daughter and their home, to the tsunami. The mother seemed unable to take her eyes off the child, who had been born since the tragedy, and she kept looking around apprehensively watching, the guide said, in case another wave came! When Willie learned that their only home was now a scattered collection of tin and wood he managed, that very day, to purchase a piece of ground and to pay for the building of a new house – the one the family now stood in front of in the photograph. I think I am correct in saying that the entire transaction cost in the region of £1,400 - a sum that was, of course, totally beyond the young couple's resources.

Closer to home, Willie bought the entire children's wear contents of the Fraserburgh and Peterhead branches of Woolworths, when they closed down. These clothes were taken into the store we stood in and Willie, with the aid of some willing helpers, sorted them all out into lots. He then invited the heads of several local schools to come along and to help themselves to whatever they wanted, for the benefit of their poorer scholars. He had been asked why he didn't send these clothes to one of the many poor developing countries but by way of reply he told us that one of these school heads had told him that several of her pupils did not own any underwear – this was in Scotland - in 2009!

In his 'spare time' Willie makes oatmeal stuffing, my mother would have called it "meal an' creish,'" a mixture of oatmeal, onion and fat with an undisclosed 'secret' ingredient. He sells this to enthusiastic buyers at many functions and the funds so generated go to swell the funds of his charity.

Willie, who is a devout Christian, told me a tale about his father that I hope he will not mind my repeating.

A few years ago Willie attended the wedding of one of his nieces and at the reception he took his place, as was his custom, not seated with his relatives but rather with people who were either strangers or at best, nodding acquaintances.

Willie's father, also William Whyte, who had been one of the top fishermen in the area, rose after the meal to make his contribution to the speeches and Willie told us that he was horrified when his father began by telling his audience that they were about to hear a speech from a millionaire!

"Aye," he continued: "I'm definitely a millionaire! Ye see, when I merrit my wife we hid nae money, but we decided tae invest all we earned intae livestock. Weel, ower the years, we hid twa sons an' fower dochters an' in time, we were blessed wi' twenty-five grandchildren an' twenty-five great-grandchildren. Noo jist last week this lass here that's jeest merrit an' who is een o' these grandchildren, cam tae oor hoose an' said that she hid jeest called tae see hoo we were keepin'. Noo – hoo much is that worth? Millions!"

I don't believe that there would have been many dry eyes in his audience when they realised what his definition of a 'millionaire' was

Willie's father died not long after this and his family were amazed to discover that he had left no money at all. "He left this world wi nithin', jeest the same wye as he cam intae it!" said Willie.

I believe that the family later discovered that he had given away all the money he had, to what he thought were deserving causes.

Since Ina and I returned, just a couple of days ago, from this trip we have been bombarded with more media revelations about the host of criminals among our politicians who are lining their pockets by lying and stealing – people who then stand unabashedly before us and attempt to lie their way out of the mess they have made.

Celebrities? I believe that very few of them are fit to tie the laces of the people I was privileged to meet and about whom I have written, but they most certainly will stand before God some day. I doubt that they will have the required answers then! I'd much rather be in William Whyte's shoes on that day than in theirs, that's for sure.

I think I have now completed the list of guests that I have presumed to invite to share a dram by Angus's fireside, but no doubt another tale about someone else – equally deserving of mention – will come to mind later. Too often our forgiving human nature dictates to us that 'late' is synonymous with 'great'. I have tried to resist this failing, if indeed it is a failing. Not all of the people I have nominated as Captains or Commanders are 'late' - fortunately some are still with us. If I have conveyed to you, the reader, just a fraction of the joy I have had in recalling my memories of these wonderful men, many of whom were giants to me, then perhaps this sharing will help to ensure that they will not be forgotten.

Ring-net men

What happened to the ring net and what caused its demise?

The ring net fishermen had their time and in my opinion, that time passed. It met with rival and superior forms of catching, in the shape of the purse net and the mid-water trawl, methods that were used to catch herring where a ring net would fail. The trawl was used by day as well as by night, and was certainly a more efficient way of reaping the shoals. No longer could the herring evade capture by diving deep; the trawl proved just as efficient at catching fish at fifty fathoms as it was at twenty.

The real improvement in landing more marketable fish, however, came with the advent and development of keeping the herring in better condition in the tanks of the purse seiners. When I was at the fishing most of the herring was carried by the drifters and ringers in bulk – not the best way of maintaining the quality of the catch. In summer months in the North fishing we boxed the herring, but that was done in wooden boxes, and we didn't carry ice to cool them. The result was that the bellies of the herring, which were filled with the plankton they had fed on, were prone to burst. I shudder to think of the prime quality herring we landed for pet food or to be converted to fishmeal, simply because they had become soft and unusable as kippers in the few hours after we had caught them.

Nowadays it is common practice for pursers and super trawlers to part fill their holding tanks with sea water, which they then chill down to almost freezing, before pumping their catch out of the net, into this excellent keeping medium. Pursers can also, if the skipper thinks it necessary, allow the captured herring to swim in the nets for many hours, or even days, until their bellies are purged of the feeding that would cause the deterioration in their quality.

Purse-seining is now itself outdated, having been largely superseded by the highly sophisticated trawl. The scene keeps on changing!

In the days of the ring-net fleet if there was a landing of 6,000 crans into Mallaig in one day, the port would almost certainly either be closed, or a quota imposed by the fishermen themselves, in order to let the market recover. Now, that amount can be landed by one 'super purser/trawler' alone, in one day and is sometimes sold over the radio by the skippers themselves. It is then delivered to whichever country, never mind port, that the successful bidder requires!

The marketing of the catches of herring and mackerel has changed completely now also. The fishermen have formed their own fish selling companies and in many cases they land into their own cold stores, from which they sell the frozen products all over the world. Relatively little money is now going to buyers – it is nearly all going into the catchers' banks. I am quite certain that Sammy Gemmell would give his whole hearted approval to this change. There are still serious malpractices on the catching side, but this is not where they should be aired. The malpractices that took place on the buyers side have disappeared along with the buyers themselves!

Does this mean that all is now well?

Certainly quite a few fishermen have joined the ranks of the 'super rich'. One of them, just this year, told me of one of his boats (he has two) that had grossed over one million pounds for one landing of mackerel but nothing in this life comes free. The price paid by others for the success of these fishermen can be seen in just about every fishing port in Scotland. Where once there were fleets of fishing boats there are now only pleasure craft. In

Anstruther, just along the coast from where I now live, the only fishing boats to be seen are the ones that have been converted into motor yachts! I used to sit on piers all over the West Coast and watch the wee 'cuddies' swimming by. You won't see them now, they are just about extinct! At certain times I would catch as many 'gleshins' – large siblings of the cuddies – and mackerel as I wanted to on handlines. They too have gone from their old haunts. I stated one night, when in company with Cecil Finn and cousin Robert Gillies in Campbeltown, that in my opinion a Clyde whiting was as tasty a fish as you could wish to eat only to hear Cecil say, "Aye, but where would you catch one now? They're all dead!"

The Modern Way of fishing
Forever Grateful FR249 and *Ocean Quest* BF77 in Fraserburgh harbour

I read of the strides being made in fish farming. Well, I was in at the very beginning of the White Fish Authority's fish farming experimental unit at Ardtoe, south of Mallaig, and for some time supplied it with minced up fish so I will not eat farmed fish. I will leave my consumption of antibiotics and chemicals to be decided by doctors, but although I will not live to see it, I can foresee the day coming when it will no longer be possible to buy wild fish. This fact makes me recall, again, the wise words of the late Ian Stewart, the lawyer in Campbeltown who one day said to me, "I'd rather be going, than coming, in today's world, Tommy!"

I clearly recall the day of the last landing of herring in Mallaig before the closure of the West Coast fishery. A ban on all fishing – I think it was supposed to last for six years – had been imposed and now the day of the last landing before the ban took effect, had arrived. I had bought 80 units of prime summer herring for Fred Buchan, of Scotprime, in Ayr, but was busy with the auction of prawns when it came time to put Fred's lorry in position to take its load aboard. I did this, however, saw the start of the unloading process and had just returned to the prawn market when it dawned on me that I should get a few herring for my freezer at home (when would I get more?) so off I galloped down the pier again. Asking the fishermen who were loading the lorry to "put a few into this box," resulted in their half-filling the box which I then lugged up the pier, putting them into the boot of my car.

When I got home, at around 1 am, I made myself a cup of tea – my wife was away in Edinburgh – but before I sat down, I remembered that the herring were still in the car boot. I was very tired, and it took a wee while to convince myself that I really had to get them gutted and packed into the freezer before I went to bed.

I sat outside the back door, gutting away while thinking of the comfortable bed that awaited me.

At last I picked up the last herring in the box and then it dawned on me – this *was* the last! We had known for some time, of course, that the fishery was to be closed but only now did the full realisation of what was coming, dawn on me. Since I was a wee boy I had been used to having herring scales mixed through every handful of coins that I took from my pocket. Herring had ruled my life, my father's life and my grandfather's life. This was the end of the road and of hundreds of years of tradition.

I sat and looked at this, the last prime, plump herring, then dropped it into the box again. I went into the house, filled a very large measure of Glenlivet into a glass and went back outside again. I took the herring in one hand, the whisky in the other, drank the whisky in one gulp and then I threw the herring and the now empty glass as far as I could down the brae toward the harbour and went to my bed.

The glass is probably still there somewhere.

Clyde herring being caught for tagging by the *Shemaron* in February 1990
This was the last known use of the ring-net in the Clyde.

We are now left with the few, and rapidly dwindling remnants of a time gone by: men - or rather, giants among men who, like Willie Jackson, scan the waters off Tarbert, seeing the ghosts of men and boats – long gone. Like Gary Voce of Ballantrae who looks in vain every March for the 'white water' that used to come ashore there when the herring spawned just offshore, on the Ballantrae Banks; like Bob McCutcheon of Dunure who recently spent a week in a rented caravan in Carradale so that he could get a yarn with his old fishing friends and like Jim Campbell, whose house now overlooks the bay where he took 1,400 baskets – around 70 tons – of herring in one ring, many years ago. John 'The Shore' McConnachie still spends many of his leisure hours gazing out to sea watching, in vain, for an 'appearance' of herring off Carradale.

My late, and very dear friend Dod Alexander, when we were on our way back to my house some years ago having had a rare afternoon yarning in Edinburgh with the late Pat Croan, remarked to me after I commented on how much I had enjoyed the time: "Mak the best o't – there'll soon be naebuddy left that kens whit ye're talking aboot!"

As usual, Dod was correct. The time is very near, now.

An old Arab saying would certainly apply to the current scene. "Take what you want." said Allah, "Take what you want - and pay for it!"

By the time I wrote the closing poem Mallaig - in common with almost all the fishing ports in Scotland - had become a pale shadow of its former self and it now is, to those who knew it in better days, a very depressing place to visit.

Of the once great fishing strongholds on the West Coast, Maidens and Dunure are now near-derelict harbours for yachts and punts. There are no fishing boats in them and although a few fishermen remain in Dunure, as far as I am aware none now live in Maidens. Girvan, Tarbert, Carradale and Campbeltown have greatly depleted fleets.

I will end then as I began, with a poem; this time one I wrote myself, several years ago. It could have been written about any one of the places mentioned in this book. Mallaig harbour is, like them, filled with ghosts. The old days will not return.

The years go past and I've now reached my 'three score years and ten'.
So I sit today, my mind goes back, and I remember when
A callow lad of just fifteen, I first smelt the acrid smoke,
From the kipper yards around the Point – the smouldering chips of oak.

The harbour then seemed always filled with boats from near and far,
The ringers brilliant varnished, and the drifters, black as tar.
Their derricks rose above the gulls, the squalling, screaming flock
That fought to catch the herring spills, before they hit the dock.

The BAs, CNs, TTs too, among the OBs lay,
The BFs, FRs and PDs - the herring was their prey.
They all came here with one intent, with but one thing in mind,
To find the silver darlings – to all else they were blind.

The time has flickered past, I fear, since I left the 'Kipper Town',
So I came back to reminisce and, as the sun went down
I wandered to the darkening pier, alone and feeling sad,
To see the spaces that were filled, when I was just a lad.

As I sat alone there came a mist, deep lit by ghostly hue,
There's a figure striding down the pier – first of a silent crew.
Who is that man? I know him well – Black Jim, of that I'm sure!
"Is that you, Jim, what like?" I cried, but silence did endure.

He walked right past, his piercing eyes, beneath that shock of hair,
Were searching still for herring signs, his shoulders strong and square.
But he didn't seem to notice me as he strode on down the pier,
And I realised that I was making sounds he couldn't hear.

The basin's filled with boats, I see; their varnish shining bright.
Their names I scan with raptured eye –it seems no longer night.
And Jary's Wharf is littered still with ring nets piled on high,
With barrels and with boxes lying scattered all awry.

The pier is growing busy now; the crowds are all around.
But though I sit and listen hard, I cannot hear a sound.
Hey, there's Big Willie, large as life, and Willum John, I swear.
Auld Petey, aye and Smithy too, now there's a royal pair!

There's 'Porter' with his rolling gait, the Mallaig Mor his aim.
And Ronnie follows hard behind; his goal is just the same.
And there's auld Robbie Hepburn; whose guiding hand, I know,
Has helped so many young lads on, and shown the way to go.

There's Clainey, with his cheery grin, and Charlie Duncan too.
The Martins, and Jimmy Henderson, come striding into view.
That's old Manson there, I see, he gave this place a start.
He's at the root of most of this, a Thurso chiel at heart.

Then Jimmy Aitchison comes by, with Ecky at his side,
They're in a fearful hurry, are they trying to catch the tide?
There's Alec Duncan too, I see, he's in an awful state.
Ah, they're seeking after Black Jim aye, they're needing lobster bait!

The ghostly mist grew lighter then, the figures ceased to come
And I realised that my visions of the nearby past were done.
Where are these men? Where have they gone? We need them sorely now
To lead us forward. "Light your torch! We'll follow. There's the lowe!"

It cannot happen, that I know; their time I fear has passed.
The harbour lies near empty now – I cannot see a mast.
The way of life I knew has gone; so many men have died.
I sat alone on Mallaig Pier. I sat alone - and cried.